SANTERÍA:
The Religion

SANTERÍA:
The Religion
A Legacy of Faith, Rites, and Magic

Migene González-Wippler

Foreword
by
Charles Wetli, M.D.

Harmony Books/New York

This book is for Beau

Photographs 3 and 5 are from *Yoruba: Sculpture of West Africa*, by William Fagg, et al.
Copyright © 1982 by Pack Editions, Inc. Reprinted by permission of Alfred A. Knopf, Inc.

Portions of this book previously appeared in *Santería: African Magic in Latin America*,
© 1973 by Migene González-Wippler, and *The Santería Experience*, © 1982 by Migene
González-Wippler.

Published by Harmony Books, a division of Crown Publishers, Inc., 225 Park Avenue
South, New York, New York 10003

HARMONY and colophon are trademarks of Crown Publishers, Inc.

Book design by Jennifer Harper

Manufactured in the United States of America

Library of Congress Cataloging-in-Publication Data

González-Wippler, Migene.
   Santería: the religion/by Migene González-Wippler; foreword by
Charles Wetli.
   Bibliography
   Includes index.
   1. Santería (Cultus)   I. Title.
BL2532.S3G674   1989
299'.67—dc19

ISBN 0-517-57154-4
10 9 8 7 6 5 4 3 2 1

First Edition

Contents

Foreword

As a Medical Examiner in South Florida, I am frequently brought into close contact with the large Hispanic, mostly Cuban, population now indigenous to this area. Impressed by the frequent depictions of Catholic saints (in the form of statues, jewelry, candles, and other items), I readily concluded there was a deep devotion to Catholicism among Hispanics. But as time went on I began to notice things that appeared to be more than just cultural variations of Catholicism: statues of Saint Barbara and an American Indian next to each other, cigars and pennies for Saint Lazarus, colored beads, glasses of water in a row, and so forth. Occasionally, I encountered decapitated animals or a whole room filled with mysterious objects (drums, stones in bowls, animal skins, objects covered with colored beads, pieces of coconut, etc.). My inquiries as to what all this meant were usually met with silence or a pronouncement that this was "Cuban Voodoo—don't worry about it."

One day, I responded to a call to examine some skeletal remains. The object in question was a bloodied skull atop a large iron cauldron filled with dirt and an amazing array of objects (railroad spikes, knives, machetes, animal skulls). The context

was obviously religious. Because of threats to destroy the cauldron, I confiscated all the items and had them transported to our
office. For the next ten weeks, the cauldron attracted a steady
stream of visitors. Most were curious and others were obviously
fearful—but none were informative.

Finally, a few knowledgeable people began grudgingly to relin-
quish some information. From them I learned that the cauldron
was an *nganga* of Palo Mayombe. Through it, I was eventually able
to discover the phenomenon of Santería, which, incidentally, has
nothing to do with Palo and does not use human remains in its
practices. For me this was an astounding discovery, as Santería is
probably the best-kept secret of Hispanic culture.

It is amazing that a religion so widely accepted and practiced is
so effectively cloaked in secrecy. When I "discovered" Santería, I
found there was very little written about this religion in English.
Most practitioners were reluctant to divulge any information,
especially to a non-Hispanic cultural outsider like myself. By
serendipity, I finally met a Cuban-born cultural anthropologist,
Rafael Martinez, who helped tremendously with field observa-
tions and interviews. I learned other basic concepts from a few
dissertations given in Florida universities, and from the earlier
writings of Migene González-Wippler. Since then, field observa-
tions have continued, and more works on Santería have appeared
in English.

Over the past ten years it has become evident that many
non-Hispanics, like myself, have a genuine desire to learn more
about Santería. For some, the interest is generated through
University-based academia and research; others want a better
understanding of the cultural values of Caribbean and South
American immigrants. Still others are interested because they
suspect the belief system of Santería may be valuable for personal
reasons.

Despite this growing interest in Santería, much remains shrouded
in a secrecy that is now unnecessary. Centuries ago, African
slaves brought to the New World were forbidden to practice their

native religion and were forced to learn Christianity. They resisted, and the result was the creation of Santería, replete with syncretic depictions of African deities as Catholic saints and a secrecy necessary, at the time, for survival. Today, however, this secrecy results in distrust and misunderstanding of Santería by the general public. Most who have only casually heard of Santería picture "voodoo dolls" pierced with needles, the ritualistic sacrifice of defenseless animals, and totally incomprehensible states of possession. And those who make a genuine effort to learn about Santería are quickly frustrated. Many are thereby deprived of the knowledge of a fascinating religion with a most interesting history, colorful ceremonies, a rich mythology, and a profound philosophy. Clearly, both factual information and meaningful dialogue are needed if Santería is to gain acceptance in modern-day America.

The issue of animal sacrifice is perhaps the most volatile and emotional issue of the Religion. Again, this is partly due to a lack of information (certainly, a lack of understanding) and variations among state laws and local ordinances regarding cruelty to animals and religious exemption. For example, in New Jersey some Santería practitioners were convicted of animal cruelty, while in Florida the statutes provided an exemption of animal sacrifice for religious purposes. More recently, a Florida Attorney General opinion stated that animal sacrifice for religious purposes was valid only if the animal is ultimately eaten. Obviously, there is a need for intelligent, nonemotional, and nonconfrontational dialogue and compromise to avert religious and legal conflict.

Fortunately, the current trend (at least in South Florida) is to promote a better understanding of Santería. This has taken the form of seminars at local colleges as well as specific training sessions. These are often directed at law enforcement officers who frequently come into contact with Santería. Also, the news media occasionally takes an interest in the Religion, with both detrimental as well as beneficial results. In general, news stories often do not provide an accurate or adequate depiction of Santería, and they usually, often erroneously, attribute the deeds of paleros to Santería. In-depth investigative reports are often quite good, but like most media events, they tend to focus on what they perceive as sensational, (e.g., use of skulls by the paleros or animal sacrifice).

Within the past several years, two major trends have emerged that promise to bring a better understanding of Santería to America. One is the advent of American-born Hispanics (and non-Hispanics) being initiated into Santería. These individuals seem to be more willing to engage in a meaningful dialogue. They have a good command of the English language and appear to be willing to ignore the traditional code of silence.

The second trend has been the appearance, in English, of scholarly works on Afro-American culture in general, and Santería in particular. These publications have gone far in revealing much of the lore of Santería and have elucidated its origins, meanings, and widespread appeal. This thesis by Migene González-Wippler will help immeasurably in furthering an understanding of The Religion, Santería.

Charles Wetli, M.D.
Deputy Chief Medical Examiner
Dade County, Florida

Preface

When I wrote my first book on Santería (*Santería: African Magic in Latin America*), I had a great deal of difficulty researching the subject. Most of the santeros (priests of the religion), who are notoriously secretive, were very reluctant to discuss their beliefs and practices with me. Those who were willing to talk did so in a veiled way, and very often misled me or gave me wrong information about their religious practices. This was done purposely in order to preserve the traditional mystery that has always pervaded the practices of Santería. As a result, several of the beliefs and rites that I described in that first book were incomplete and, in some instances, incorrect. From a sociological and anthropological point of view, these errors are significant because they underline the zealousness with which the santeros protect the mysteries of their religion.

By the time I wrote my second book (*The Santería Experience*), I had received several of the initiations of Santería and the santeros had learned that my respect for their religion was genuine, and that my desire to introduce it to an English-reading audience was rooted in my firm conviction that Santería was as viable and dynamic as any of the world's major religions. They were far more cooperative and truthful this second time around, and although a few still resented my persistent prodding, they seemed to realize the importance of revealing at least some of the practices that have made Santería so well known. They did not open the door completely, but rather left it ajar so that some of the wonders within might be glimpsed by observers standing outside. The second book contained very few errors, and those that crept in were largely the result of secondhand information.

Several other books followed the first two, and academic and public interest grew with each one. When Harmony approached me about the possibility of reprinting *Santería* and *The Santería Experience,* it seemed clear that what was really needed was a comprehensive volume that encompassed the most vital portions of the first two books and presented additional material that heretofore had not been published. That is how this new book came into being. In the interest of conciseness and accuracy, some of the old material has been excised and many necessary corrections have been incorporated into the original texts. The new material and the extraordinary photographs—many of them previously unpublished—help make the book far more thorough and informative than the first two.

I am deeply indebted to the many santeros, babalawos, and paleros who helped me in my continuing research on Santería, among them the late Fernando Sierra (O-Yeye-I, Obatalá), the late babalawo Pancho Mora (Ifá Moro, Orúnmila), Lillian Ramírez (Oshún), Lucila Rivera (Obatalá), Margot Torres (Oyá), and most especially my padrino, Eduardo Pastoriza (Changó Larí). Special thanks to Dr. Charles V. Wetli, Deputy Chief Medical Examiner of Dade County, Florida, who wrote the foreword, for many stunning photographs; to Rafael Martinez, research assistant in the Department of Psychiatry, University of Miami School of Medicine; to Dr. Stanley Dean, also of the Department of Psychiatry of the University of Miami School of Medicine and author/editor of the book *Psychiatry and Mysticism;* and to Dr. Andrés Pérez y Mena of Rutgers University. My deep gratitude also to my first editor and publisher, Arthur Ceppos, who published my first book on Santería; to Tam Mossman, my editor at Prentice-Hall, without whose gentle prodding *The Santería Experience* would have never been written; to Milton Benezra, of Original Publications, whose faith in my work has never diminished; and, last but not least, to Esther Mitgang, formerly at Harmony, who conceived the idea of a fusion of the first two books. To all of them, ashé and modupués.

Migene González-Wippler
New York City

Ashé d'owo Oloddumare

Introduction ▰▰▰▰▰▰▰▰▰▰▰▰▰▰▰▰▰

Santería was born in Nigeria, along the banks of the Niger River. This is the country of origin of the Yoruba people, many of whom, along with members of other African tribes, were brought to the New World by slave traders over four centuries ago. The Yoruba brought with them the colorful mythology of their religion, known in Cuba as *Lucumí* and in Brazil as *Macumba* and *Candomblé*.

The Yoruba people originated in southwestern Nigeria. At one time they had a powerful and complex social structure organized in a series of kingdoms, the most important of which was Benin. The kingdom of Benin lasted from the twelfth century until 1896, when it was dispersed by English colonists. Benin was a form of theocratic autocracy where the *oba*, or king, had absolute power. The advanced culture of the Benin civilization can be appreciated in the beautiful works of bronze and ivory, dating from archaic times to the seventeenth century, that can be found in many museums throughout the world. At the beginning of the seventeenth century, the Ewe people invaded the region of Dahomey and the neighboring kingdoms, forcing the Yoruba tribes to migrate to the Nigerian coast, where many of them were captured by slave traders and brought to the New World.

The most interesting and important aspects of the Yoruba culture are its mythology and religious practices. Extensive studies of the Yoruba cult, notably those by William Bascom and Roger Bastide, have shown that the Yoruba pantheon is extremely complex and sophisticated and strongly reminiscent of the ancient Greeks. Their deities, known as *orishas*, are believable and extraordinarily human in their behavior. The term *orisha* is of uncertain origin. Some anthropologists believe it is derived from the word *asha,* meaning "religious ceremony." Others claim it is formed of the roots *ri* (to see) and *sha* (to choose). There are many orishas in the pantheon. Some authorities believe that in Africa their number exceeds six hundred. In Latin America their number fluctuates between twenty and twenty-five.

As members of the various African tribes were scattered throughout the New World by the slave trade, their religious practices were influenced by their new surroundings and the strange languages spoken in the lands of their exile. Each tribe borrowed freely from the customs, ideas, and religious beliefs of its adopted land. This brought great diversity into the magic ceremonies of black people. The rites varied with each tribe. In Haiti, Voodoo (or Voudun), was propagated by the Fon, the Nago, the Kongo, the Ibo, the Dahomeans, and other tribes. In the Spanish and Portuguese colonies, similar magic rites were transmitted by the Yoruba, Bantu, and Kongo people. There are some similarities between Santería and Voodoo, notably the worship of some of the same deities, such as Changó, Oggún (known as Oggou in Voodoo), and Elegguá (called Legba in Voodoo). The similarities are the result of the fusion of beliefs when different tribes intermixed. But in general the divergences between the two religions are far greater than the similarities, largely because in Santería the Yoruba influence supersedes that of any other culture. Also, Haiti was under French rule during the slave trade, while other Caribbean countries, such as Cuba, Puerto Rico, and the Dominican Republic, were dominated by Spain.

In Cuba, where Santería originated, the Yoruba became known

as *Lucumí,* a word that means "friendship." Some researchers
believe that this term is derived from *akumi,* which means "I
am Aku." In Sierra Leone, where the Yoruba are also found, they
are known as Aku. This may indicate that many of the Yoruba
who were brought to Cuba came from Sierra Leone.

The Cuban Lucumís were deeply influenced by the Catholic
iconolatry of their Spanish masters. In their efforts to hide their
magical and religious practices from the eyes of the Spaniards, they
identified their deities with the saints of the Catholic Church.
This was the beginning of Santería, which is a term derived from
the Spanish word *santo* (saint), and literally means "the worship
of saints." Santería is a typical case of syncretism, the spontaneous, popular combination or reconciliation of different religious
beliefs. This syncretism can be appreciated in the fact that all of
the Yoruba deities worshiped in Santería have been identified
with Catholic saints.

Santería is therefore a mixture of the magic rites of the Yoruba
and some of the traditions of the Catholic Church. All the legends that surround the lives of Jesus, Mary, and the Catholic
saints are of great importance to the santero because they help
delineate the personalities of the saints, making it easier to identify them with the appropriate Yoruba deities. But in spite of the
influence of the Catholic Church, Santería is mostly primitive
magic, and its roots are deeply buried in the heart of Africa.

Although the Yoruba were successful in hiding their orishas
under the guise of Catholic saints, it did not take long for the
Spanish settlers to realize what the slaves were doing. The Yoruba
religion comprises an intricate system of rituals and ceremonies
of a distinct magical nature, all of which the slaves conducted in
the woods. This resulted in a great deal of persecution, which
forced the slaves to cloak their religion in secrecy. All the rituals,
especially the initiations, were conducted under stringent vows of
secrecy. This secrecy, which never existed in Nigeria, is still
observed by the practitioners of Santería today and is one of the
reasons the religion is so closed to outsiders. The vows of se-

crecy, which once meant the difference between life and death to the Yoruba, became an intrinsic part of the Santería tradition, and the santeros are adamant about observing it, even though it is no longer necessary.

Santería is an earth religion, a magico-religious system that has its roots in nature and natural forces. Each orisha or saint is identified with a force of nature and with a human interest or endeavor. Changó, for instance, is the orisha who controls fire, thunder, and lightning, but he also symbolizes raw power and control over enemies and general difficulties. Because of his tremendous dynamism, he is also seen as the embodiment of passion and virility and is often invoked in works of seduction. Oshún, on the other hand, symbolizes river waters but is also the patron of love and marriage, fertility, and gold. She is essentially the archetype of joy and pleasure. Yemayá is identified with the sea but is also the symbol of motherhood and protects women in their endeavors. Elegguá is the orisha of the crossroads and controls change and destiny. He is the one who makes things possible or impossible and symbolizes the balance of things. Obatalá is the father, the symbol of peace and purity, and is the creator of mankind on a physical level. Everything white belongs to him. Oyá symbolizes the winds and is the owner of the cemetery, the watcher of the doorway between life and death. She is not death but the awareness of its existence. She is also the owner of the thunderbolt, and many santeros believe she was the one who gave Changó power over thunder and lightning. Oggún, the last orisha to be considered here, is the patron of all metals and protects farmers, carpenters, butchers, surgeons, mechanics, policemen, and all who work with or near metals or metal weapons. He also rules over accidents, which he often causes.

In Yoruba tradition, the orishas were divided into two groups: the white (*orisha fun-fun*) and the dark. The white orishas are "cool" and have life-giving powers. Among them are Obatalá, Osain (the orisha of herbs), Orisha-Oko (the orisha of farming), Oshún, and Yemayá. The dark orishas are "hot," and their powers are present in war or when blood is shed in battle or in the hunt. Among them are Changó, Oggún, and Oyá.

Santería, like the ancient Yoruba tradition, is based on the concepts of *ashé* and *ebbó*. *Ashé* is a Yoruba word that means, literally, "so be it," but it is also a symbol of divine power. It is the power with which God Almighty—Oloddumare—created the universe. Everything is made of ashé, and through ashé everything is possible. The orishas are the repositories of Oloddumare's ashé. All the invocations, propitiations, spells, and rituals of Santería are conducted to acquire ashé from the orishas. With ashé, all problems can be solved, enemies can be subdued, love and money can be acquired. Ashé is also authority, power of action.

Ebbó, on the other hand, is the concept of sacrifice, the way in which the orishas are propitiated so that they will give us their ashé. All the rites and spells of Santería are part of the ebbó concept.

According to the Yoruba, the universe is divided into two camps—one dominated by the orishas, seen as forces of good, and the other by the *ajogun*, seen as forces of evil. Among the latter are *ikú* (death), *arun* (disease), *ofo* (loss), *eqba* (paralysis), *epe* (curse), and *ewon* (prison). The Yoruba believe that the ajogun must be propitiated so that they leave us in peace, and the orishas must be propitiated so that they remain with us and grant us their ashé. In Santería, only the orishas are propitiated. With their ashé, the ajogun can be safely vanquished. But this can only be accomplished through sacrifice, ebbó.

Sacrifice does not always require a sacrificial victim. Blood is the essence of life and is not to be shed lightly. Ebbó can be an offering of fruits, flowers, candles, or any of the favorite foods of the orishas. In Santería, these small offerings are called *addimús*. The larger offerings are usually given for the solution of big problems. When blood is called for, great forces are invariably in play, and often the life of a person is in danger or a major undertaking is involved. Ebbós are never offered indiscriminately or whimsically. An orisha is always the one to mark an ebbó; that is, the orisha always determines what type of ebbó he or she requires to solve a specific problem. The santero ascertains what the orisha wants by questioning him or her through the *Diloggún,* the divination system known also as "the seashells."

Central to the practice of Santería is ancestor worship. The dead in one's family, known collectively as *eggun,* must be fed periodically. At these times, water, coffee, bits of one's food, flowers, and a candle are placed either on the bathroom floor or in another specific place in the house, often behind doors. Before every ceremony, the eggun must be honored because, according to the santeros, the dead come before the saints (the orishas). This is one of the strongest precepts of Santería.

Santeros are also known by the Yoruba name of *omo-orisha,* which means "child of an orisha." Usually a santero or santera takes the name of the orisha or saint into whose mysteries he or she has been initiated. For example, a son or daughter of Changó is an omo-Changó, a child of Oshún is an omo-Oshún, and so on. When a santero or omo-orisha initiates another person as a santero, that person becomes a *babalocha* or *iyalocha,* meaning, respectively, the father or mother of a saint. The high priest of the religion is known as a *babalawo,* and he conducts sacrifices during the initiation ceremonies, confers certain of the initiations, and settles points of contention or doubt among santeros.

Therefore we have in Santería a religious system that honors the ancestors and recognizes a direct contact between mankind and the forces of nature, which are seen as direct manifestations of God Himself. This contact between God and mankind—through nature—is enforced through ebbó, sacrifice, for the purpose of receiving ashé, power. This is what Santería is all about, in essence. But although Santería is immersed deeply in African tradition, there is a very definite difference between the actual Yoruba religion and Santería. This is not only because of the pronounced influence of Catholicism in Santería, but also because the original Yoruba practices underwent many changes and adaptations in the New World. For that reason we have to consider Santería as a religion entirely independent from that of the Yoruba, even though its general structure is largely based on the Yoruba tradition. This is also true of other Yoruba-based religions of the New World, such as Candomblé or Macumba in Brazil and Shango in Trinidad.

It is surprising how strongly Santería has influenced the inhabitants of the Latin American countries. From Cuba it migrated to Puerto Rico, the Dominican Republic, Venezuela, Colombia, Panama, and other countries. The primitive beliefs and customs, with their "barbarous words of evocation," have found their way to the busy, sophisticated streets of New York, Chicago, Los Angeles, and Miami, where Santería flourishes now as powerfully as in the Caribbean islands. According to a conservative estimate, there are more than a hundred million practitioners of the religion in Latin America and the United States.

1.

The Orisha
Tradition ◿◿◿◿◿◿◿◿◿◿◿◿◿◿◿◿◿◿◿◿◿◿◿◿◿◿◿◿

The Yoruba people of southwestern Nigeria and the neighboring republics of Benin (Dahomey) and Togo number more than 10 million. They are subdivided into more than twenty subgroups, each of which was traditionally an autonomous kingdom. In spite of the many differences between the various subgroups, enough cultural links remain to indicate that they all belong to the same ethnic group. This is particularly true of their language, which, according to scholars, has been spoken by the Yoruba for several thousand years.

The antiquity of the Yoruba is reckoned not only on linguistic evidence, but also on archeological studies that seem to indicate that the tribes migrated from the east, perhaps from the Upper Nile, at the beginning of the Christian era. It is during this period that we begin to trace the extraordinary complexity of the economic, political, artistic, and religious aspects of the Yoruba culture, which ranks among the most developed in West Africa.

One of the most outstanding characteristics of Yoruba culture was the formation of city-state kingdoms in a process of urbanization unique among so-called primitive peoples. The center of their civilization, both politically and religiously, has traditionally been the holy city of Ile-Ife.

All the various city-states or kingdoms formed a pyramidal sociopolitical structure, at the apex of which was the city of Ile-Ife. The word *ilé* means "home," and indeed Ife is considered the ancestral home of the Yoruba people.

The head of Ife was the *ooni,* or divine king, from whom all the other Yoruba kings or *oba*s received the right to wear the beaded crown that was the symbol of their power. The ooni was said to be a direct descendant of Oddudúa, the orisha founder of Ife and one of the three deities sent to earth by the Creator, Oloddumare, to oversee the destinies of mankind. Today the ooni's dynasty is still very much in power in Nigeria, and he still traces his ancestry to Oddudúa.

The integral unity of Yoruba culture is directly related to the powerful religious beliefs that throughout the centuries have influenced and permeated their art and sociopolitical structures. Ife soon became a center of pilgrimage for all Yoruba people who came to consult the priest-chiefs who were dedicated to the worship of the principal deities or orishas. Ife became an oracle city, very much like Delphi in ancient Greece. And indeed, the complexity of the Yoruba pantheon is not unlike that of Greek mythology. Like the Olympians, the Yoruba gods were anthropomorphized and identified with natural forces. They were also invoked in times of need and propitiated through sacrifice. The one important difference between Greek and Yoruba deities is that while the worship of the Olympians was soon relegated to books of mythology and ancient history, that of the orishas is still very much alive today, not only in Nigeria but also in the Western hemisphere.

In the Americas, the worship of the orishas is known collectively as the Orisha Tradition. Most of the 100 million people who practice it are concentrated in Brazil. In the United States the number of worshipers, mostly practitioners of Santería, fluctuates around 5 million. These are mostly Cubans, Puerto Ricans,

Venezuelans, Colombians, Dominicans, and other people of Latin American extraction. But the numbers of both black and white American practitioners is increasing.

The Orisha Tradition teaches the importance of religious tolerance. Many Yoruba believe that this is the reason why Islam and Christianity were so readily welcome when they arrived in Nigeria. Today the vast majority of Yoruba are Muslims or Christians, but the ancient beliefs are so deeply rooted that they often revert to traditional practices, especially during times of dire need.

The tremendous impact of orisha worship in the New World has created a revival of the ancient beliefs in Nigeria, and many Yoruba scholars are coming to the Americas to teach Yoruba lore and religion in American universities. Notable among these is Professor Wande Abimbola, of the University of Ile-Ife, who teaches courses in Yoruba tradition and culture at the University of Puerto Rico. There is also a yearly conference on the Orisha Tradition sponsored by the Caribbean Cultural Center in New York, which is largely responsible for these cultural exchanges. The conference is held in a different country each year; thus far there have been conferences in Nigeria, Brazil, and New York City.

Some Yoruba scholars believe that the Yoruba-based religions of the New World, like Candomblé and Santería, are not the result of syncretism but rather of the acceptance by the Yoruba slaves of the Catholic religion. This acceptance, according to them, was rooted in the traditional Yoruba respect for other religions. I do not agree with this theory. Syncretism is the combination or reconciliation of different religious or philosophical beliefs. The Yoruba did not simply accept the Catholic saints— they *identified* them with the orishas. Santería means literally "the worship of saints," and these saints are identified with the orishas of the Yoruba pantheon. This is a typical case of syncretism. It is most important that Candomblé, Shango, or Santería never be identified as part of the traditional Yoruba religion.

They are Yoruba-based, but because of the syncretism and other changes that took place throughout the centuries, they should be considered as independent religions, different not only from the original Yoruba belief system, but also from one another. They are all part of the Orisha Tradition, but each one is an individual phenomenon. Their roots are intrinsically Yoruba, but each one has taken the special flavor of the country where it was born. Candomblé is strictly Brazilian, Shango is typically Trinidadian, and Santería could only have arisen in Cuba.

2.

What Is Santería? ⟁⟁⟁⟁⟁⟁⟁⟁

To the santeros and to its millions of practitioners, Santería is known simply as the Religion. My own extensive research into the subject has convinced me that this is exactly what Santería is. In the beginning of my studies, I thought of Santería as a cult, which is the way many researchers see it. But this is a view I no longer share. A cult often uses a central figure or leader as either an object of worship or to provide spiritual guidance. In Santería there are no leaders who are viewed as central to the religion or as objects of worship. The santeros and santeras, who are the priests and priestesses, are seen only as the mouthpieces of the orishas, or saints, and as the instructors in the mysteries of Santería. Those santeros who become imbued with a sense of their own importance are said to be *endiosados*—that is, self-deified—and are harshly criticized by other santeros.

Like most established religions, Santería worships a central creative force, known as Oloddumare, who corresponds to the concept of God. The orishas were created by Oloddumare to manifest his will and express his essence in nature. They are also the guides and protectors of mankind. The orishas are not really gods, but the children and servants of Oloddumare. In this sense,

Santería is a monotheistic religion, rather than a polytheistic one. The orishas are not worshiped as gods but as "guardian angels."

One of the central beliefs of Santería is that every individual's life is overseen by one of the orishas. It does not matter whether the person believes or not in the orishas. He or she has that divine protection and guidance all of his or her life. This orisha is known as that person's guardian angel or, alternatively, as his or her father or mother, depending on whether the orisha is male or female.

When an individual chooses Santería as his religion, one of the first things he does is to ascertain who is his personal orisha. This is done through one of the divination systems used in the religion. From the moment he learns the name of his orisha, the practitioner of Santería petitions that particular deity constantly and assiduously for help and guidance in his life. He considers himself the child of that orisha, and if he ever decides to become a santero, he can only be initiated into the mysteries of that particular orisha.

When the Yoruba slaves identified their orishas with the saints of the Catholic faith, the saints became invested with the same supernatural powers of the African deities. They were invoked by the Yoruba priests to undertake cures, cast spells, and do the same type of magic usually ascribed to the orishas. Each orisha-saint was credited with certain specific attributes and was believed to control some aspects of human life. All natural phenomena and the common occurrences of everyday living were under the direct influence of the deities.

No one really knows when a culture starts to leave its imprint on another—or how. Throughout the centuries, the Spanish settlers and their descendants became increasingly interested in the ritualistic magic of the Yoruba. The initial interest may have been kindled by a slave being able to cure an illness that an accredited physician was unable to conquer—or maybe by the accuracy of his predictions and spell-casting. Whatever the reason, the white man began to attend the primitive rites of the African slaves and occasionally to take part in them.

As the magical rituals of the Yoruba became more popular, the Spaniards, slowly overcoming the natural reticence of the African priests, managed to learn most of the intricate legends and rites of the cult, until they were allowed to participate in the initiation ceremonies. As soon as the initiate reached adepthood, he re-named the Yoruba practices and called them Santería. He himself became known as a santero. He preserved the African names of the orishas and used them in conjunction with the names of the Catholic saints with which they had become identified. Most important, he continued to observe all the various rituals, espe-cially the divination systems and the major initiation ceremony, which he renamed *asiento,* a Spanish word that means "seat." The choice of this word may be explained by the fact that the saints are believed to take possession of their initiates and liter-ally "mount" them. The santero is known commonly as the "horse" of the saints. During the initiation, the "seat" of the saints—that is, the mind of the initiate, (*iyawó*)—is conditioned for future work. The asiento is also known as *hacer el santo,* which means literally "to make the saint."

The modern santero practices very nearly the same type of primitive magic as the old Yoruba priests did but with marked Catholic overtones. Most of the Yoruba words that he uses in his rituals have been so heavily influenced by the Spanish language that a native Yoruba often has difficulties in recognizing them as part of the Yoruba lexicon. There have been other changes. In Nigeria, for example, each city-kingdom worships its own orisha, and the king or *oba* of each city often claims direct descendancy from that orisha. During the slave trade, the inhabitants of differ-ent city-kingdoms were gathered together and brought to the New World. The various orishas worshiped in those city-kingdoms also came together, and that is why Santería pays homage to many deities instead of one, as is done in Nigeria. There were cases when an entire city-kingdom was captured and its inhabi-tants brought to the Americas as slaves. In such cases, the orisha who was worshiped by that city no longer exists in Nigeria. A typical example is that of Ochosi, the divine hunter, syncretized in Santería as San Isidro Labrador. Ochosi is very popular in Santería and is a member of the powerful triad known as the Warriors, composed of him, Elegguá, and Oggún. But Ochosi is no longer worshiped in Nigeria because all the inhabitants of the city he ruled were brought to the New World.

In the traditional Yoruba religion, the various orishas come in contact with each other. Sometimes they love each other, sometimes they battle each other, but their contacts always take place on a supernal level. Human beings never interact with or petition more than one orisha.

In Santería, the santeros and their followers interact with and petition all of the orishas, not just the one in whose mysteries they are initiated. They also take an active part in the relationships between the orishas. For instance, those orishas who are antagonistic toward one another, like Yemayá and Oyá or Changó and Oggún, are carefully kept apart in the ceremonies and are never "fed" together. In other words, the santeros participate in the feud between these orishas, observing and respecting it, but never attempting to alter it. Likewise, a santero can never initiate the child of an orisha who is the lover or mate of his own orisha. For example, a son of Changó should never initiate a son or daughter of Oshún because Oshún and Changó are lovers. Since the santero is considered to be the spiritual father of the initiate, such an initiation would be considered an incestuous act.

To the santero the orishas are not remote divinities, ensconced in their heavenly niches, far removed from worldly matters. On the contrary, they are vibrant, living entities who take an active part in his everyday life. One does not pray to an orisha on bent knees. One confronts him or her face to face, either as a force of nature—in the wind, in the fire, in the sea—or, better yet, when the orisha has taken possession of one of his or her children. For at this time, it is not only possible to talk to an orisha; the orisha can also answer back. There is something very moving and strangely comforting in speaking face to face with an orisha. It reminds us that somehow God is near, that He cares, that we are not alone. It is this strong interaction with the orishas that makes Santería such a powerful and dynamic religion and explains its growing popularity.

In Cuba, the ancient traditions were transmitted orally by the old priests to their descendants and followers in special meeting places called *cabildos*. During the course of these meetings the santeros established the laws and practices of their religion, and made them known to the new initiates. Still another method of transmitting the legends and practices was by means of handwritten notebooks called *libretas*. Although the cabildos no longer exist (there are rumors that some still survive in Cuba in secret), the custom of keeping a written record of the spells and rites of Santería is still observed. Every santero has a libreta where his *padrino*, or godfather, has written down the most important practices of the religion, as well as all the acts he must either avoid or undertake during his lifetime. The libreta also includes predictions of events that will take place in the initiate's future, with painstaking directions as to how he can avoid calamities and save himself from harm. This notebook is handed over to the santero exactly one year and seven days from the day he "made the saint."

Santería is based largely on a progressive system of initiations by means of which the neophyte gains not only the protection of the orishas, but also increasing knowledge of the various practices and beliefs of the religion. The first two of these initiations are the Necklaces (*collares* or *elekes*) and the Warriors. The Necklaces are five strands of beads in the colors of the five major orishas. They are given as protection against all forms of evil. The Warriors are the orishas Elegguá, Oggún, and Ochosi, and they are said to fight all the human battles faced by the initiate and to give him help and guidance in all his endeavors. When a person has received these two initiations, he is said to have acquired half of the major initiation known as the asiento. Such a person is believed to be *prendido en el santo,* that is, he is now expected to make the saint. According to the santeros, not every person is called to make the saint. In fact, there are some individuals for whom it would be spiritually dangerous to undertake this initiation. But there are others who are specially chosen by the orishas to be priests and priestesses. If they ignore this call, the orishas may punish their disobedience by visiting them with all sorts of calamities, even death.

Central to the religion are the various divination systems by means of which the santeros and babalawos ascertain the will of the orishas. The babalawo is the high priest of Santería, the one to whom the santero turns in especially difficult cases. The babalawo and the santero have different divination systems. The santero uses a set of sixteen cowrie shells to conduct his consultations with his clients. These cowrie shells are known in Spanish as *los caracoles* and in the Yoruba as the *Erindinlogún* (Diloggún in Santería). By means of the Diloggún the santero can speak with the orishas and in this manner determine the best solutions for his client's problems. With the Diloggún he can also find out who is the ruling orisha of an individual.

The Babalawo uses two forms of divination. The most common one is known as the *opelé* (pronounced *okuelé*), and is a long chain with eight equidistant medallions made of coconut rinds. The other is used only during initiations and to determine who is the ruling orisha of an individual. It is called the Table of Ifá (*opón-Ifá* in Yoruba) and is composed of a wooden tray upon which the babalawo sprinkles a secret powder known as *yefá*. On this powder the babalawo draws a series of vertical lines that he then interprets according to a series of versicles known as *oddu*. Both the santero and the babalawo share the most common of the divination systems of Santería. This is known as *darle coco al santo*. It employs four pieces of coconut that are cast on the floor to determine the wishes of a particular orisha. The coconut is not used in consultations but only to determine whether the orishas are pleased or displeased with a particular offer and how such an offer is to be disposed of.

In Santería the coconut is known as *obi,* which is the name given by the Yoruba to the kola nut. Since the kola nut is not as easily available in the Americas as in Nigeria, the original Yoruba slaves substituted the coconut for it. The kola nut breaks naturally into four parts, which are cast on the ground and then interpreted according to which side falls uppermost. Since the coconut does not break apart in this manner, the Yoruba cut four pieces out of the rind and used them as a substitute for the obi oracle.

The basic difference between the Yoruba priest and the santero is that the latter practices his magic in the asphalt jungles of the big cities instead of the African wilderness. In many ways, Santería is jungle magic adapted to city living. Its ritual practices are based on sympathetic magic. That is, they are natural magic based on what the Scottish anthropologist Sir James George Frazer called the laws of similarity and contact.

In 1890, Frazer published his monumental work, *The Golden Bough,* which had a great impact on twentieth-century anthropology. In this work Frazer showed definite parallels between the rites and beliefs of primitive cultures and those of Christianity. His definition of sympathetic magic and its laws is extremely illuminating in understanding the magical practices of Santería.

According to Frazer, the law of similarity may be expressed by the magical principle that "likes produces like." On the other hand, the law of contact says that "things which have been in contact with each other continue to affect each other long after the physical contact has been broken." When the type of magic used hinges on the law of similarity, it is known as *homeopathic magic.* In this system, the magician believes he can create virtually any kind of natural phenomenon by acting it out beforehand, often by using natural objects that are in sympathetic alliance with the purpose of the ceremony. The most familiar example of this type of magic is that of a wax doll that has been molded in the image of the person to be affected. The magician believes that whatever happens to the doll will also happen to the intended victim. Another example of homeopathic magic, fairly common in Latin American witchcraft, makes use of a small stone that may be found in a park or an ordinary garden. The stone is picked up and named after the person one desires to influence. It is then brought into one's house and thrown on the floor by the door. It is then kicked lightly throughout the house until it rolls under one's bed. As the stone rolls, one should stress that it is not a stone that is being kicked, but the person one wishes to dominate. There are many variations of this spell, and a coconut, an orange, or another object may be substituted for the stone. The intention, however, is always the same: to abase, humiliate, and in general dominate the person represented by the object used. From these two simple examples it is easy to understand the basic principles behind imitative or homeopathic magic.

Contagious magic assumes that things that have been in contact with each other are always in contact. It is thus possible to exert influence on a person if one can only procure something that has been in contact with that person. It may be a piece of clothing, some hair, or nail parings. These materials can be used to bewitch their previous owner in a very real and effective way. For example, hair strands from the victim can be knotted together with hair from the person casting the spell in the form of a bracelet. This bracelet is then worn on the right wrist for nine days, and all the while the wearer wills the victim to come to the magician and bend to his or her desires. Nail parings can be used in perfumes, and used clothing can be craftily employed in making rag dolls that represent the victim.

All forms of sympathetic magic assume that things act on each other at a distance through an unidentified and unexplainable attraction, the initial contact being sparked by the will of the magician. This belief in the sympathetic influence exerted on each other by objects or individuals separated by a distance is of tremendous importance in Santería, and indeed in any form of natural magic.

The English magician Aleister Crowley defined magic as the

ability to effect changes in consciousness in accordance with the will of the magician. This definition agrees in principle with the magical practices of Santería. But it is not enough to have a strong will to bring about the reaction desired. One must also have faith—the burning conviction that the magic will work. Whether this faith transcends human consciousness and stems from nonhuman entities or whether it is rooted in an unshakable self-assurance is immaterial. What matters is its influence and the sometimes incredible phenomena it can create. In Santería this faith is firmly placed in the mighty powers of the saints or orishas. The supernatural powers of the saints, in close alliance with the sympathetic magic of the santeros, and their strong determination to succeed, bring about the changes in consciousness described by Crowley. Naturally the saints do not grant their favors without a suitable offering. This may range from a nine-day candle or a dish of honey to a basket of fruit or an animal sacrifice. The orishas usually "mark the ebbó" themselves; that is, they determine the type of offering necessary to accomplish what is desired. The offering itself is not given to the orishas as a kind of bribe to attain one's wishes, for the orishas are not interested in material things. Whatever is offered to an orisha is transformed by that deity into pure energy—ashé—which is then used by him or her to carry out the needs of the supplicant. Any type of magic requiring the help of a saint must employ materials that are attributes of that particular orisha. For example, any love magic enlisting the aid of Oshún would be worked with seashells, honey, mirrors, pumpkins, or other attributes of the orisha.

According to one of the best santeros I have ever known, the late Fernando Sierra, Santería is basically four things: water, herbs, seashells (cowries), and stones. Without these, there can be no Santería. Stones (*ota* in Yoruba and *otanes* in the santero's language) are of vital importance because the spiritual essence of the orishas is gathered in the groups of ritual stones that are believed to represent them. These sacred stones are kept inside fancy tureens in the colors of each orisha. Each time the orisha is "fed," the food offering is placed on a dish that is then balanced on top of the open tureen. If an animal offering is given to the orisha, the blood of the ritual sacrifice is poured directly on the stones. After a suitable time, the stones and the tureen are rinsed and the cover is then replaced. Under no circumstances can an *aleyo* (an uninitiated person) see what is inside the tureen, nor can these sacred contents be photographed. The photographs herein, some of which reveal the actual contents of the tureens, are both rare and extraordinary in that this is the first time the stones and other ritualistic objects of Santería have been photographed and published in a book. The photographs were part of field work undertaken by Dr. Charles Wetli, Deputy Chief Medical Examiner of Dade County, Florida, who is deeply interested in the subject of Santería and who kindly made them available to me for the present work.

The seashells (cowries) constitute the second vital part of Santería. Their importance is obvious, as they are the mouthpieces of the orishas in the divination system known as the Diloggún. Each orisha possesses his or her own set of twenty-one cowrie shells, which is kept with the otanes inside the tureen. If a santero wishes to speak with a specific orisha, he must reach inside the tureen, remove the shells, and then proceed to use them in the Diloggún. Of the twenty-one shells, only sixteen are used in the interpretation of the oracle. During important occasions, such as the determination of someone's saint or when a person's life is in danger, the santero spreads a traditional straw mat on the floor and reads the shells on the mat instead of his working table. If he wishes to speak to his own orisha, he must ask another santero to read his orisha's shells, as he cannot read the shells of his own saint.

Water, the third essential constituent of Santería, is used by the santero during all the rituals. Water is asperged on the floor before the reading of the Diloggún, before the interpretation of the coconut and during each and every ceremony. Water is used basically to "refresh" the saints. *Omi tutu* (fresh water) is truly the elixir of the saints.

Herbs are the fourth of Santería's important elements: plants, roots, leaves, and flowers (*ewe*). Every santero is a competent herbalist who can cure practically every disease with an herbal brew or cast a tremendous spell with a few leaves. Every plant is "owned" by one or more of the orishas and can be used for cures or for magic. Lustral, or purifying, baths using combinations of plants are often recommended by the santeros to their clients for the removal of negative influences and evil spirits. Sometimes the plants are gathered together in bunches and used in rubbing rituals for the same purposes. These cleansing ceremonies are known as *despojos*. Among the most popular plants are spearmint, sage, rue, vervain, elm leaves, marjoram, and rosemary. Artemisia is used in teas against appendicitis and also in purifying baths. *Anamú (Petiveria alliacea)* is used as an abortive and also to cause trouble and dissension. Some santeros, like Fernando, are so leery of *anamú* that they will not even touch it. Another extremely popular plant in Santería is *escoba amarga (Partenium hysterophorus)*, which is used in cleansing baths and to drive away the *abikús*. An abikú is a mischievous spirit who is believed to reincarnate in a human child, who then often dies in early childhood. Whenever a child is very sickly and cries constantly, his body is said to be inhabited by an abikú, particularly if the family has suffered the death of another child. Some old santeros believe that the best way to drive away the abikú is to rub the ailing child's body with escoba amarga or to thrash it lightly with the plant, especially on Wednesdays. Plants such as *rompezaragüey (Eupatorium odoratum)*, *salvadera (Hura crepitans)*, *espanta muerto* and *quita maldición* (Latin denominations unknown) are of great importance to the santeros in the removal of curses, evil spirits and general bad luck. But undoubtedly the most important use of plants in Santería is in the preparation of the *omiero*.

The omiero is the sacred liquid used by the santero during

initiations. It is prepared in large receptacles where a certain number of the plants sacred to each orisha are crushed in fresh water. The crushing of the leaves, all of which must be fresh, is known as *ripiar*. Only initiated santeros and santeras can crush the herbs. During the asiento, only the santeros who have been initiated in the mysteries of an orisha can crush his or her plants. After the ritual crushing of the leaves, the resulting liquid, tinted green with the plants' chlorophyll, is gathered together and mixed with other sacred ingredients, among which are rainwater, holy water, and some of the blood of the sacrificial animals. The omiero is used for many ritual purposes. During the investment of the Necklaces and during the ceremony of the asiento, the initiate drinks of the omiero by the glassful. So wonderful are the properties of this liquid that the santeros often drink it as a cure for many illnesses, especially stomach complaints.

As we have seen, Santería is largely natural magic. But, more than that, it is a system that seeks to find the divine in the most common, ordinary things. It is childlike and often naïve, but it is this simple and total faith that makes it so powerful. There are no sophisticated tenets in Santería. Its wisdom is the wisdom of the earth. All that Santería wants to do is to embrace nature, but in so doing it embraces the soul of all things.

3.

The Orishas///////////////////////////
Gods of Santería

To the santeros as well as to the Yoruba, God is known as Oloddumare. The origin of this name is difficult to trace, but its connotation is that of One whose essence transcends our ability to comprehend it. Oloddumare is immanent, omnipotent, and omniscient. He is the All, and greater than the All. Oloddumare is not an orisha because He was never created. He has always existed.

There are other names associated with Oloddumare. As Olorun, He is the owner of *orun* (the heavens), as well as the deity whose abode is in heaven. According to the Yoruba scholar J. Omosade Awolalu, the Yoruba use Olorun Oloddumare as a composite name for the Creator, but never Oloddumare Olorun. The double name means the Supreme Being whose abode is in heaven and who is almighty and dependable. To the santeros, Oloddumare is God as the Almighty and Olorun is God as the Creator on the material world. *Orun* in Santería is identified with both heaven and the sun. There is a special ceremony known as *ñangale* or *ñangare*, which is a mystical greeting to the sun, usually conducted very early in the morning. The babalawos never forget to greet the sun each morning with extended arms. The greeting is usually accompanied with a petition.

Another name used by the Yoruba to define God is *Eledáa*. This name means "Creator" and implies a being who is the source of all things. In Santería, Eledáa is the spark of God that lives in each human being. It is often associated with one's guardian angel, and many santeros associate it with an individual's ruling orisha.

The Yoruba may use the names Oloddumare, Olorun, and Eledáa interchangeably, but each name denotes a different aspect of God. The name Ori, which is also used by the Yoruba in connection with the Supreme Deity, is far more complex. Ori is the physical head, as well as the driving force that guides it. It derives from Oloddumare, but it is not identical with Him. Ori is not the soul, which can be more easily equated with Eledáa; rather it is awareness, consciousness, pure being. To the Yoruba, a lucky person or one who is unusually wise is *olorí-iré*, one who has a good ori (*iré* means good luck). On the other hand, someone who is not very clever, or who is unlucky, is *olori-buruku*, one who has a bad ori (*buruku* means "bad" or "evil"). The santeros give a similar definition to Ori but do not associate it as closely with Oloddumare.

In Santería, there is another name given to the Deity, which is not used by the Yoruba. This name is Olofi or Olofin, and is the most common name used to refer to God. The origin of Olofi, like that of Oloddumare, is obscure. The santeros make a distinction between Oloddumare and Olofi. Oloddumare is a transcendent being, who is the essence of all there is and more. Olofi is the creation itself, rather than the Creator. He is Oloddumare manifested through Olorun, the true Creator. Oloddumare, Olorun, and Olofi are different aspects of the same supernal being. Oloddumare is divine essence, the creative will; Olorun is the creative act; and Olofi is the creation. Eledáa is God's spirit manifested in man. Ori is the driving force, the awareness of that spirit.

The best way to define the concept of Olofi in Santería is as man's personal god, a manifested force that is in charge of creation, being creation itself. The santeros refer to Oloddumare rather vaguely and obliquely. They recognize Him as the central, ruling force of the universe but do not deal with Him directly. Their work is conducted with Olofi through the powers of the orishas. Olofi is syncretized as Jesus Christ.

According to one of the legends—*patakís*—of Santería, Olofi created the orishas by gathering together a number of flat, smooth stones (otanes), and projecting some of his ashé into them. From these otanes, filled with Olofi's ashé (divine power, energy), the orishas were born. Among the first orishas created in this manner by Olofi were Orúnmila, Oriṣa-nlá (also known as Obatalá), Olokun, and Eshu (known also as Elegguá in Santería). All of these orishas except Olokun lived in heaven in the company of Olofi. Olokun lived on earth, which was at this time a marshy waste.

When Olofi decided to create the solid ground, he delegated this work to the archdivinity Obatalá, a symbol of pure intellect and purity. To aid Obatalá in this task, he assigned to him the orisha Orúnmila, the personification of wisdom, who could divine the future by means of sixteen palm nuts (*ikin*).

Orúnmila consulted his oracle and told Obatalá that in order to accomplish his task he needed some loose earth in a snail shell; a hen; a cat; a palm nut; and a long gold chain. Through the gold chain Obatalá descended to the marshy ground beneath the sky. Holding on to the chain with one hand, he used the other to spill some of the earth inside the snail shell onto the wet terrain. He immediately let go of the hen, which started to dig into the spilled earth, dispersing it in all directions. Wherever the earth touched the water, it became solid land. Soon there was a great expanse of dry ground over the water, and Obatalá let go of the chain and fell down on the new earth.

The new ground created by Obatalá with Orúnmila's help became known as the holy city of Ile-Ife, which is, to this day, sacred to Obatalá. The palm nut he brought with him was planted immediately and soon became a tall, shady palm tree.

The cat was thoughtfully provided by Orúnmila to be Obatalá's companion until the city of Ile-Ife would become populated with other life.

Soon after Obatalá's descent from the sky, other orishas became curious about the new land, and one after another came down to visit Obatalá. Many of them returned to the sky, but enough remained in Ile-Ife to give the city the beginning of the population it needed.

Some time after the creation of Ile-Ife, Olofi called Obatalá to heaven to instruct him in the creation of mankind. He told Obatalá to mold figures—both male and female—out of clay and lay them on the ground to dry. Later on, Olofi would come down and breathe some of his life force into them. Obatalá followed Olofi's instructions carefully, but after working for some time with the figures, he became thirsty and decided to drink some palm wine to quench his thirst. Very soon his hands became clumsy through the effects of the liquor, and the figures he then produced were twisted and malformed. He set these figures out to dry next to the well-formed ones. He then called out to Olofi and put the breath of life into the clay figures. Olofi, who trusted Obatalá implicitly, did not examine the figures but gave them life immediately. They instantly became living beings, full of human feelings and emotions. That is why there are deformed people in the world. When Obatalá's intoxication wore off, he felt very unhappy at what he had done and swore that from that moment on, he would never touch liquor again. He also became the patron of those who are deformed or abnormal in some way. This pataki is also the basis of the Yoruba belief that Obatalá shapes the newborn in their mothers' wombs.

Among the orishas who came down to earth were Aganyú, Orisha-Oko, Osain, and Babalú-Ayé (Ṣonponno [Shanpanna] to the Yoruba). At first they did not receive any special powers from Olofi. But with time, Olofi decided to divide his powers among them. He gave Aganyú the power to melt stones with his breath, thus creating the volcano. He gave the Orisha-Oko the secret of the harvests, thus creating the four seasons and all growing things. To Osain he gave the secrets of the herbs and plants, thus creating the woods. And to Babalú-Ayé he gave the power to cause and cure illnesses, especially smallpox. Olofi had many other powers, but he kept most of them because he knew that in time other orishas would come into being.

ELEGGUÁ

In Nigeria this orisha is known as Eṣu (pronounced Eshu). He is one of the most important deities and almost every household or village reveres him, regardless of the orisha it worships traditionally. He must be propitiated before any other divinity because he is the one who is said to carry the offerings to the other orishas, and he will do not so unless he is honored first. According to Awolalu, without Eṣu the dynamics of ritual would not exist: "If he did not receive the necessary elements needed to fulfill his constructive function, he would retaliate by blocking the way of goodness and opening up the ways that are inimical and destructive to human beings. Hence he is both feared and revered." Because of this orisha's ambivalent nature, in some traditions, such as the Brazilian Candomblé, where he is known as Exu, he is associated with the devil. But the Yorubas do not see Eṣu as an evil entity. Neither do they acknowledge the concept of radically opposing forces, such as good and evil. Eṣu is one of the "functionaries" of Oloddumare, and he is simply out to try to test the human heart. His chief function is to carry messages between human beings and the other orishas and to report human actions to Oloddumare.

In Santería, Eṣu is known as Eleggua, Elegbara, and Eshu. As Eleggua, he is the essence of potentiality; as Elegbara, he is the wielder of power; and as Eshu, he is the eternal wanderer, moving with the swiftness of Mercury from place to place, and appearing where he is least expected. In reality, Elegguá is beyond good and evil. He is justice personified, and punishes or rewards with perfect equanimity. In many ways Elegguá is a symbol of destiny and of perfect balance in nature. Whereas he can be propitiated to help his followers in their human endeavors, he can create havoc in a person's life if that individual behaves improperly. Elegguá's vision surpasses that of the other orishas. Only he knows past, present, and future without recourse to divination systems. He knows the ills that affect mankind, and he knows the cures. He is always justified in what he does. Although his actions may be difficult to understand at times, Elegguá never acts irrationally. It is simply that he knows things that nobody else knows, and always acts according to his own invariably perfect judgment.

In Santería, Elegguá is a trickster who stands in corners and at crossroads and guards the home against dangers. Some santeros keep Elegguá's image in their courtyards in a small house built especially for him, but most keep him inside the house, near the front door, so that he can keep away evil.

Elegguá's punishments are usually mischievous in nature, not unlike the pranks that a naughty child may play. But in extreme cases, when the orisha wants to show his displeasure with a wrongdoer, he will deal with the culprit with a heavy hand. That person may find himself the victim of a theft or an accident, or he may even wind up in jail, all distinctive punishments of Elegguá.

Elegguá's rewards are equally distinctive, usually accompanied by a special sign of the orisha, such as his colors (red and black) or his number (three or any multiple of three, especially twenty-one).

Elegguá is said to have twenty-one paths, and in each one he has a different set of characteristics. Each of these names is preceded by the name Eshu. There is an Eshu Alabwanna, an Eshu Laroye, an Eshu Bi, an Eshu Ayé, an Eshu Afra, an Eshu Barakeño, and so on. Eshu Alabwanna lives in the woods, Eshu Laroye hides behind doors, Eshu Ayé works with Olokun, an aspect of Yemayá, and Eshu Barakeño, the youngest of the

Elegguás, creates confusion wherever he goes. In some of his aspects, Elegguá is very old, as with Eshu Elufe and Eshu Anagüi, but for the most part Elegguá is conceived of as a youthful deity with a dynamic and jovial personality. When a person receives Elegguá, he is told the name of the aspect of the orisha that "walks" with him, so that he may invoke the orisha by his special name and develop a closer relationship with him.

Most of the orishas also have many paths—aspects—also known by the santeros as *avatares,* a Sanskrit word obviously borrowed from Santería's spiritualist roots, which in turn are largely indebted to theosophy. Only some of the paths of the orishas will be discussed here, as an entire volume would be necessary to discuss them all in detail. In each path, the orishas are syncretized with a different Catholic saint.

In Santería, Monday is Elegguá's special day. On Mondays, santeros and those who have received Elegguá honor the orisha by making him an offering of a small dish of candies, rum, and a cigar. Some people like to give him an additional present of corn, smoked fish, and opossum (*pescado y jutía*). The orisha is also offered a white candle. Three drops of cool water are then poured on the floor in front of his image, which is carefully rubbed with palm oil—an orange grease known as *manteca de corojo* or *epó*. These ritual actions are usually accompanied by a short prayer in Yoruba.

Elegguá is received as part of the initiation known as *Los Guerreros,* that is, "the Warriors." The initiation, which can be given either by a santero or a babalawo, includes the implements and attributes of Elegguá, Ochosi and Oggún. These three orishas work together in a powerful combination that is believed to protect the recipient against all evil and help him in all worldly matters. Oggún and Ochosi are given to the initiate inside a cauldron that holds their implements. Oggún's attributes include seven implements of labor, such as a hoe, an awl, a spade, and a hammer, symbolizing Oggún's patronage of work. Ochosi, who is the divine hunter, is symbolized by a crossbow. Elegguá's symbol is usually a clay or cement head with cowrie shells to denote the eyes, the mouth, and sometimes the ears. In some instances, Elegguá is given in the form of a porous stone, a coconut, a *ñame* (a type of yam), or a large seashell. When Elegguá is given in the form of a cement head, there is always a small blade protruding from its top. This blade is a symbol of his awesome power and of his inexhaustible ashé.

There are distinct differences between the Elegguás given by the santero and those given by the babalawo. The most important difference is that the Elegguá given by the babalawo cannot be presented to the head of the initiate when he is making the saint. Only the Elegguá given by the santero can be used during this major initiation. Nevertheless, many santeros believe that the initiation of the Warriors should be given by a babalawo and that a second Elegguá should be prepared by the padrino prior to the ceremony of the asiento.

The ceremony during which a person receives Elegguá and the Warriors should not be confused with the initiation of an individual into Elegguá's mysteries during the asiento. This initiation can only be received by those people who are Elegguá's children, and is one of the most complicated in Santería. It includes a ceremony in the woods and a party for small children, as there is a very childish side to Elegguá's nature.

In Santería, Elegguá has been syncretized with several saints of the Catholic Church, one for each of his twenty-one paths. Among them are Saint Anthony of Padua, the Holy Infant of Prague, Saint Martin of Porres, and Saint Benito.

The origins of Elegguá are vague. Some santeros say that he is the child of Alabwanna—the Lonely Spirit—which is also believed to be one of his aspects. According to this tradition, as soon as he was old enough to walk, Elegguá chained his mother's hands, and took off on his own to explore the woods, where he is often found. But the most popular legend or pataki explaining his origins says that at one time Elegguá was a prince, the son of a king called Oquiboru and his queen Añaqüi. One day the young prince found a coconut that was radiating strange lights, picked it up, and brought it to the palace to show to his parents. But as soon as Elegguá lifted the coconut off the ground, it stopped emitting light and his parents refused to believe his story. Distraught at the coconut's failure to continue radiating light, Elegguá threw it behind a door and forgot about it. Shortly thereafter, the young prince died. The kingdom, which had been immensely wealthy, soon became desperately poor. People were dying of hunger, and finally the king ordered the wise men of the city to determine the cause of the problem. After much deliberation, they came to the conclusion that the reason for the tragedies facing the kingdom was the coconut that was still lying behind the door where Elegguá had thrown it. When they went to look for the coconut they found that it was covered with insects and worms. The wise men decided to replace the coconut with a stone—*otán*—that was also placed behind the door. As soon as they did this, the kingdom regained its former prosperity. The otán became a symbol of Elegguá, who was then deified. This story explains the tradition of offering coconut to Elegguá and the other saints and provides another explanation of why the orishas are identified with the otanes.

Elegguá is propitiated with candles, toys, fruits, rum, and cigars. Among the animals offered to him are black male chickens, roosters, and he-goats. Most of all, he loves palm oil—*epó*—and many santeros believe that when epó is not given to the orisha, and his image is dry, he will create all sorts of disturbances. Among his many attributes are a twisted branch in the shape of a fork, a whistle, and mousetraps.

Elegguá is the first of the orishas to be honored during the ceremonies of Santería, and the first to be "fed," a tradition easily traced to its Yoruba roots. Before santeros undertake any work, they must ask Elegguá's blessing and permission, for without his goodwill no work can prosper. Even the other orishas have to count on Elegguá before doing any of their cosmic work.

According to one of the patakís, Elegguá's preeminence among the orishas is due to the fact that at one time he cured Oloddumare of a grave illness. In gratitude for Elegguá's help, the Almighty gave him the keys to all doors and ordered that he be honored over the other orishas. In still another pataki, all the orishas decided to come to Oloddumare to ask Him to choose the most powerful among them. Each orisha came to the presence of the Deity carrying a rich sacrificial offering on his or her head. The only exception was Elegguá, who carried no offering on his head but boasted instead a bright red parrot feather upon his forehead. (The legend says he did this following the advice of Orúnmila.) Based on the symbolism of the feather, which represents the full power of the cosmic energy known as ashé, Oloddumare chose Elegguá as the most powerful of the orishas and granted him the ability to make things happen, making him the largest repository of ashé. The parrot feather, known as *ekodide,* is an important part of the ceremony of the asiento, and all initiates must wear it upon their foreheads as a remembrance that they must never carry anything on their heads, as well as a symbol of ashé.

As an archetype, Elegguá can be identified as opportunity, chance, and the unexpected. He is the grim reminder that we reap what we sow. Elegguá comes from the region of Ketu in Nigeria, where he is still specially worshiped.

ORÚNMILA

According to the Yoruba tradition, when Oloddumare commissioned Obatalá to create the earth, he asked Orúnmila to accompany him to give him the necessary guidance. After the world came into being, Orúnmila divided his time equally between heaven and earth, returning to Ile-Ife whenever his help was needed. For this reason he became known as Gbaye-Gborun, a name that means "one who lives both in heaven and earth." After the slave trade, the name became corrupted into Iboru-Iboya. A third name—Ibochiche—was added from unknown sources. The combination, Iboru-Iboya-Ibochiche, became the common salutation that is given to the babalawo or high priest of Santería, whose patron is Orúnmila.

Among the Yoruba, Orúnmila is known as Ibikeji Edumare, which means "next in rank to Oloddumare." Because Orúnmila was present when man was created, he knows the ultimate destiny of each individual and therefore can give guidance as to how one can improve his fate. He also knows what is pleasant and unpleasant to the other orishas, and can help mankind in their propitiation as well as in communication with them. This he does through the oracle known as opon-Ifá, or Table of Ifá.

According to the Yorubas, the one who taught Orúnmila the art of divination was Eṣu (Elegguá). The patakí that tells the story says that at one time Orúnmila was living on earth, barely surviving on the offerings of human beings. Eṣu offered to teach Orúnmila the techniques of divination if he promised to share with Eṣu a portion of every offering he received. Orúnmila agreed. Eṣu then told him to procure sixteen palm nuts. These palm nuts—known as *ikin*—have a series of holes or "eyes" on their hard rinds. The more holes a nut has, the more powerful and valuable it is believed to be.

Orúnmila went to the orisha Orungán (not commonly worshiped in Santería), who owned the palm tree, and begged him for sixteen nuts. Orungán complied with Orúnmila's wishes and gave him the nuts, which Orúnmila immediately brought to Eṣu. In no time, Eṣu revealed to Orúnmila the secrets of the palm nuts and how to divine with them. That is why the babalawos say that Eṣu (Elegguá in Santería) is Orúnmila's best friend and also why only the babalawo, as a priest of Orúnmila, should give the initiation of Elegguá and the Warriors.

Among the Yoruba, Orúnmila's emblems are sixteen palm nuts, plain or engraved pieces of elephant tusks, cowrie shells, the divining tray (opon-Ifá), and several conical bells known as *Irofa*. In Nigeria the babalawo (the word means "father of mysteries") shaves his head and carries a fly whisk and an amulet made of palm fiber.

In Santería, Orúnmila is most commonly known as Orúnla, although the babalawos also call him Ifá, a custom bitterly criticized by Yoruba scholars, who oppose the identification of Orúnmila with the divination system.

Orúnla is syncretized with Saint Francis of Assisi, and his colors are green and yellow. According to one of the patakís, Orúnla tricked Death (Ikú) into sparing the life of anyone who wears Orúnla's *idé*—a bracelet made with green and yellow beads. Babalawos usually give the idé and Orunla's necklace—also made of green and yellow beads—when they confer upon someone the initiation of Eleggúa and the Warriors.

Anther pataki says that Orúnla exchanged the gift of the dance, a proficiency he had received from Olofi, for the Table of Ifá, which originally belonged to Changó. Since Changó loves to dance, he was happy to make the exchange.

According to Santería tradition, only a man can become a babalawo, as Orúnla refuses to share his secrets with any woman. (This has been recently challenged, as will be related in chapter 7.) The reason for this is explained by a pataki, as we will see later on.

Unlike the other orishas, Orúnla does not take possession of his priests, the babalawos. He manifests himself only in an intellectual manner, never physically. The initiation of the babalawo—one of the costliest in Santería—requires a formidable memory on the part of the initiate, who is required to learn an immense quantity of legends and secret teachings. The legends are classified according to the 256 *oddus* or signs (*letras*) of Ifá, which are the combinations formed by the divination procedure of Orúnla. Together they form a kind of oral encyclopedia of the traditional knowledge of the Yoruba.

Orúnla's day is celebrated on October 4, the day of Saint Francis in the Catholic Church. On that day the babalawo's "godchildren," the ones who have received initiations from him, come to his house to pay their respects to Orúnla. They must bring with them two coconuts, a ñame, two white candles, and a *derecho* or offering of $1.05 or whatever they wish to give.

Although the Yoruba have not syncretized the orishas with Catholic saints, they also celebrate their festivals once a year, which naturally do not coincide with the dates observed in the New World. For example, Changó's festival is celebrated by the Yoruba in July, while the santeros observe his "birthday" in December. The Yoruba have a traditional four-day week in which each day is sacred to one of the major orishas. The first day, Ojo Awo, is dedicated to Orúnmila; the second day, Ojo Ógún, is dedicated to Oggún; the third day, Ojo Jakuta, is sacred to Changó; and the fourth, Ojo Óbatalá, is dedicated to Obatalá.

Orúnla is consulted in Santería on important matters, particularly to determine an individual's patron saint. At least five babalawos are required to "bring down" Orúnla and ask him through the Table of Ifá which of the orishas claims an individual's head. This usually takes place during the initiation known as the *Cofá de Orúnla* (for women) and the *Mano de Orúnla* (for men).

Like all the orishas, Orúnla has many legends. He is a close friend of Elegguá and at one time he had a feud with Osain, the patron of herbs. The dispute literally cost Osain an arm and a leg. Since that day, Osain hops about the woods holding a crutch with his one arm. The babalawos give a talisman of Osain that is said to attract great wealth and prosperity.

One of the most important offices of the babalawo is the *matanza* or ritual slaying of the sacrificial animals during the asiento. There are some santeros who resent the authority of the babalawo and seldom consult him, but most practitioners of Santería agree that the babalawo, as Orúnla's mouthpiece, is of great importance to the religion and should be an integral part of every initiation.

OBATALÁ

Obatalá is known as the King of the White Cloth, as he is always dressed in impeccable white clothes. He is a symbol of peace and purity. He is also the father of mankind and the messenger of Olofi. As we have seen, in Nigeria he is also known as Órishanlá. This name is pronounced Orichanlá or Ochanlá in Santería.

Santería recognizes twenty-four paths or avatares for Obatalá. Among them are Ochanlá, Ochacriñán and Ochalufón. Ocha is another name given by the santeros to an orisha and to Santería in general. *Asentado en ocha* is a common title given by Cuban santeros to those who have made the saint. *La Ocha* is simply Santería. In reality, *ocha* is a shorter version of the *orisha*. The *ch* sound is substituted for *sh* because there is no *sh* sound in Spanish. The same is true of Changó, whose real name is Ṣangó (pronounced Shangó) in Yoruba.

In some of Obatalá's aspects, the orisha is female. The most common example is Ochanlá, who is said to be the oldest of the Obatalás. This idiosyncrasy of the orisha may be traced to an ancient Yoruba tradition according to which Obatalá (Órishanlá) and the orisha Oddudúa are androgynous deities who are two in one, male and female. They are represented by a white-washed calabash; the lid or upper half is Obatalá (male), and the calabash itself—the bottom half—is Oddudúa (female). They symbolize heaven and earth. This tradition is disputed by some Yoruba, especially those who come from the city of Ile-Ife. They argue that Oddudúa is a male orisha who battled Obatalá ferociously on several occasions.

Obatalá is believed to control the mind and all thought. He is the owner of all heads, all bone structures, and all white substances. The animals sacred to him are pigeons, especially doves, and snails. Among his offerings are coconut, cotton, cocoa butter, cornstarch (*eko tutu*), *cascarilla* (powdered eggshell), and bitter kola (*orogbo*). Because he owns all heads, he is the only orisha who can be received by any person, even if he or she has another ruling orisha. Very often, when there is doubt as to which orisha is the initiate's "guardian angel," the person is initiated into the mysteries of Obatalá. That is why Obatalá is the most common orisha that is "made" in Santería.

Obatalá is generally identified with Our Lady of Mercy, although in his other aspects he is syncretized with other saints. Obbamoro, one of the oldest, is identified with Jesus Christ. Obatalá Ochacriñán, who is said to be so old that he trembles constantly, is identified with Saint Joseph. There are many other paths with unclear or controversial syncretisms, such as Ochalufón and Alláguna, who is considered to be the youngest and a fierce warrior who always fights on horseback. Among the female aspects of Obatalá are Yemmu, Oremu, Aggüeme, and Ochanlá.

The santeros often say that all of Obatalá's attributes emanate from a combination of the orisha's male and female aspects, but that it is important to remember that Obatalá is one entity. He is the owner of the world, *cabeza grande,* the first orisha, and for that reason, his tureen or *sopera* is placed above those of all the other orishas in the *canastillero* or cabinet where they are kept.

Obatalá is said to live in the mountaintops—*oke*—and many of the offerings given to him are brought there. The santeros recommend that all the offerings to Obatalá be covered with cotton, as the orisha will not accept any offer that is contaminated in any way.

One of Obatalá's emblems is a horse's tail with a handle studded with cowrie shells, known as *iruke.* During the time of war and personal conflicts, the santeros place small white flags around their houses so that Obatalá may bring peace.

Obatalá's sacred numbers are eight, sixteen, and twenty-four. His feast is celebrated on September 24, the day of Our Lady of Mercy in the Catholic Church.

ODDUDÚA

Oddudúa is one of the most controversial of all the deities in the Yoruba pantheon. According to one tradition, the orisha is both a central divinity and a deified ancestor. The Yoruba of Ile-Ife insist that it was Oddudúa and not Obatalá who created the earth and mankind and the city of Ife. They claim that when Obatalá became drunk with palm wine, Oddudúa took over his creative work and completed what Obatalá had barely started. But another pataki says that Oddudúa arrived in Ile-Ife long after the city had been created and peopled, conquered the original inhabitants, and settled there. In this legend, Oddudúa is not an orisha but a powerful warrior. To complicate things further, there is still another pataki that identifies Oddudúa as the wife of Obatalá and the chief female deity.

In Santería there are no controversies surrounding Obatalá and Oddudúa. To the santeros, Obatalá was the creator of earth and of mankind. Oddudúa is seen as one of the oldest aspects of Obatalá, and his wife is known as Odduaremu. Some of the elders make a distinction between Oddudúa, as a male, and Oddúa, as a female. But it is clear that Oddudúa and Oddúa are in all probability the same deity, male and female aspects of the androgynous Obatalá. Odduaremu is probably a conjunction between Oddúa and Yemmu, also a female aspect of Obatalá. Some santeros say that Oddúa is a fearful warrior, who fights on horseback and wears an *obe* (machete) on the side.

Oddúa's necklace is made of sixteen white beads and eight red ones. Some santeros identify her with Saint Anne and others with Saint Manuel.

CHANGÓ

Among the Yoruba, as mentioned earlier, Changó's name is Ṣangó (pronounced Shangó). Changó is the legendary fourth *oba* (king) of the city of Oyo in Nigeria. According to tradition, his reign lasted seven violent years. One of the patakís says that Changó was fascinated with magic and had great magical powers. One day he inadvertently caused a thunderstorm that destroyed his palace, killing many of his wives and children. Full of sorrow and remorse, he abdicated his throne and hanged himself. His enemies rejoiced at his disgrace and heaped scorn upon his name. Soon afterward a series of thunderstorms devastated large parts of the city of Oyo, and his former followers immediately proclaimed that the storms were caused by Changó's anger against his enemies. Many sacrifices were made in his honor, and his followers cried, *"Oba ko so!"* ("The king did not hang!") From this point on, Changó was proclaimed an orisha and his worship was instituted. In New Oyo, the central shrine in Changó's honor is in the palace of the Alafin or king, who claims direct descendancy from Changó. Alafin, Alafia, and Alafina are all titles given to Changó in Santería.

In ancient times, all the king's messengers, or *ilari*, were initiated Changó priests, or were accompanied by Changó priests when they traveled to the coast. Anyone who wanted to become a Changó priest had to travel to Oyo to be specially initiated by the *Mogba*, who were the Changó priests at the royal shrine. In this manner, the spread of the kingdom of Oyo was accompanied by the worship of the deified king.

All of Changó's legends, and the central theme of his cult, is power, be it procreative, authoritative, destructive, medicinal, or moral. This power is visualized or centralized in Changó's staff—*oshé Changó*—which generally depicts a woman with a double-edged ax (*edun ara*) balanced upon her head. This ax is a symbol of Changó's thunderbolt, which is also his power. It is double-edged because power can either create or destroy. In Santería, the *oshé Changó* is a large, double-edged ax made of wood and painted red and white. Sometimes the ax is adorned with cowrie shells.

Among the Yoruba, women worship Changó by kneeling down

and lifting their breasts with their hands in supplication. Traditionally, it is also the women who sing the praise songs—*oriki*—in Changó's honor. The orisha's "horses" are known as *elegún Changó* and wear their hair braided on one side in the style of women or don beaded veils. This custom is also observed by the Alafin of Oyo, who also wears a beaded veil when he is in full regalia. Santería does not observe this tradition, but Candomblé does. These traditions are based on Changó's legendary love for women and on his great vanity; he is said to be extremely beautiful.

As in Santería, the shrines of Changó in Oyo preserve the orisha's power in his thunderstones (*piedras de rayo* in Santería), which are collected by his priests when lightning falls. The thunderstones are kept inside a calabash (a wooden *batea* or bowl in Santería), which sits upon a wooden mortar or *odo Changó* (known as *pilón* in Santería). On the orisha's festival, the mortar is washed in water containing the crushed leaves of several plants sacred to Changó, the juice of a snail, and palm oil (*epó*). Then a rooster is sacrificed and its blood poured upon the thunderstones. Later on, the blood of a ram, which is Changó's sacred animal, is also poured on the stones. During the sacrificial offering, the priest touches the mortar and asks Eṣu (Elegguá), who is the bearer of the sacrifices, to carry the sacrifice to Changó. These practices have survived, with very few changes, in Santería.

The deification of Changó and his identification with thunder and lightning may be traced to a Yoruba solar deity known as Jakuta (the stone thrower), who was a guardian of morality and goodness. Whenever people did evil in the eyes of Oloddumare, Jakuta would hurl down stones of fire. Undoubtedly a syncretism took place between Changó, the deified king, and Jakuta, and now they are both worshiped as one. This theory is based on the fact that the Yoruba worship Changó on the day sacred to Jakuta. Thunder and lightning is greeted among the Yoruba with cries of *"Kabiesi!"* ("Hail, Your Majesty!"), which is the same greeting given to all Yoruba kings. This tradition stems from the belief that whenever there is thunder, Changó has come down for a visit. In Santería, Changó is also greeted with cries of *"Kabiesi!"* or *"Kabiesile!"*

In Nigeria, the principal means of divination by the priests of Changó is the *orogbo,* or bitter kola nut. The orogbo is cut into two halves, lengthwise, and cast upon the ground for interpretation. The sixteen cowrie shells (*Erindinlogún*) are used as an alternate divination system.

At the annual Changó festival in Oyo, the ritual *batáa* drums play in honor of the orisha, and his devotees dance to their rhythms until one or more of them become possessed by him. The elegún Changó wear a red cotton coat, to which are fastened many cowrie shells and miniature symbols of Changó. Most of the elegún are male, but in some places, such as the Egba section of Nigeria, the elegún are female.

The elegún usually carry the oshé Changó and imitate with violent gestures the devastating powers of the deity of thunder and lightning. Sometimes they sit on the tip of an iron spear, carry a pot of live coals upon their heads, pierce their tongues and cheeks with knives or iron rods, swallow fire, or catch bullets with their teeth. These violent actions depict Changó's power, which can be unleashed not only against others, but also against the self. The lesson is that power, when ill used, can go beyond rational and moral limits, destroying the good instead of the evil. This is the meaning of the edun ara, the double-edged ax that symbolizes Changó's power, and that his devotee carries suspended over his head all of his life. To be able to control that power is power itself.

Santería does not carry the worship of Changó to the violent extremes of the Yoruba, but the santeros are careful never to light fire or smoke cigars or cigarettes when one of Changó's initiates is possessed by the orisha. I have seen a santero possessed by Changó take a lit cigar from the hand of an unwary devotee and eat and swallow the glowing end with much relish, without burning his mouth.

The santeros recognize the power of the orisha and the dangers one incurs in offending him or one of his children. Changó will kill and destroy for his children and often gives them power over fire. Thunderstorms are generally good omens for Changó's children (his initiates or devotees), who often gather strength and energy during these times.

According to Santería tradition, Changó's colors are red and white and his numbers are four and six. He is said to be the son of the orisha Aganyú—symbolized by the volcano—and Yemmu—one of the female aspects of Obatalá. Yemayá, the ocean deity, is said to have raised him.

Changó is said to have twelve *caminos* (paths or aspects). Some of the names of these caminos are Changó Ogodo, Alufina Crueco, Alafia, Larde, Yoda, Obakoso, Ochongo, and Ogomi Oni. Although his major syncretism is with Saint Barbara, in some of his other aspects he has been syncretized with Saint Patrick, Saint Expeditus, Saint Mark, Saint Daniel, and Saint George.

In Yoruba tradition, Changó has three wives: the orishas Oba, Oshún, and Oyá, all of them river deities. His servant is the rainbow, Ochumare. His sacred tree is known as *ayan*, which is said to be the tree where he hanged himself.

In Santería, Changó is depicted as an incorrigible woman-chaser and a lover of food and dance. He is a great friend of Elegguá, with whom he has had many adventures. The santeros say that Changó's "legal" wife is Oba, but that he abandoned her when she cut off her ears and served them to him in a soup (*cararu*). This ill-fated action was prompted by Oshún's malicious advice. Madly in love with Changó, Oshún wanted the orisha of fire and thunder for herself and told Oba that if she performed this unusual deed she would never lose Changó. Oshún knew, of course, that the opposite would prove true. Oshún is forever vying for Changó's favors with the tempestuous Oyá, the wind deity and keeper of the cemetery, whom santeros say is Changó's favorite concubine.

In Santería, Changó's sacred tree is the palm tree and his favorite food is *amalá,* a dish prepared with okra and cornmeal. His symbols are his mortar, in which he is said to prepare his thunderbolts and magic spells, his castle, and his double-edged ax. The şeeree (shere) Changó, or gourd rattle, used by the Yoruba to call the orisha, has been exchanged in Santería for a maraca painted red and white. Whenever a santero wants to attract Changó's attention, he shakes this maraca, which is always kept with the sacred implements of the deity of thunder. Saint Barbara, the most popular of Changó's syncretisms, was probably identified with Changó because she has a cup in one hand (Changó's mortar), a sword (his ax) in the other, and a castle at her feet. Her mantle is red and her tunic white, and she is traditionally associated with thunder and lightning. Changó's feast day in Santería is celebrated on December 4, Saint Barbara's day in the Catholic Church.

Changó's control over fire makes him the patron of firemen. He is invoked for works of dominion, passion, and many other endeavors. He is the most popular of the orishas, and his followers are counted in the millions. At the mention of Changó's name, his followers lift themselves off their seats and mutter a hasty *"Kabiesile"* in honor of the orisha. Changó is propitiated with apples, bananas, roosters, and, on special occasions, with a ram, his sacred animal.

OGGÚN

Oggún is the ironworker and patron of all metals. He is also the overseer of surgeons, policemen, and soldiers. Oggún is one of the orishas received during the initiation of the Warriors. The other two are Elegguá and Ochosi, Oggún's constant companions. Oggún provides employment and protection against criminals, but he is also said to be responsible for all car and railroad accidents where blood is shed. Violent crimes where metal weapons are used also fall within Oggún's province. One of Elegguá's aspects, Eshu Oggüanilebbe, is Oggún's faithful friend. He is said to cause car accidents and derailments so that Oggún may feed on the blood thus spilled.

As a symbol of war, Oggún is much feared and respected in Santería. Some santeros say that he is the father of tragedy, a symbol of all the pain and horror caused by war and violence. The orisha is worshiped and propitiated so that he will protect his followers from the very things he represents.

In Santería, Oggún symbolizes the sacrificial knife and the act of slaying. And although Elegguá is the first orisha to be honored in all the ceremonies of the religion, Oggún is the first one who "eats." This is because Oggún is the only orisha who works without rest, twenty-four hours a day, and since Oggún represents the sacrificial knife, when the santero slays the animal offering, the blood first touches the knife's blade before falling on the stones of the orisha being fed. For that reason, upon slaying the animal the santero says, *"Oggún choro choro,"* meaning, "Oggún devours this offering." Therefore, as the knife, Oggún "eats" first. Even in cases where the santero kills the sacrificial animal with his hand, Oggún is said to be responsible for the actual slaying, as he is the force and violence associated with bloodletting and all violent acts (*alagbara*).

Oggún's violent nature has resulted in a certain disrepute for the iron worker, and some people are terrified by him. But Oggún is not an evil entity; he is simply the archetype of the violent occurrences that result from man's weaknesses and lack of control. Santeros believe that when a tragic event takes place, it is the result of the excess of evil in our society. Evil concentrates in our midst and then manifests itself in physical violence. Oggún is the orisha in charge of these violent manifestations for which we, through our lack of respect for divine and human laws, are directly responsible.

Oggún lives in the woods and is said to represent the woods themselves. According to legend, at one time he became so disgusted with the ways of mankind that he abandoned his forge and refused to come out of the woods. Without his metalwork, the advancement of society came to a standstill and Olofi was very concerned. One after another, all of the orishas went into the woods to try to talk Oggún into returning to the world of man, but to no avail. Finally it was Oshún's turn to talk to Oggún. She walked into the woods wearing five yellow handkerchiefs around her waist and carrying a gourd of honey dangling from her side. Unlike the other orishas, she did not try to talk to the ironworker. Instead, she waited until she saw him hiding behind some bushes and then began to sing and dance. As she danced, she tied the five handkerchiefs together, forming a silken rope. Oggún was so fascinated by her unearthly beauty that he slowly crept out from behind his bush and stood out in the open. Oshún still paid no attention to him, but kept right on dancing. Seeing that she did not try to approach him, Oggún came a little closer. Quick as lightning, Oshún dipped her fingers into the gourd and spread some of her honey on Oggún's lips. The ironworker licked the honey and was dumbfounded. Never had he tasted anything so sweet and delicious. He came even closer to Oshún and again she spread some honey on his lips. While he savored the honey, Oshún tied the handkerchiefs around his waist and gently pulled him toward her. Oggún was unresisting, so enthralled was he by her beauty, her dancing, and her honey (a covert symbol of her sexuality). In this fashion, dancing and feeding Oggún honey, Oshún was able to pull him out of the woods and bring him back to society. Ever since, Oggún has been madly in love with Oshún, and although he was at one time married to Oshún's sister, Yemayá, it is Oshún whom he pines for.

For the love of Oshún, Changó and Oggún have had some ferocious battles. But Oshún has eyes only for Changó. It is understandable that Oshún, who represents love, should favor Changó, who symbolizes passion and desire, over Oggún, who symbolizes war.

Oggún has seven known paths in Santería, according to some santeros. Among them are Oggún Sarabanda and Baumba. Oggún's colors are black and green, although originally his color was red, the color of blood. But according to one of the legends, Oggún lost that color to Changó. Oggún usually wears a skirt made of *mariwó* (palm fronds) and a large straw hat; a machete hangs from his waist. Dogs are sacred to him, among both the Yoruba and the santeros. His necklace is made of black and green beads. In Santería, Oggún is syncretized with Saint Peter. Two of the numbers most closely associated with him are seven and three. Among his seven implements are a rake, a spade, an awl, a pick, and a hoe. Sometimes santeros add three large railroad nails (*clavos de linea*) to the cauldron he shares with Ochosi.

Among the Yoruba, Oggún (Ogún) is worshiped sometimes as one of the first orishas and sometimes as a deified ancestor. According to the Orisha Tradition, when the deities first came down to inhabit the earth, they were unable to pass through a dense thicket that obstructed their pathway. Oggún brought out the sharp machete that is his trademark and cut through the unyielding shrubbery as if it were cotton. As a result of this simple deed, the other orishas hailed him as great, and ever since then he has been the deity invoked to clear the way or to remove heavy obstacles. According to another legend, he is the son of Oddudúa, whom he helped to win many battles and defeat many enemies, including Obatalá. (This Yoruba legend is disputed by Santería, which sees Oggún as Obatalá's son.) In recognition of his many prowesses, Oddudúa gave him the city of Iré to rule and set him there as the oba. Oggún thus became the first king of Iré (Ogún-Oniré). The present king of this city, the Oliré or Iré, claims direct descent from Oggún. There are many Yoruba today whose family name is Oggún.

To the Yoruba, Oggún is the patron of iron and of war, and is said to protect hunters, blacksmiths, barbers, butchers, and all those who work with iron and steel. He is also said to be the absolute symbol of justice, and he is often called upon to witness a pact between people. In Nigeria, so strong is this belief in Oggún's symbology as justice that whenever a devotee of the orisha religion appears in a court of law, he is asked to swear upon Oggún (represented by a piece of iron) instead of the Bible or the Koran. The individual will kiss the iron and swear to speak the truth. No one would dare to break this solemn oath, as Oggún is said to inflict the most terrible punishments on those who swear falsely upon his name.

Oggún shrines are usually found in the open air, at the roots of sacred trees, near a smithy, or facing a river (often the Oshún River in Nigeria, as he is said to adore Oshún). Among the offerings given to Oggún by the Yoruba are small bags of salt, palm wine, dogs, roasted yams, and tortoises.

OCHOSI

Ochosi's name is derived from the Yoruba title Osowusi, meaning "the night watchman is popular." As we have already seen, when someone receives the initiation known as the Warriors—Los Guerreros—he or she gets the powers of protection of three of the major orishas of Santería: Elegguá, Oggún, and Ochosi. Osun, symbolized by a metal rooster, guards the home and advises the initiate when danger is near and is also received with the initiation, but he is not one of the Warriors.

Ochosi is the divine hunter and is syncretized in Santería as Saint Norberto. In Brazil, he's identified with both Saint Sebastian and Saint George, and his necklace is made of blue-green beads. In Santería his colors are blue and yellow, and his numbers are three and seven. His symbol is a crossbow made of iron.

In Nigeria his cult is almost nonexistent because the region of Ketu, where the worship of Ochosi was mostly concentrated, was ravaged by the kingdom of Dahomey and its inhabitants sold as slaves and brought to the New World. Ochosi owes his importance to several factors. First, he is the patron of hunters, whom he protects and helps in locating their prey. Second, he is said to have medical and healing powers, since he is forever in the woods in the company of Osain, the god of herbs, from whom he has learned their magical and curative properties. Third, he is reputed to have power over new houses and over cities, therefore people who wish to move to new locations or wish to buy a house often invoke his help in their quest. And finally, he has judicial and administrative powers, so that people who find themselves in trouble with the police, or who are facing a trial, often ask his help in overcoming their difficulties. The santeros prepare a special powder with Ochosi's help, which they give to those of their clients who have to stand in front of a judge. The powder is to be scattered discreetly inside the courtroom and the remnants rubbed over the defendant's forehead. Invariably, people who use this powder are released from custody and win their trials.

Ochosi is an orisha of many legends. In one of these, very popular in Brazil, he was the son of Yemayá and the brother of Elegguá (called Exu in Brazil) and Oggún. Elegguá was very disobedient toward his mother, and Yemayá finally threw him out of the house. Oggún and Ochosi remained with their mother and they all lived in relative peace. Oggún worked the fields and Ochosi hunted, so there was always plenty of food in the house. But Yemayá worried about Ochosi because he had no interests other than the hunt and often took unnecessary risks. One day she went to see a babalawo, who told her that she should try to dissuade Ochosi from the hunt because he ran the risk of meeting Osain in the woods and becoming the victim of one of Osain's magical tricks. Yemayá was naturally alarmed by this prognostication and immediately told Ochosi what the babalawo had said. Ochosi did not have much use for oracles and told his mother the babalawo was an impostor and that nothing would ever stop him from pursuing his favorite pastime. Undaunted, he continued to hunt, and for a while nothing happened. Then one day he did come across Osain in the woods, and the god of herbs, who was looking for a steady companion, gave Ochosi a magical potion to drink, which brought on a state of total amnesia. Ochosi forgot not only where he lived, but also who he was. In the meantime, Oggún became worried by his brother's prolonged absence and went to look for Ochosi in the forest. After a long search, he finally found him with Osain and succeeded in helping him regain his memory. He brought Ochosi back to their home, but when Yemayá saw them, she refused to allow Ochosi to return to the house in punishment for his disobedience. Oggún was angry with his mother for her severity and decided to leave as well. So Ochosi returned to the woods to live with Osain, and Oggún went to live in the open fields. Yemayá, brokenhearted over the loss of her sons, transformed herself into a river. This legend, well known in Brazil, is not accepted by Afro-Cuban Santería, in which Yemayá is not seen as the mother of the three Warriors. On the contrary, in some of the legends of Santería, Yemayá is romantically linked to both Oggún and Ochosi.

The most poignant of Ochosi's legends tells how Olofi, who wanted an *acuaro*—a pheasant—sent Obatalá to search for the bird. Obatalá had heard of Ochosi's prowess as a hunter and went to the woods to look for him. At first he could not find him because Ochosi was very elusive, but finally he located the divine hunter resting under a giant mahogany tree. When Ochosi learned that Olofi wanted an acuaro, he told Obatalá he would immediately set out to find the bird. As soon as he had done so, he would let Obatalá know through the batáa drums.

Ochosi began a long, diligent search for the most beautiful acuaro he could find. He wanted the bird to be perfect because it was to be presented to Olofi. Finally he came upon a small grove in the woods, and there he saw a truly spectacular acuaro with glorious iridescent plumage. This, Ochosi felt, was the only acuaro worthy of being presented to the Almighty. He skillfully set his trap, and soon the magnificent specimen was in his possession. Full of joy, Ochosi built a cage outside his hut and placed the bird inside. Immediately he let Obatalá know through the drums that the acuaro had been found. But when Obatalá arrived to claim the pheasant, Ochosi found to his dismay that someone had stolen the bird. The divine hunter was enraged at the theft and promptly took an arrow from his quiver and shot it high in the air. "Let this arrow fly swiftly," he cried, "and let it embed itself in the heart of the thief who stole my pheasant."

What Ochosi did not know was that his mother had found the cage with the bird by her son's hut and, coveting it herself, had assumed he would not mind if she took it. She was nestling the beautiful creature in her arms when Ochosi's arrow, guided by the magical force of his curse, came whistling through the air and pierced her heart. With a great cry she fell dead to the ground, and the acuaro, frightened by her scream, flew swiftly away.

His mother's cry reached Ochosi's ears as soon as it was uttered, and a horrible foreboding filled his soul. He quickly rushed to her house and found her lying on the ground with his arrow embedded in her heart. Ochosi's grief was indescribable, and he swore that from that moment on he would have no further contact with another being.

In Santería, Ochosi and Oggún generally "eat" and "live" together. That is, their implements are kept together inside a small cauldron, and when one receives a sacrifice, the other usually partakes of it. But Ochosi is for the most part a solitary being who shuns others.

Ochosi's initiation is one of the most expensive and spectacular in Santería, and his iyawó usually wears a violet cassock in satin or silk, richly embroidered in colored stones, gold braid, and seashells. A violet cap with a long feather, Robin Hood–style, completes the outfit, which also includes white satin breeches, a bow and arrow, and a brace of pheasants across the back.

Like most of the other orishas, Ochosi is partial to fruit and candy offerings and a special drink made of milk, honey, and cornmeal. Animal sacrifices usually consist of male fowl, although in Brazil he is offered pigs and other animals.

AGANYÚ

Aganyú is symbolized by the volcano. Although he is one of the most powerful orishas, he is not very well known. He is said to be Changó's father through a brief dalliance with Yemmu, one of the female aspects of Obatalá. According to legend, Aganyú was in charge of rowing people back and forth across a large river. Yemmu came one day in a great hurry and asked Aganyú to ferry her across. Since she did not have any money, she offered to lie with Aganyú in payment for the trip. He accepted, and the result of this encounter was Changó. All during his growing years, Changó pestered Yemmu with questions about his father. At first Yemmu did not want to tell him who his father was, but finally she tired of the boy's insistence and revealed Aganyú's identity. Although he was still a small child, Changó left home to search for his father. But when Changó finally found him, Aganyú refused to recognize his paternity and, enraged by the boy's insistence, blasted Changó with a mouthful of fire and melted lava. The impact blew Changó all the way up to the sky, where Olofi lived. The Almighty was both touched by the youngster's plight and surprised by his immunity to fire. Aware that Yemayá was childless and longing for a son, he gave her Changó to raise as her own.

Aganyú and Changó reconciled after a while and later became very close. When someone receives Aganyú's initiation, he must undergo the initiation of Changó, for only through Changó can Aganyú be received. Similarly, when someone receives Changó, Aganyú has to be honored at a special ceremony conducted by the riverside. Aganyú's colors are red and green, and his numbers, like Changó's, are six and four. He is syncretized with Saint Christopher.

BABALÚ-AYÉ

In Nigeria, Babalú-Ayé is known as Obaluaye (King Who Owns the Earth), as Omolu (Son of the Lord), and as Sonponno, the god of smallpox and contagious diseases. He is represented as an infirm old man leaning on a large staff. In Santería he is syncretized with Saint Lazarus, and his feast is celebrated on December 17. Babalú-Ayé is said to dress in sackcloth like a beggar, with a shoulder bag (*alforja*) crisscrossed upon his chest, carrying his favorite food, toasted corn.

Santeros believe Babalú-Ayé comes from the land of Arara (Dahomey). According to legend, he was originally from Yoruba territory but had to leave when he contracted smallpox, caused by his disrepect for the elder orishas. Everyone despised and rejected him and threw water behind him as a sign of their contempt. The only orisha who expressed sympathy for Babalú-Ayé was Elegguá, who took him to Orúnla, in the land of Ife, for a consultation. Orunla told Babalú-Ayé that his condition was the result of his disobedience but that he would be venerated again as an orisha if he went to Dahomey. To achieve this, however, Babalú-Ayé had to cleanse himself with different types of grain, beans, and corn and always keep a dog by his side. Elegguá found a dog for Babalú-Ayé, which he acquired through the help of his good friends Oggún and Ochosi. Babalú-Ayé followed Orúnla's advice, cleansed himself, and, full of remorse for his past actions, went to live in Dahomey. As soon as he arrived there, Olofi sent down some rain, which washed away all of the impurities from Babalú-Ayé's body, signifying that he was forgiven for his past errors. Babalú-Ayé established his kingdom in Dahomey, where he was greatly venerated. He still remains a close friend of Elegguá and Orúnla, who alone share his secrets.

Babalú-Ayé is one of the most respected and well-loved of all the orishas in Santería. His powers are so great that he is never initiated on the head of an individual. During the tambors, or drum parties, Babalú-Ayé and Obatalá are the only orishas who can come down and take possession of any santero, even if that person has been initiated into the mysteries of another orisha.

Babalú-Ayé can either heal or bring about the most dreadful diseases, from cancer and paralysis to syphilis, leprosy, and epidemics of all kinds. His many followers also believe him to be very helpful during financial difficulties. The shoulder bag he carries is filled with corn, a symbol of material prosperity, which the orisha generously shares with his devotees. He is also said to be partial to lovers because he has great sexual powers.

Babalú-Ayé is propitiated with bread soaked in olive oil, toasted corn on the cob, bread spread with honey and *manteca de corojo* or *epó* (palm oil) and different types of grain (*minestras*). His necklace is made of white beads with blue stripes, and his number is seventeen. People with leg ailments wear a small pair of crutches in his honor, and he is said to heal them speedily. One of his favorite herbs is *cundiamor,* which is used in teas by diabetics to bring down their sugar level. Among his other herbs are *albahaca, apasote,* and *zarzaparrilla,* which are used in his name to prepare personal baths or to cleanse a house.

OSAIN

The magic of Santería is natural magic. Its power is the power of herbs and trees that are found in the steaming, tropical forests of the Antilles. In these dark, brooding woods live the spiritual entities of the Yoruba. Everything comes from the forest, from the fertile womb of the earth, say the santeros. Magic cannot be practiced without the help of the woods. The most basic rite or spell in Santería will always require a plant, an herb, a stone, a flower, a fruit, a seed, or an animal. With *ewe* (the Yoruba term for herbs, trees, fruits, and plants), the santero can cure a simple headache or a malignant tumor. He can also undo an evil spell, drive away bad luck, and neutralize the evil work of an enemy.

The woods have everything the santero needs to preserve his health and to defend himself against evil. But he must always remember to ask the woods' permission before removing a stone or a leaf from a tree. Above all, he must pay the forest for whatever he takes, with rum, tobacco, or a few copper coins. Sometimes, when the occasion demands it, a young chicken is sacrificed to the woods, usually at the foot of a large tree. In the United States, where the climate does not allow the survival of tropical plants, santeros must import the fresh herbs they need for their magical ceremonies. Most of the plants come from Puerto Rico and the Dominican Republic, although Miami is beginning to get into the market, owing to its semitropical climate.

The owner of the woods is Osain, a one-eyed, one-armed one-legged deity whose symbol is a twisted tree branch. Osain has an enormous ear through which he hears absolutely nothing, and a tiny ear through which he can hear the rustling of the grass two miles away. All the ewe is the property of Osain, and without enlisting his aid beforehand, it is not possible to do any work in Santería.

Osain was never born. He sprang from the bowels of the earth like Athena from Zeus's forehead. There are countless stories about how Osain lost the missing members of his body. In one of these stories, he was left in this sad condition during a fight with Changó, who became enraged when Osain pressed his unwelcome advances upon the orisha Oyá. Infuriated with Osain's audacity, Changó blasted him with a shaft of lightning, leaving him lame and half blind for all eternity. But some santeros disclaim this story on the basis that Osain is a very pure deity who is not interested in sexual activities and who is also a very good friend of Changó. These santeros explain the missing limbs of Osain with the following story.

At one time, Osain was constantly at war with Orúnla, the owner of the Table of Ifá. Orúnla, who is a very peaceful orisha, did not want to fight with Osain but was unable to convey his desire for peace to the recalcitrant orisha. Finally growing tired of Osain's constant animosity, Orúnla appealed to Changó to help him with his magic. Changó advised Orunla to prepare an *ebbó* (a spell) with twelve torches that had to be lit with twelve flints (*odduarás*). While Orúnla was preparing the ebbó, Osain was in the woods looking for herbs with which to harm Orúnla. But the god of divination proved to be the quicker of the two, and he managed to light the torches before Osain came out of the woods. Immediately a bolt of lightning flashed across the sky and fell on the woods, setting it on fire and trapping Osain among the flames. This was how the god of herbs and plants lost his missing limbs.

The twisted tree branch, which is Osain's special attribute, is used by the orisha to lean on as he hops about on his one remaining foot. Many santeros keep a twisted tree branch in their houses in honor of Osain and as a safety measure against danger. The branch is believed to whistle when peril is near. It is often lent to young girls who want to "ensnare" a husband. The branch is also used to invoke the aid of Elegguá, who is said to be a good friend of Osain.

Although Osain is the accepted owner of the woods and the keeper of all secrets of herbal magic, he has to share his natural treasures with the other orishas. How this came about is the subject of still another legend. Changó, who is a great magician and master of witchcraft, complained one day to his concubine Oyá that his ebbós and *bilongos* (black magic spells) were lacking in effectiveness because he needed some herbs to strengthen his spells, and Osain would not let him have any. Oyá, who is also a very powerful witch, stood up and began to fan her skirts until a great gale was created. Osain kept all his herbs in a gigantic gourd that hung from a high tree branch. The wind made the gourd sway violently until it fell to the ground, scattering all the ewe to the four cardinal points. All the orishas hastened to pick up the herbs, which they divided among themselves.

From that day on, although Osain is still considered the official deity of the woods, the other gods have been able to work with herbs as well.

Both the santeros and the babalawos prepare an "Osain," a talisman of the orisha, which is used mostly to acquire money. Naturally, the santeros and the babalawos do not prepare the talisman in the same way. The santeros prepare the talisman inside a hollow gourd, which is then hung from a high place. The babalawos place the "secrets" contained by the amulet in a hairy piece of animal skin. On the first of the month, the Osain is sprinkled with rum and a few mouthfuls of cigar smoke are blown on it. Men are supposed to keep it in the pocket where they put their money and must not ever let a woman touch the talisman. Likewise, women must not let men touch their Osains. This is usually the case with all amulets; no one but the owner should be allowed to touch them, regardless of sex. The Osain talismans are extremely popular in Santería, especially for people who run their own businesses.

YEMAYÁ

Yemayá is the goddess of the sea waters and a symbol of maternity. Her name is derived from the Yoruba title *Yeyeomo eja,* which means "The Mother Whose Children Are the Fish." Her cult comes from the city of Abeokuta. She is represented as a beautiful matron with prominent breasts. Her colors are blue and white, and her number is seven. In Santería she has been syncretized with Our Lady of Regla. (Regla is a region of Cuba.) In Nigeria she is associated with the Ogun River.

According to the legends, Yemayá has been married to several of the orishas, including Orunla and Oggún, and has had love affairs with others. She has seven paths, among which are Okutti, her most violent aspect; Awoyo, the oldest; Malewo, who lives in the lakes; and Asesu, who lives in murky water and is slow to answer prayers.

Yemayá's favorite foods are melons, guinea hens, ducks, and rams. Santeros prepare a special dish of fried pork rinds and green plantains to propitiate her. She is also said to be partial to coconut balls and sugar-cane syrup.

Olokun is one of the most powerful aspects of Yemayá. Some santeros say that Olokun symbolizes the depths of the oceans and see her as either a hermaphrodite or a siren. As Olokun, Yemayá is not initiated on a person's head; santeros say that the vastness of the seas cannot fit inside a human brain. Her initiation is still conducted, but not as part of the asiento.

Yemayá is one of the most revered and popular of the orishas in Santería. Her otanes are seashells or stones found by the seaside. Her initiation is one of the less complicated and less expensive in the religion. When Yemayá comes down at a tambor and takes possession of one of her children, she imitates the waves of the sea and circles around very fast, swaying like the sea waters.

There is a strong link between Yemayá and her sister Oshún, the goddess of river waters. Santeros say that Yemayá is the source of Oshún's riches, because the sea goddess has a soft spot in her heart for her younger sister and gives her everything she wants. In fact, according to santeros, Yemayá even raises Oshún's children, since the beautiful river goddess is too busy with her tambors and her love affairs to care for her young ones properly. It is not, santeros hasten to add, that Oshún is a bad mother. It is simply that she knows her sister loves children and can take care of them better than anyone else; thus she leaves her children in Yemayá's care with complete confidence. Oshún always comes to Yemayá, as the river comes to the sea.

One of Yemayá's greatest loves is her adopted son, Changó. According to legend, the god of thunder at one time had a love affair with Yemayá. This happened long after he left her home. When he met her again he did not recognize her and fell in love with her. In the tambors, when both Changó and Yemayá take possession of their children, they salute each other in an ambiguous way that suggests there is more between them than the simple love between mother and son. Santeros also say that it is not advisable to wear Changó's and Yemayá's necklaces alone. It is always important to wear Obatalá's necklace with the other two, so that there will be no quarrel between Yemayá and Changó. Obatalá, Changó's mother and a symbol of peace, can always avert violence between the orishas.

Yemayá is a symbol of womanhood and is often associated with the moon. Her necklace is made of seven white or crystal beads alternating with seven blue beads, but sometimes this color scheme varies according to the path the necklace represents.

OSHÚN

Oshún is the divinity of the river of the same name that crosses the region of Oshogbo in Nigeria. Her title of *Yalodde* (iyalode) is the highest honor that may be conferred upon a woman in those lands. It means "mother of nations." Oshún is the symbol of river waters, without which life in the earth would be impossible. In the same manner, she controls all that makes life worth living, such as love and marriage, children, money, and pleasure. In Santería she is syncretized with Our Lady of La Caridád del Cobre, the patron of Cuba. The main reason for the syncretization is that in Nigeria, copper (*cobre* in Spanish) was the most precious metal in ancient times. Oshún is said to have been passionately fond of copper jewelry, and part of her ashé is deposited on this metal. Now that copper is no longer a valuable metal, her tastes have changed and now she is partial to gold, which is one of her attributes.

Oshún's number in Santería is five, and her color is yellow. The reason for her color preference is traced to another legend. The story says that at one time Oshún was very poor and had only one dress. Meticulously clean and vain about her appearance, she used to wash her one dress in the river every day. She washed it so much that it eventually became yellow with age. From that day on, yellow was her ascribed color.

The entire abdominal area is sacred to Oshún, and for that reason women who wish to bear children propitiate the orisha to help them achieve their desires. But childbearing is only one of Oshún's concerns. The orisha is also responsible for all abdominal illnesses and operations.

As the Venus of the Yoruba pantheon, Oshún has had numerous love affairs. She has had romantic interludes with Oggún, Ochosi, and Orunla, but the greatest love of her life is Changó. According to one of the legends, she saw Changó for the first time in a tambor. As soon as she saw him, she fell in love with him. But since Changó was too busy dancing, eating, and playing drums to pay any attention to her, Oshún played the same trick on him that she had once played on Oggún. She reached for the honey gourd that always hangs at her side and quickly spread some of the sweet, sticky liquid on Changó's lips. Like Oggún before him, Changó reacted swiftly to the honey, and before long he was dancing with Oshún. After that, nature took its course, and soon Changó and Oshún were lovers. As a result of their relationship, Changó allowed Oshún the right to wear red beads in her yellow necklace. From that moment on, Oshún has had a necklace that alternates five amber or yellow beads with one red or coral bead in honor of Changó.

Among Oshún's attributes are mirrors, fans, canoes, coral, gold, copper, and a tortoiseshell comb. She is said to have five paths. Among them are Yeye Cari, Yeye Moru, and Yeye Miwa. She favors honey cakes, oranges, eggs, and, of course, honey (oñi), which must always be tested in her presence, for, according to one of her legends, someone once tried to offer her a dish of poisoned honey. Santeros prepare a special dish for her called ochinchín, consisting of a thick omelet made with shrimps and watercress. Pumpkins are sacred to her, and she uses them as her bank. Many of her spells call for the use of a pumpkin, especially in love matters.

OYÁ

Oyá, also called Yansa, is the orisha of the winds, the tempests and the Niger River, which is known in Nigeria as Odo-Oyá. In Santería she is said to be the owner of the cemetery. This dreary possession is explained in a legend in which Oyá was originally the owner of the seas while Yemayá owned the cemetery. Tired of her dismal empire, Yemayá decided to trick Oyá into exchanging the sea for the house of the dead. To carry out her malicious plan, she invited Oyá on an outing, making sure that during the course of their walk together, they would pass near the cemetery. As they passed by, Yemayá pointed out her extensive property to Oyá, bragging about its luxurious appointments. Of course, she was careful not to bring Oyá inside the cemetery walls. From outside, the cemetery looked big and airy, and Oyá sighed and commented enviously that she wished she had such a spacious and dry residence instead of her watery domain. Instantly, Yemayá offered to exchange her house for that of Oyá, and the former sea goddess joyfully agreed. Only after the agreement was consummated, with Olofi's approval, was Oyá able to enter the cemetery and realize the extent of Yemayá's treachery. Naturally she was enraged but found herself unable to change the situation. Her resentment toward Yemayá has never abated, and ever since, the two orishas are bitter enemies. Their animosity is so great that the santeros will not "feed" the two orishas together, as they refuse to share a meal. Initiates of Oyá cannot conduct Yemayá's initiation, and those who have been initiated in Yemayá's mysteries cannot initiate Oyá.

Oyá's color is wine or dark red, and her number is nine. Her initiates are the only ones whose hair is not cut off during the asiento.

According to an ancient tradition, Oyá was Changó's first wife. One day Changó was getting ready to go to battle, and before leaving his house he prepared the potion that lets him spout fire through his nose and mouth. Oyá was watching him from behind the door, and as soon as he left, she came out of her hiding place and drank what was left of the potion. All at once she was also spouting fire through mouth and nose. The effects of the potion were lasting, and when Changó returned home he found that Oyá could spout fire as he could. Naturally he was furious and immediately called her to account. But it was too late. From that moment, Oyá also had power over fire. In Santería, one of her identifications is Our Lady of La Candelaria. *Candelaria* is a Spanish word that means "conflagration."

Oyá has another well-known syncretization in Saint Teresa. Flowery designs are among her attributes, and her initiates and followers avoid wearing them in their clothing, since they are hers. Oyá is a warrior orisha, and she is very aggressive in her behavior. Sometimes she engages in ferocious battles with Changó, usually caused by his roving eye. Because they are both equally powerful, these wars usually come to an impasse. If Oyá wants to frighten Changó, she shows him a human skull, the one thing that the orisha fears. Changó, on the other hand, has the perfect way to get even, for Oyá is terrified of a ram's head, which is one of Changó's attributes and which he shows to her in order to control her.

Oyá's necklace is brown with white and red stripes. Her favorite animals are hens and goats.

The orishas that have been listed thus far are the most popular in Santería: Elegguá, Obatalá, Orunla, Babalú-Ayé, Osain, Oggún, Ochosi, Changó, Aganyú, Yemayá, Oshún, and Oyá. With the exception of Babalú-Ayé and Osain, they are the orishas initiated during the asientos. There are other important orishas, which we will discuss in lesser detail in the following pages, as they are not part of the major initiation.

ORISHA-OKO

Orisha-Oko is syncretized with Saint Isidro Labrador and is a symbol of the earth and of agriculture. Santeros say that after Oggún, the next orisha to eat and partake of the sacrificial animals is Orisha-Oko, because some of the sacrificial blood is sprinkled on the ground (Orisha-Oko) at the moment of the slaying.

In one legend, Yemayá, who was married to Oggún at the time, saw that the woods were dry and barren. Knowing that only Orisha-Oko knew how to revive the earth, Yemayá set out to seduce him. Orisha-Oko was pure and celibate and had never had a love relationship with a woman. Therefore it was not difficult for the experienced Yemayá to seduce him. As soon as she had Orisha-Oko eating out of her hand, Yemayá talked him into telling her the secrets of the earth and of fertility. As soon as she had them, she gave them to Oggún and abandoned Orisha-Oko.

Like Osain, Orisha-Oko is not "crowned" during the asiento, but there is a special initiation that is given in his name for emotional stability and material prosperity. Unlike Osain, Orisha-Oko has a necklace that is of pink and blue beads; there are no specific numbers ascribed to him.

According to an ancient Yoruba legend, Orisha-Oko was once the chieftain of the city of Irawo. He was ousted from the town because he became leprous. He and his wife settled far away from the place and began to earn their living by hunting and gathering crops. During these times, people did not know how to plant and sow. Orisha-Oko and his wife learned to do this by sheer accident. Among the crops they gathered were not only yams and fruit, but also many curative plants. By experimenting with the various herbs, Orisha-Oko was soon cured of his leprosy. He and his wife returned to Irawo, where the townspeople were happy to welcome them back. Generously, Orisha-Oko taught them his newly acquired knowledge of the land. When he and his wife died, the townspeople did not forget them and continuously spoke about them to their descendants. Eventually Orisha-Oko became deified as the patron of Yoruba farmers.

Among the Yoruba, both men and women are priests of Orisha-Oko. As a symbol of priesthood they wear a red and a white vertical line upon their foreheads. But only the priestesses become possessed by the orisha. They are known as Agegún Orişa-Oko. This deity is represented by an iron staff ornamented with cowrie shells. The honeybees are said to be his servants. Among his favorite foods are goats, melon stew, corn wine (*oti şeketé*), a special fish called *eja abori,* and powdered yams. Farmers present all their products to the orisha before bringing them to the marketplace.

Like other primitive societies, the Yoruba always offer thanksgiving sacrifices at the beginning of each harvest. During these festivals, there is a great deal of eating and drinking, following a time-honored tradition that has been observed by many cultures from the Mayans and the Egyptians to the Romans and the Greeks. The sacred names may vary among different peoples, but the belief is the same: Honor the deities of nature, and they will reward you with their protection and all the bounties of the earth.

YEWÁ

Yewá (Yeguá) is an orisha of many mysteries. She is said to symbolize death (Ikú) or the transition of death, and for that reason she is very much feared and respected in Santería.

The santeros say that Yewá "feeds" on the dead. What is left after this dark "meal" is consumed by Oyá, who only comes inside the cemetery to partake of the dead. Most of the time, Oyá hovers outside the cemetery's gates. Strangely, the santeros say that Oyá's true "home" is the marketplace.

According to Santería tradition, Yewá is a virgin orisha who is very modest and severe. Her priestesses are often women past their prime and always celibate, as Yewá will not tolerate any sexual dalliances among her "daughters." She is syncretized as Saint Claire. In Cuba she is still initiated during the asiento. In the United States her initiation is very rare. Yewá's ascribed color is pink. When she dances her ritual dance during the santero's funeral ceremony (*itutu*), she covers her face with two *irukes*, scepters made from horses' tails.

DADÁ

According to one pataki, Dadá is Changó's half brother. When their father, the king of Oyo, died, Dadá (also known as Ajaba or Bayanmi) inherited the kingdom. He was a peaceful oba, who loved and encouraged the arts. But Changó coveted his brother's kingdom and soon started a revolt that culminated in Dadá being deposed and Changó becoming the fourth king of Oyo. After Changó's mythical death, Dadá became king once more. He was therefore crowned twice.

In Santería, Dadá is the symbol of wealth and prosperity. He is not commonly "crowned" during the asiento, but his initiation is received by those who desire or need help in their business endeavors. He is commonly syncretized with Our Lady of the Rosary.

THE IBEYI

The Ibeyi, or divine twins, are also known as the Jimaguas. They are the darlings of santeros and are believed to be the children as well as the messengers of Changó. The Ibeyi are propitiated with twin dishes of candy or fruit, and are said to be very helpful in the acquisition of material prosperity. They are identified with the saints Cosme and Damian. They are not "crowned" on the head.

OBA

The symbol of the family and the virtuous wife is Oba, the long-forsaken spouse of Changó. In Nigeria there is a river bearing her name, which meets at one point with Oshún's river waters. At the point of contact between the two rivers, the waters become violent, almost as if the two orishas were reliving their eternal feud over Changó.

Oba has no number assigned to her in Santería. Her color is pink. She cannot be directly "crowned" on the initiate's head; he or she first has to undergo Oshún's initiation in order to receive Oba. This orisha is said to "partake" of the bones of the dead and to control the bone structure of the body.

INLE

A symbol of the physician, Inle is syncretized with Saint Raphael. He is not "crowned" on the initiate's head directly, but through the initiation of Yemayá. His necklace has white beads with green streaks.

Inle carries a staff with two snakes intertwined. The snakes are a symbol of Abbata, Inle's female companion. This symbol is reminiscent of the caduceus, which traditionally represents the healing arts.

OSUN

Osun is received in Santería at the same time as the Warriors. His secrets are contained in a small silvery metal cup, topped by a tiny rooster and surrounded by small bells. Osun must be placed on top of a closet or wherever he will not be in danger of falling off or turning over. If, despite all precautions, Osun falls over, there is imminent danger surrounding its owner: he must immediately contact the person who gave him the Warriors to discover what is wrong and take the proper measures to avoid trouble. In Santería, Osun represents one's personal guardian angel.

According to Santería, each year is ruled by a different orisha or orishas. Every year—around January 1—a conclave of babalawos meets in Cuba to determine what is called *la letra del año*, that is, the names of the orisha(s) who rule the new year, and the predictions of Orúnla—the orisha of divination—for the next twelve months. This event also takes places in Nigeria and in some cities in the United States, but most santeros and babalawos pay heed only to the *letra* that comes from Cuba. Whenever a year is prognosticated as "difficult," the santeros place white flags around their homes to invoke Obatalá's help in deflecting any forthcoming evil. Often, together with the *letra,* comes a series of suggestions as to what *ebbós* (offerings) should be given to the ruling orishas to placate their anger and enlist their help throughout the year.

There is much speculation as to how Santería is surviving in Cuba under the Castro regime. As far as I have been able to determine, the santeros in Cuba are relatively free to practice their religion. Whenever an initiation or a *bembé* (feast in honor of the saints) is planned, the santero who will be in charge of the ceremonies must ask special permission from the authorities. This permission is usually granted without any difficulties. Naturally, many of the ritualistic implements are hard to find, such as the orishas' attributes and the materials for the initiation clothes. Beads for the *elekes* (necklaces) are in great demand, and are practically nonexistent in Cuba.

An elder in Havana told this story to one of his godchildren, who lives in Miami. It seems a santero was getting ready to initiate someone in the asiento, the major ceremony of Santeria, and he desperately needed colored beads for the ceremonial necklaces. He had heard that in one of the best restaurants in the capital, the entrance to the dining room was ornamented with colorful beaded curtains, so he presented himself at the place with two of his godchildren, each armed with a tiny razor blade held hidden between two fingers. As soon as they were in front of the curtain, the elder santero feigned a fainting spell. He grabbed at the curtain as if he were trying to avoid falling to the ground, and the curtain immediately collapsed, at which point he and his godchildren—both seemingly trying to help him—cut the strings of the beads, which promptly scattered over the floor. In the confusion that ensued, they were able to pocket enough beads to prepare the necklaces for the asiento.

Probably the reason Fidel Castro allows the practice of Santería in Cuba has to do with its tremendous importance in the cultural, sociological, and spiritual development of the Cuban people. Santería is an intrinsic part of Cuban music, religious practices, and social structure. Our Lady of La Caridad del Cobre, the patron saint of Cuba, is syncretized with Oshún, one of the most popular orishas in the Santería pantheon. So popular is the saint, and so well known her syncretism with Oshún, that every year, on September 8, there is a high mass in her honor at St. Patrick's Cathedral in New York City. Many santeros are present during the mass, many of them wearing yellow—the orisha's color—or waving small yellow flags. More than half of those present during the mass—traditionally said in Spanish—wear Oshún's beaded necklace made of amber-colored beads.

Many santeros claim that when Castro took over the region known as El Cobre—where the shrine honoring Oshún is based—he dressed her small statue (only fifteen inches tall) in combat clothes similar to the ones he wears. Another story says that he appropriated the considerable treasures of the sanctuary of another popular orisha—Babalú-Ayé—syncretized as Saint Lazarus and immortalized by Desi Arnaz with drum and song in the TV show "I Love Lucy."

According to santeros in the United States, Castro is a firm believer in the powers of the saints and a practitioner of both Santería and Palo (the practices of Palo will be discussed in detail in a later chapter). He is reputed to be the "son" of the mighty Elegguá, one of the most formidable warriors among the orishas.

Traditionally, all the presidents of Cuba have been initiated santeros. The fabled Gerardo Machado y Morales (president from 1925 to 1933) was an initiate of Changó and was reputed to carry a red handkerchief tied around his waist, well hidden from view, to ensure Changó's protection. Cuba's former dictator, Fulgencio Batista, was also a son of Changó and a renowned santero. The santeros believe that the battle for power between Castro and Batista was fought on two levels: the physical world and the world of the orishas. Castro won the war because of the many ebbós made on his behalf, but he could not destroy Batista, who escaped from Cuba with millions of dollars and retired to Spain, where he died of natural causes many years later.

A well-known story about this magical battle tells how the defeated Batista waited alone in the Presidential Palace after Castro's victorious entrance into Havana. He held a loaded pistol close to his head, ready to pull the trigger the moment Castro's soldiers burst into his office. But the soldiers stopped in front of the locked door and did not break it down. Inside the office, Batista could hear them breathing agitatedly, as if paralyzed by unknown forces. Their hesitation saved his life. A few minutes later his own soldiers burst into the room through one of the windows and rushed him to a waiting helicopter, which flew him out of Havana and to safety.

The orishas are essentially a source of comfort and help in times of need to the practitioners of Santería, but they are also severe upholders of strictly moral behavior. Any deviation from the "straight and narrow" is swiftly and severely punished by the saints. Santeros who are zealous about their religion are usually highly respectable individuals. They must be, if they want the protection of the orishas. Those who break the strict rules set by the deities pay dearly for their actions.

The orishas punish, and sometimes kill, by means of the same things they are said to control. Any sudden or inexplicable death may be suspected to be the work of an enraged orisha. Changó, who controls fire and lightning, often punishes an erring child by burning his most precious possession (or the offender himself, if the offense is too grave). He will also take revenge on anyone who offends or hurts one of his children by destroying his property in a raging inferno. Oshún and Yemayá usually afflict the abdominal area and the reproductive system. Babalú-Ayé brings on plagues, infectious diseases, and leg injuries. Obatalá, on the other hand, causes blindness, head injuries, brain tumors, and palsy; he is often depicted as an infirm old man with shaking limbs. An example of this kind of punishment by Obatalá was pointed out to me recently.

One of this supreme orisha's children—a santero for more than twenty years—has been offending Obatalá steadily for a long time. He was carrying on all kinds of sexual excesses, using drugs, harboring drug dealers in his house, and charging exorbitant prices for his services as a santero. As a common, ordinary person, what he was doing was morally indefensible. As an elder in Santería, his conduct was unforgivable. According to other santeros, Obatalá was very patient and gave his son plenty of warning. For years the kind and long-suffering orisha withstood his son's behavior and told him, through the coconut and the seashells, that the day of reckoning was near. He was asked to repent and to do ebbó at Obatalá's feet (to ask forgiveness and give Obatalá the prescribed sacrifices). But the santero was adamant. One day he woke up with his head terribly swollen. (Obatalá rules the head.) Those who saw him say he looked monstrous, disfigured. He was rushed to the hospital, where doctors conducted a barrage of tests. Finally the diagnosis was made. The santero had contracted AIDS in its most virulent form. He lived in terrible agony for three months. Toward the end of his life, he turned from a strong, handsome, virile man into a trembling, shriveled old man, his hair becoming totally gray almost overnight. He looked, according to the santeros who knew him, like the very image of his father, Obatalá Ochacriñán. Strangely enough, after his death and when all the ritual cleansing ceremonies were done, he regained his lost beauty. In his coffin, dressed in Obatalá's clothes (when a santero dies he is dressed in his orisha's clothes), he looked as he had before his illness. In death, Obatalá had given him both peace and forgiveness.

Stories like the preceding one are abundant in Santería. The orishas will not tolerate disobedience or any type of antisocial behavior on the part of their initiates or followers. They are generous with their protection and bounties, but terribly severe with their punishments. The santero is, after all, a priest, the representative of a divine force; as such, he is expected to be an example, a role model for the community, and a servant of the orishas and of mankind. When he fails in this lofty task, he becomes the recipient of the orishas' divine wrath, often expressed in the most terrifying ways.

In all of my books on Santería, I have expressed my belief that, in reality, the orishas are certain points of contact that the Yoruba—and later on, the santeros—were able to establish within the collective unconscious. Each orisha seems to be what Carl Gustav Jung called an archetype, which he defined as an autonomous complex within the human personality. Because each archetype is independent from the rest of the personality and exhibits intensely individualistic characteristics, it often behaves as if it were a separate, supernatural entity.

According to Jung, each archetype controls a different aspect of the personality and/or a different human endeavor—a definition that could just as well describe the functions of the orishas. For the perfect balance of the personality (and therefore for mental health), it is vital that each archetype be well developed and also well assimilated by the individual. When one archetype is allowed to overpower the rest of the personality (as in the case of Nietzsche's Zarathustra), the result can be a mental disturbance or dissociation of the personality—a leading symptom of psychosis.

Each orisha can be seen as an archetype or autonomous complex that has been perfectly developed and balanced into the personality of the santero. Because each individual has specific characteristics that set him apart from others, he is said to be under the protection of the orisha who shares those same characteristics.

When an orisha descends to take possession of a santero or a believer, that particular archetype's overpowering psychic energies are temporarily unleashed within the conscious personality. The possessed person then displays strange powers and unusual precognitive abilities, the natural attributes of an archetype formed of pure energy, directed into a specific channel.

The anthropomorphism of the orishas by the santeros is not mere delusion, but a useful tool by means of which the various elements of the personality become easier to understand and come to terms with.

Elegguá, for example, is the most important orisha because he is the "moderator" of social behavior. Elegguá brings all the other orisha archetypes together into a harmonious whole, and helps complete what Jung calls the individuation process, bringing about a personality that is perfectly integrated, mature, and well balanced. When Elegguá's proddings are heeded, the psychic energies of the individual are directed along constructive channels and he is in control of his destiny.

ATTRIBUTES OF MAJOR ORISHAS

Orisha	Principal Colors	Function or Power	Force in Nature	Weapon or Symbol	Numbers
Elegguá	red and black	messages; controls fate, the unexpected; justice personified	corners, cross-roads	clay or cement head with eyes and mouth made of cowrie shells	3
Orúnmila	green and yellow	divination		Table of Ifá	16
Obatalá	white	peace, purity	father-hood, all white substances	*iruke* (horsetail with a beaded handle)	8
Changó	red and white	power, passion, control of enemies	fire, thunder and lightning	double-edged ax, mortar castle	4, 6
Oggún	green and black	employ-ment, war, hospitals	iron, steel	metal weapons and knives	7
Ochosi	violet	hunting, jails	all game animals	crossbow	7
Aganyú	red and green	control of enemies	volcanoes	ax	9
Babalú-Ayé	sackcloth	causes and cures illness	smallpox, leg ailments	crutches	17
Yemayá	blue and white	maternity, woman-hood	the ocean	seashells, canoes, corals	7
Oshún	white and yellow	love, marriage, gold	rivers	fans, mirrors, boats	5
Oyá	maroon and white	protection against death	wind, burial grounds, thunder-bolt	horsetail	9

MAJOR ORISHA-CATHOLIC SYNCRETISMS

Orisha	Saint	Feast Day	Propitiation
Elegguá	Anthony	June 13	male chickens, *epó*, rum, cigars, coconuts, toasted corn, smoked fish and opossum, toys, candy
Orúnmila	Francis of Assisi	October 4	kola nuts, yams, black hens
Obatalá	Our Lady of Mercy	September 24	cotton, *cascarilla*, yams, white doves, coconuts
Changó	Barbara	December 4	apples, bananas, red rooster, rams
Oggún	Peter	June 29	roosters, pigeons, green plantains, rum, cigars
Ochosi	Norbert	June 6	roosters, pigeons
Aganyú	Christopher	November 16	roosters, plantains, unsalted crackers with palm oil
Babalú-Ayé	Lazarus	December 17	toasted corn, pigeons, all types of beans
Yemayá	Our Lady of Regla	September 7	watermelon, sugar cane syrup, she-goats, ducks, hens
Oshún	Our Lady of Charity	September 8	honey, pumpkins, white wine, rum cakes, jewelry, hens
Oyá	Our Lady of La Candelaria	February 2	eggplant, hens, she-goats

THE ORISHAS IN THE NEW WORLD

Yoruba	Santería	Candomblé (Macumba)
Eṣu	Eshu, Elegguá	Exu
Oriṣa-nla	Obatalá	Orixalá, Oxalá, Obatalá
Orúnmila	Orúnmila, Orunla	Orunmilá
Ṣangó	Changó	Xangô
Ogún	Oggún	Ogum
—	Ochosi	Oxossi
Ṣonponno	Babalú-Ayé	Obaluaê, Omolu, Xanpanã
Yemojá	Yemayá	Iemanjá
Osún	Oshún	Oxum
Oyá	Oyá, Yansa	Oiá-Iansã

4.

Eggun ///
Spirits of the Dead

The santeros always say that the dead—*eggun*—"go before the saints." This means that the dead must be honored before the orishas. The eggun are the spirits of one's ancestors. In Santería they include not only the spirits of relatives, but also the dead *santeros mayores*—that is, the elders who belonged to the same "house" or "family" in which one has been initiated. Every santero belongs to the "house" of his *padrino* or *madrina,* the individual who initiated him into the mysteries of the orishas. Those people who have also been initiated by the santero's padrino are his *abure,* that is, his brothers and sisters "in the saint." In this manner, an elder in Santería has "children" (his godchildren), "grandchildren," "brothers and sisters," "grandparents," and even "nephews" and "nieces." This "family" is formed of Santería initiates who share a common padrino or godfather. The members of a *casa de santo*—the house of an elder—are expected to help and protect each other, in the same way they would help and protect their real families.

Among the eggun are also included those spiritual entities that were assigned to an individual as his guides and protectors when he was born.

Every ceremony, ritual, and divination procedure starts with an invocation or an offering to the eggun. When a santero prays or invokes the blessing of the dead or of the orishas, the ritual is known as *moyubbar*. The prayers or invocations are known as *suyeres*.

Because of the great importance given to the worship of the ancestors, the santeros believe it is important to ensure that the eggun are happy and enlightened so that they may be able to grant their protection to their devotees. For this reason, every santero or practitioner of Santería keeps a special place in his home known as the *bóveda*. This is usually a small table covered with a white tablecloth upon which are placed several water goblets—often seven or nine—each of which is dedicated to one or more of the eggun. The largest of the goblets is placed in the center and is sacred to the main spiritual guide of the santero.

These central guides are usually African entities. One of the most popular is El Negrito José, who seems to protect a great many santeros and spiritualists. José may be identified in a special way by each santero. For example, a santero of my acquaintance called his guide José de Dios and identified him as an old African slave who had lived several centuries before. José is depicted as an old black man leaning on a crooked staff. There are many statues of José in the *botánicas* or religious-goods stores catering to the needs of the santeros. In some of the representations José is sitting down and in others he is standing up. As soon as they purchase the statue, the santeros dress it, sometimes in red and white, as José is said to work with Changó/Saint Barbara. They also place a knapsack crisscrossed over the statue's chest, usually sewn out of sackcloth. In this shoulder bag José carries the herbs he uses for his ebbós, and other paraphernalia required to carry on his magical work. The last emblem that the santeros place in José's hand is a crooked staff that is the symbol of his superiority. Every santero has his own crooked staff, sometimes with a carved African face as a handle; other times the staff is an ordinary tree branch tied with many colored ribbons and tiny bells. This staff is "fed" the blood of a small chicken as soon as it is acquired and is used exclusively to summon or to invoke the eggun. It is known as a *palo*.

On the bóveda the santeros place flowers, cigars, rum, a bottle of the aromatic alcohol known as Florida Water—a staple in Santería—candies, and sometimes a dish of food specially prepared for the eggun. A small cup of espresso coffee is usually a part of the offerings. Often a red rose and a crucifix are placed inside the largest of the goblets to ensure the blessings of God for the house. The santeros believe that whenever a goblet—or more than one—fills with air bubbles, it is an indication that there are spiritual entities—often of a negative nature—in the vicinity. The water therefore acts as a kind of spiritual cleansing and as a subtle "trap" for impure spirits.

Some santeros keep the bóveda for what they call their *cuadro espiritual* (their spiritual guides), but do not "feed" the eggun at the bóveda. These santeros prefer to propitiate the dead either behind a door or on the bathroom floor. That is where they place the coffee, rum, cigars, and food offerings for the eggun. They use the bóveda for meditation purposes only, or to invoke the eggun directly.

Whenever there are disturbing influences around a santero or a practitioner of the religion, the eggun may ask for a "spiritual mass." This is sometimes ascertained by means of the Diloggún or seashells, and sometimes by a telepathic "prompting" of the eggun.

A spiritual mass is an "open" séance. In most séances, the participants sit at a table, often joining hands. In the spiritual mass an altar is set at one end of the room where the séance is to take place. The altar is very much like a bóveda, with goblets of water, many flower vases, several bottles of rum, and cigars upon its surface. A large basin filled with Florida Water, tap water, and flower petals is placed on the floor facing the altar. The participants sit on several rows of chairs in front of the altar. The mediums and the santero who directs the ceremony sit on both sides of the altar. Before the ceremony begins, everyone must dip his fingers in the basin, cleanse himself with the liquid, and then knock three times on the altar. Those who wish to do so may light a cigar and start to smoke. The cigars are said to attract spiritual entities, especially those of African spirits. The officiating santero then starts to read a number of prayers from a book known as *La Colección*, a compilation of invocations to the dead by the famed French spiritualist Allan Kardec.

After a long prayer period, the spirits of the various eggun begin to make their appearance. Unlike the spirits that manifest themselves through the average séance, the African eggun walk around the room, with eyes opened, talking to those present very much as if they were living entities. Their speech is invariably guttural, often interspersed with African words. The Spanish they do speak is largely broken and of an archaic style. Their treatment of those present at the mass is that of a slave to a white person. For example, in several masses I attended where José de Dios took possession of his "horse" (the santero whom he protected) he invariably referred to me as "Niña Mineen." The term *niña*, meaning "child," was used by the slaves to address white women. José de Dios obviously had trouble pronouncing my name; that is why he called me "Niña Mineen."

The transformation suffered by a person possessed by an African eggun is often extraordinary. I have seen a santero possessed by such an eggun munch contentedly on a lit cigar, which he then *swallowed*. This was then merrily chased by an entire bottle of 151-proof Bacardi. Several hours later, when the eggun had left, the santero was as sober as if he had been drinking water all night.

Any ceremony dedicated to the eggun must be conducted after sunset. This is true not just of the spiritual masses, but also of the *toques de muerto*, the ritual drum rhythms played in the eggun's honor. During these ceremonies, the santeros recommend that those present cover their heads with white caps or handkerchiefs. The santeros always wear ritual headgear, usually African-style caps in the colors of the orishas, during all major rituals. For ceremonies conducted in the eggun's honor, white is the prescribed color. Black is frowned upon by most santeros, who believe it attracts dark spirits.

Sometimes the santeros use a black doll to represent the spirit of an African entity or eggun. These dolls are dressed in gingham, the colors of the orisha to whom the eggun was devoted when he or she was alive. The dolls are addressed with the name of the eggun and are considered to be the repositories of the eggun's powers. For that reason they are often kept on the bóveda, where they are given various food offerings and small presents. The doll is not the eggun, and it is not worshiped as such. Rather it is seen as a *dynamic representation* of the eggun, by means of which the spirit may be contacted. This custom is so prevalent in Santería that most santeros have one or more of these dolls to which they are very attached.

Some santeros are more adept at working with the eggun than others. Sometimes, during a consultation, or *registro,* a santero will become possessed by his personal eggun, who will then conduct a special ritualistic cleansing of the santero's client. During this cleansing, the eggun will stand back to back with the person to be cleansed and lock arms with that individual, who will then be lifted bodily onto the possessed santero's back. The eggun will carry the person around the room on his back for a while, praying in Yoruba. In this manner, all the negative influences surrounding an individual will be transferred to the eggun, who will then dispel them by means of his spiritual powers. At other times the eggun may simply grab the person by the waist and lift him or her high over his head, as he would a rag doll. This is another form of cleansing. I have seen a frail, elderly santera possessed by her eggun do this type of cleansing on a man at least double her weight, with no visible effort.

As mentioned earlier, every major ritual or ceremony begins with a prayer or propitiatory offer to the eggun. During the ritual cleansing of the head—*rogación de cabeza*—the coconut rinds must be read to determine what the eggun and the orishas have to say about the rite. The eggun are questioned first. At this point the santero conducting the ritual asks the person being cleansed to turn his back so that he does not see the coconut rinds as they fall on the floor. When the rinds have touched the floor and one of the divination patterns has been formed, the person is asked to turn around and see the eggun's response to the question asked. This is done because the person's fate at that moment is being decided by the dead, and it is considered dangerous to witness the decision before it is made. But when the orishas—who are symbols of eternal life—are questioned, the person can witness the fall of the coconut on the floor.

There are times when it may be necessary for a person to "feed" his spirit guide. This may necessitate the sacrifice of a rooster, particularly if the individual's life is believed to be endangered. The santero officiating in this ritual places nine bits of coconut on a white plate. Upon each bit of coconut he places a dab of palm oil (epó or manteca de corojo). On top of the palm oil he places a grain of guinea pepper (pimienta de guinea), a staple in Santería. He puts the plate on the floor and surrounds it with several crosses drawn with cascarilla (powdered egg shell). He then proceeds to invoke the eggun and sacrifices the chicken or rooster over a clay vessel. As the blood falls on the vessel, he prays to the eggun and offers the blood to God—Oloddumare—through the eggun. Later he uses his ritual palo while he chants the suyeres required during the ritual known as moyubbar.

Sometimes the blood sacrifice is given to an individual's "shadow" instead of to his eggun. This ritual, which was common among the Egyptians, has led some researchers to believe that the Yoruba have Egyptian roots. During the "feeding" of the shadow, the santero passes the ritual animal along the person's shadow before he sacrifices it. The ritual is conducted only when the orishas indicate that it is necessary to improve a person's lot.

Lesser cleansing rituals, using the eggun's benevolent powers, may be conducted by an individual without the santero's help.

These are "rubbing rituals," during which an individual rubs his body from head to foot with a small paper bag inside of which he has placed a piece of meat or a raw soup bone that has been previously smeared with palm oil and asperged with rum and cigar smoke. After the rubbing, the bag may be brought to the door of the cemetery or to the railroad tracks with nine cents. The eggun who work in these rituals are connected with Oyá, the owner of the cemetery, or with Oggún, who owns the railroad.

Among the most common complaints brought to the santero are hauntings and bewitchments. Very often, people come to the santero for a registro and find, to their intense discomfort, that there is a spirit, usually of the opposite sex, following them around. This is ascertained by the santero's reading of the seashells. Sometimes the santero finds that the spirit has been "hired" by an enemy of the consultant to harm him in every possible way. This is known as an *enviación*, or "sending." The spirit, usually the disembodied soul of a madman or a criminal, is invoked and then hired, usually with a white candle and a few copper coins.

There are also several spiritual entities that are often used in Latin magic to overcome a person, usually in love spells. The three most popular ones are the Restless Spirit (Espíritu Intranquilo), the Dominant Spirit (Espíritu Dominante), and the Lonely Spirit (Anima Sola). This last is also known in Santería as Alabbwana, who, according to one of the Yoruba myths, is the mother of Elegguá. There are special prayers to these spirits, and often artists' conceptions of them, available at botánicas.

Ancestor worship and belief in the powers of the eggun in Santería can be traced to a similar belief among the Yoruba. In Nigeria, the spirits of the ancestors are believed to take possession of the living. The ceremonies for the invocation of the dead are conducted in ancestral shrines known as *Ojubo baba, Oju eegun,* or *Oju orori.* They can also take place in sacred groves known as *Igbo igbale.* The priest in charge of the ceremony is called the *Alagbaa.* When a spirit takes possession of a person, that individual becomes known as *Egungún*. This is believed to be the materialized spirit, not just a person possessed by the dead. Because the *Egungún* is believed to have returned from *orun* (heaven), it is known as *ara orun* (a citizen of heaven).

The Egungún is dressed in special vestments made of variously colored cloths that are sewn together so that they cover the entire body, as no part of the Egungún may be seen by human eyes. This cocoonlike garment is known as the *ago*. The feet are also covered, as is the face, which is concealed by a thick veil. This is entirely different from the practices of Santería, in which the eggun are always barefoot.

Among the Yoruba, many families who worship the Egungún keep their own family agos, which are worn only by their own ancestors. Some of these agos have become blackened with many years of sacrificial blood. When the Egungún materialize, they speak with the living and pray for their needs. The people often make offerings to the Egungún, who accept them gratefully and grant their blessings in return. Women and the uninitiated in the Egungún mysteries are not allowed to come too near the spirit. Those who are permitted to do so must uncover their heads and pay their respects by prostrating themselves on the ground. So widespread is the worship of the Egungún among the Yoruba that in many parts of Nigeria the annual festival in honor of the ancestors is the principal event of the year.

In Santería the ritual worship of the ancestors is as important as among the Yoruba, although the rites have varied through the influence of the Catholic faith. There is no annual festival in honor of the eggun in Santería, but the santeros do observe November 2 as the Day of the Dead, as does the Catholic Church.

5.

The Santero ////////////////////////////
Priest of Santería

Devotees of Santería are organized into ranks. At the top of the hierarchy are those high priests or babalawos who have received the consecration of Ifá and the initiation known as Olofi, or "God's mysteries." These high initiates are known as *omokolobas*. There are very few people who hold this elevated rank.

The second rank comprises those babalawos who have been consecrated to Ifá and who have received the initiation known as the *Cuanaldo* or *Wanaldo*, during which they receive the babalawo's sacrificial knife.

In the third rank are the men (never women) who have been consecrated to Ifá during a ceremony known as coronation or asiento. They are known as *oluwos*.

The fourth rank are those men (never women) who have been consecrated to Ifá without undergoing the asiento ceremony. They are known as babalawos.

In the fifth rank are those santeros (men and women) who have received the initiation known as the *Pinaldo*, during which they receive the santero's sacrificial knife or *cuchillo*.

The sixth rank consists of those people who have received the initiation known as *karioriocha* or asiento. They are the santeros and santeras.

The seventh rank includes those people who have received the *Abo-Facá* (*mano de Orúnla*), which is only given to men, or the *Ico-Fa* (*Cofá de Orúnla*), which is given only to women. These initiations can be conferred only by the babalawo.

In the eighth rank are those people who have received the initiation known as *Los Guerreros,* comprising Elegguá, Ochosi, and Oggún. This is a very basic and important initiation because without it an individual may not receive the higher initiations.

In the ninth rank are those people who have received the initiation known as the Necklaces (*los collares* or *elekes*).

The tenth rank consists of those people who have received an Osain amulet.

In the eleventh rank are those people who believe in Santería, but who do not have any of the initiations or amulets.

The twelfth and last category comprises those people who do not believe in the orishas or in Santería.

People in the seventh to tenth categories are known as *aleyos.* Those aleyos who have the Necklaces and the Warriors are said to have received the *fundamento* or "foundation" of Santería and half of the asiento ceremony. Most of these people are believed to be *prendidos en el santo*—that is, they are spiritually committed to "make the saint" and to become santeros or santeras.

There are several categories of santeros. An *iyalocha* is a santera who has initiated one or more persons as a priest or priestess during the asiento ceremony. The term means mother (*iyá*) of an orisha (*ocha*).

A *babalocha* is a santero who likewise has presided during the asiento ceremony. *Baba* means "father," and the whole term means "father of an orisha." Santería believes that upon initiation into the religion, the santero becomes his deity's physical counterpart. Since he then has the power to initiate others, he is said to "give birth" to other santeros, providing the orishas with new channels of manifestation. This belief is sustained by the central purpose of the asiento, which is to cause the initiate to be born anew. The initiate is thought of and treated as a young child. He is even given a new name, which is then used in all subsequent ceremonies. In this sense, Santería is very much a "born again" religion.

There are other orders of priests among the santeros. The *oriaté* is the master of ceremonies during the asiento, and the *italero* is a santero who is highly skilled in the reading of the seashells. The *ayugbona,* on the other hand, is the assistant to the presiding iyalocha or babalocha during the asiento. The ayugbona is the one in charge of the training and guidance of the initiate, or *iyawó,* during the year following the asiento.

The santero or santera is also known as an *omo-orisha,* that is the child (*omo*) of an orisha or saint. He takes the name of his presiding saint immediately after the ceremony of the asiento. A santero who is a son of Changó is known as an omo-Changó; a son or daughter to Yemayá is an omo-Yemayá, and so on.

Santería's most basic belief is that destiny begins before birth in Ilé-Olofi, the house of God, heaven. Like the ancient Babylonians, the Yoruba believe that we are the children of the gods. Race, language, and place of birth are of no importance to the orishas, who encompass the entire world with their divine powers and claim all human beings as their children.

Long before Obatalá finishes his work of shaping the child in the womb, the child's life has been preordained by Olofi and the other orishas. Also determined before birth is the orisha who is going to be the *iyá-Oru* or *babá-Oru,* the newborn's heavenly mother or father. Sometimes (as when a person does not believe in the Yoruba faith) the child never learns he is the offspring of an orisha. Nevertheless, the orisha who claims that person as his *omo-mi*—one of his children—will guide and protect him all through his life. Of course, should the child get out of hand and offend his orisha with his bad behavior, the orisha will withdraw his protection and unleash heavenly rage upon his omo-mi. The punishment may sometimes be slow in coming, but it will come inexorably.

Santería believes that it is possible to foretell the protecting orisha of a child before it is born. When a woman desires to learn which orisha will preside over her unborn child's destiny, she visits a santero or a babalawo so that he may provide her with this vital information. This lets her pray to that orisha for her safe delivery, and teach her child to honor his heavenly protector from an early age. The child will often be dressed in the colors of his saint and will not be allowed to eat the foods sacred to his protector.

Sometimes the orishas indicate that the child is meant to be a santero or santera, and that it must be initiated before its birth. This causes a minor commotion, as it means the child must be initiated in the mysteries of Santería while still in its mother's womb. The ritual involved, known as *medio asiento* or "half of the asiento," is conducted over the mother's abdomen. When the child is born, it is immediately presented to the otanes or sacred stones that represent his orisha, and washed in the *omiero,* or ritual liquid prepared with the favorite ewe (herbs) of the saint. The remnants of the liquid are usually thrown under a large tree with an ample shadow, so that the child may be always protected from harm.

Santería is a highly ritualistic religion in which the strictest protocol is constantly observed. The elders of the religion—both male and female—are known as *santeros mayores,* and they are treated with the greatest respect and reverence by the younger santeros as well as the aleyos. This respect—*tingüi agüo*—is shown by doing *foribale* at the feet of the elder. This is a ritual greeting that is conducted in one of two ways. If the santero who is doing foribale at the feet of an elder is a son or daughter of a male orisha, such as Elegguá, he lies facedown on the ground, his arms kept straight and close to his body. If his orisha is female, he lies on one side on the floor, one elbow on the ground, the other arm akimbo on the waist. He repeats this motion, lying on the other side. When the santero finishes the greeting, the elder touches him lightly on the shoulders and says, "Wo-Agbó Wo

Ató [and the name of the santero's orisha], *Agbó O Didé.*"
("May you live long and well, we beg your orisha.") He or she
then helps the santero stand up, and they both cross their arms in
front of their chests and then touch shoulders. At this point the
santero asks the elder's blessing, *"Bendición,"* and the elder
answers, *"Santo,"* which means "saint" or orisha.

After a babalocha or an iyalocha has initiated several individuals as santeros, his or her house becomes known as a *casa de
santo,* that is, an orisha house. In every Santería community there
are many *casas,* and very often there are variations in the ritual
observances from house to house. These variations sometimes
create dissension among the leading santeros and santeras, each
of whom claims that his or her house follows the true teachings
of the ancients. But most of the elders agree that it does not
matter to which casa de santo a person belongs. The important
thing is that he or she has proper respect for the orishas. There is
a popular saying among the elders, "The saints eat hearts." It
simply means that the saints or orishas can see into people's
hearts and divine their true intentions. It is a person's intention
that the saints care about; how he carries out that intention is
secondary.

When a person receives any of the Santería initiations from a
santero or santera, that individual becomes known as his *padrino*
(godfather) or *madrina* (godmother). The initiate becomes the
santero's *ahijado* (godson) or *ahijada* (goddaughter). The relationship between a santero and his or her godchild is character-
ized by the godchild's respect, reverence, and obedience for his
godparent and the godparent's protection and guidance of the
godchild. It is a remarkable relationship, based on mutual trust.
The ahijado is expected to obey his godparent without hesitation.
The padrino or madrina is expected to help and protect the
godchild and advise him in all his problems. This ideal relationship sometimes fails. The failure may be caused by the godchild's
open disobedience of the godparent. Other failures may be caused
by the godchild's dissatisfaction with his padrino or madrina.

Whatever the reason, such a failure can lead to a parting of the ways between a santero and a godchild. If the godchild is an initiated santero himself, he may or may not decide to join the house of another elder. If he is knowledgeable in the mysteries of the religion, he may decide to start a casa of his own. But if the person is not a santero and has only one or more of the lesser initiations, he will need to find another house and another padrino or madrina, especially if he has the intention of making the saint sometime in his life. But generally, both the padrino and the ahijado make every effort for their relationship to be harmonious, because dissension between a godfather and his godchild is a source of great unhappiness to both.

The relationship between a santero and his godchildren is considered a sacred trust. A santero may not marry or have a love affair with a godchild; to do so is to risk the anger of the orishas and the criticism of other santeros. And it is to the santero's best advantage to have a prestigious and respectable house. This is the only way he can win the respect and support of his peers, and the acquisition of more prospective godchildren.

There are two all-important dates in the santero's calendar. The first is the "birthday" of his orisha, celebrated on the day assigned by the Catholic Church to the Catholic aspect of the deity. The second is the anniversary of the day he made the saint. On those days most santeros prepare a *trono* ("throne") in the *igbodu* or room where they keep the tureens with the orishas' *otanes*. The trono is the seat on top of which is placed the tureen where the otanes of the santero's orisha are kept. The trono is draped with silk or brocaded cloth in the colors of the orisha. The walls are often similarly draped, giving an impression of barbaric splendor. The floor in front of the throne is covered with an immense variety of fruits, often arranged in geometric patterns. Cakes, candies, and huge flower vases complete the arrangement. The lavishness of the display depends upon the purse of the santero.

On both of these days the santero holds an open house. Everyone, even the uninitiated, is welcome to his house to celebrate these important dates. The santero's godchildren are obligated to visit their padrino's house at these times and to pay foribale to him and to his orisha. Even *aleyos* (the uninitiated) are expected to pay foribale to the throne and to the santero. The godchildren must bring with them an offering of a coconut and two white candles, as well as a *derecho* (a money offering) ranging from a dollar upwards, depending on what they can or want to give. The most respected and best-known elders are visited by hundreds of people on these days. They are all treated to a plentiful and splendid repast consisting of several types of Cuban delicacies. When they leave, the santero fills a paper bag with several of the fruits and candies from the throne and hands them to the departing guests. In this way the visitors partake of the offerings to the saint, which are filled with the orisha's blessings. The larger the number of people who come to his house and the greater the number he feeds, the happier the santero is, for he believes that feeding great masses of people will result in multiple blessings for himself and for his family and godchildren.

Among the initiations conferred by the santero are the Necklaces, the Warriors, and the asiento. Both santeros and santeras can give the Necklaces and the asiento, but santeras cannot give the Warriors. There is much controversy surrounding this initiation, which the babalawos claim that only they should give. But most santeros argue against the babalawos' claim and insist that they can also give the Warriors. If a babalawo confers this initiation upon an individual and this person later makes the saint, he must receive another Eleggua from a santero, as the babalawo's Eleggua cannot be used during the asiento.

The people who consult a santero do so for a great variety of reasons. Some are ill or are suffering from nervous conditions; others believe they are being attacked psychically by some deadly enemy; still others need help in securing employment, in starting a business venture, or in controlling a wandering spouse or lover. The santero has an answer and a remedy for everyone.

The consultation with a santero, known as a *registro,* does not differ very much from a visit to a psychologist or therapist. The santero's client sits across from him at his consulting table and tells him all of his or her problems and needs. The santero listens quietly, without interrupting the client. Then he proceeds to find out the reasons for the problems and their appropriate solutions. The only difference between a santero and a consulting psychologist lies in methodology. And very often the santero succeeds where a psychologist might fail. In fact, some psychologists in New York City hospitals refer some of their clients to santeros for consultation. Among these are Bellevue Hospital, Lincoln Hospital, and the Columbia Presbyterian Medical Center. These clinical psychologists have the names of several well-known santeros with whom they work on a steady basis. Most of the clients referred by psychologists to santeros are Hispanics with mental or nervous disorders. They are referred to the santero because they often believe in Santeria and in the santero's powers. Therefore they respond better psychologically to the santero's treatment than to that of a conventional psychologist alone.

A typical registro is conducted by the santero through the Diloggún, or reading of the seashells. Through the seashells the orishas "speak" to the santero and tell him what ails the client and the steps that must be taken to remedy his condition. The solution to the problem may range from very simple to extremely complicated. The santero informs his client step by step of the orishas' message. (Sometimes the eggun also speak through the Diloggún.) He then tells his client what he must do in order to solve his problem. The solution may lie in a series of lustral baths, a ritual cleansing (*despojo*) the acquisition of an initiation such as the Necklaces, an offering of fruits or candies to the orishas, a Catholic mass for the dead, or an animal sacrifice. Sometimes the client can carry out the orishas' instructions on his own, as in the case of the lustral baths or the mass. On other occasions he must have the help of the santero, as in the case of ritual cleansings or animal sacrifices. At no time does the santero decide on his own what ails his clients or what he has to do to solve his problem. Each time it is the orishas—through the interpretation of the seashells—who decide what is to be done. All the santero does is to carry out the will of the orishas.

Not all santeros read the seashells, and not all who read them are equally proficient. The reason for this is that some are said to have more ashé—vision, blessings, power—than others. This is why it is important to choose a santero well when one desires a registro. A santero should be recommended by someone who knows him well before one undertakes a consultation with that individual.

A competent santero is usually easy to pinpoint because his waiting room is generally packed with his clients and ahijados, all trusting completely in his wisdom. Those waiting often pass the time exchanging anecdotes involving the santero and his "supernatural" powers. Undoubtedly, a reputable, well-known santero is apt to earn a reasonably good living from his registros, but most santeros have other jobs or private businesses and do not live exclusively on their registros. Because they do not depend on their consultations to make a living, they can afford to be charitable and truthful to their clients. But the main reason a serious santero does not dare to take advantage of his powers is his fear of retribution on the part of the orishas. Such is the respect and the supernatural awe evoked by the saints that only the most disreputable and faithless of santeros will dare to offend them. Still, there are many who do. These are the santeros who charge outrageous prices for the tiniest amulet, who confer initiations when none are needed, who cheat and lie to their clients, and who take part in all sorts of forbidden activities, such as drug dealing and sexual debaucheries. Inevitably, these bad priests pay for their crimes, often in the most terrifying ways. For, according to the santeros, the orishas are loving friends but terrible enemies.

Santeros are notoriously reticent about their practices and beliefs. This reticence is not based on fear of public opinion, because the santeros are not in the least interested in public relations. The secrecy arises partly from ancient traditions and partly from the santero's desire to preserve his religion in all its purity, free from outside influences. The controversy and condemnation caused by some of his practices, notably the animal sacrifices, have done little to help bring the santero out of his self-imposed concealment. And although many members of the Santería are beginning to take legal steps to protect their religious freedom, it is unlikely that the tenets or practices of the religion will change in the future.

6.

The Babalawo
High Priest of Santería

The word *babalawo*—pronounced baba-*lah*-gwo among the Yoruba, and baba-*lah*-oh among santeros—means father (baba) of divination (awo). In Nigeria these priests are more commonly known as *awos*, or diviners.

In Santería the babalawo is the high priest of the religion. His office is largely judicial, and he is usually consulted by santeros and their clients in extremely difficult situations. A babalawo can also determine who is the ruling orisha of an individual, but to do so he must work in conjunction with at least five more babalawos in the ceremony known as *bajar a Orunla*, the "bringing down of Orunla." Orunla or Orúnmila is the patron saint of the babalawo and the orisha of divination. As we have seen, he is syncretized in Santería with Saint Francis of Assisi, and his day is celebrated by the babalawo and his godchildren on October 4.

In the Santería tradition, only men can become babalawos. This belief is traced to one of the patakís, according to which at one time Orúnla was married to Yemayá. In those early times, Orúnla divined by means of the seashells. One day he went away on a prolonged trip, and Yemayá—who had been watching him conduct the divination and knew how to do it—decided to

94

start consulting people so that her husband would not lose his business. She was so proficient in her consultations, and her prognostications proved so accurate, that she soon became more popular than Orúnla himself. When Orúnla returned and saw what his wife had been doing, he became so enraged that he abandoned her. He also swore that he would never again read the Diloggún and that he would find a divination system that would forever be forbidden to women. That is the reason why women cannot be babalawos, because they are the priests of Orúnla and the ones empowered by him to interpret his oracles. So entrenched is this belief in Santería that in the house of the babalawo, only he can divine. His wife—who is usually a santera—is not allowed to read the seashells. After many years of service, the babalawo's wife becomes known as Orúnla's *akpetebí*, or handmaiden.

The reason Orúnla is the orisha of divination and "owner of the secrets" is that, according to tradition, he is the only deity who is present when the ori of an individual chooses his destiny on earth. That is why Orúnla is known as *eleri-ipin*, or "witness of the ori" in its choice of fate. Orúnla is therefore the only orisha who knows the truth about each human being and what is best for him or her. For that reason he is often the speaker for the other orishas. Reincarnation is therefore an intrinsic belief of Santería, as each person comes to earth with a specific destiny to fulfill. Sometimes the person fails to carry out the work and duties that he or she chose before birth. That individual then suffers the punishments of the orishas for his failure. He or she must then reincarnate until those duties have been fulfilled. Sometimes an individual's life is shortened by his inability to carry on with his chosen destiny. Only Orúnla can help these persons ameliorate their fates. One of the most fascinating of the patakís surrounding Orúnla tells how the orisha at one time tricked Ikú (Death) into prolonging any individual's life who wears Orúnla's colors in an *idé* or *ildé* (bracelet) with alternating green and yellow beads. Because of his pact with Death, Orúnla also knows an infinite number of *ebbós* by means of which a person's life may be extended.

The babalawo uses three divination systems, the *opelé*, the *opón Ifá* (the Table of Ifá), and the *ikin*. The opelé (pronounced "okuelé") consists of an iron chain that connects eight oval medallions usually made of coconut rinds, although they can be also made of tortoiseshell, ivory, bone, copper, or tin. Each medallion has a different design on either of its two sides. The babalawo interprets the oracle according to which sides of the eight medallions fall down when he throws the opelé on his working table.

When the babalawo throws down the opelé, he holds the chain by the middle. In this way he ensures that the medallions fall four on each side, parallel to each other. There are sixteen different designs that can be made by the opelé. Each design is known as an *oddu*. The combination of the sixteen oddus forms 256 new designs, each of which is accompanied by a verse and by one or more patakís. The babalawo interprets the person's fate according to the verse and the pataki. Each oddu is also accompanied by one or more of the prayers known as *suyeres*.

According to the babalawos, the divination of Ifá (the various oracles of Orúnla) comprises all the knowledge of the universe and the entire past, present, and future of mankind. Some babalawos see more than 256 oddus in the opelé. If both sides of the opelé show the same design they are known as *melli*, or twins. These are subdivided into sixteen compound oddus known as *amulúos*. These form 256 oddus (sixteen times sixteen). But each amulúo is also subdivided into sixteen "subjects," forming a total of 4,096 oddus. Each of the "subjects" subdivides into sixteen sub-subjects for a total of 65,536 oddus. Each of these oddus has 1,680 patakís, for a grand total of 110,100,480 patakís. Not all babalawos agree with this mathematical computation of the opelé, but the more learned a babalawo is, the more patakís and suyeres he will know. The more patakís he knows, the more accurate his prognostications will be.

The babalawo uses the opelé for most of his consultations. He begins the ceremony with the ritual known as *moyubbar*, during which he prays to all the eggun and the orishas. Then he touches the opelé to the forehead of his client to ask the permission of the person's guardian angel to conduct the divination procedure. After this, the babalawo throws the opelé three times in a row to determine the principal oddu or *letra*. He then throws the chain a few more times to clarify the first oddu. As each oddu is formed, the babalawo writes it down in the form of either a numeral one or a zero. Each oddu is written underneath the preceding one until four lines have been formed. The combination of lines yields a numerical minimum of 256, as we have already seen. An example of an oracle follows:

$$
\begin{array}{cc}
1 & 1 \\
1 & 0 \\
0 & 1 \\
1 & 1
\end{array}
$$

This oracle is then interpreted by the babalawo in accordance with the verses and the patakís that belong to that particular design. The first time I consulted a babalawo and I saw him write down the oddu, I realized that I was looking at a binary system. The 1 and the 0 that the babalawo used in the oracle were the same digits used in computer calculations. Furthermore, the babalawo was using the binary code in the same manner as the computer does, a system handed down to him through countless years of African religious tradition. After the consultation, when I told the babalawo about the similarities between the opelé and the computer system, he shrugged his shoulders.

"It's the simplest system in the world," he said. "And the most complete. It's a combination—or series of combinations—between *something*, the one, and *nothing*, the zero. The entire universe is made of somethings and nothings. With those two ciphers, worlds can be made and destroyed. But we're now in

Orúnla's province," he added with a smile. "I cannot tell you any more. Except the Yoruba were not the only ones who used the binary system. Many other ancient civilizations knew it. Computer technology chose it simply because it is the best and the simplest. All the knowledge that can be had lies between the one and the zero."

Once the babalawo has written down the oddus, he must find out if they come with good luck—*iré*—or bad luck—*osogbo*. To determine this, he hands his client a small seashell and a tiny stone. These two implements are known as *igbo*. The person takes the igbo, rubs them between his hands, and divides them so that each falls into a different hand. He closes his hands and offers his fists to the babalawo, who then throws the opelé again to determine which hand he must choose. If the hand chosen has the stone, the oracle is accompanied by *iré*; if the hand has the seashell, the answer is *osogbo*.

Whether the answer is good or bad luck, the babalawo now must determine how this iré or osogbo is coming to his client. The good luck or iré may come in many ways, including the following:

Ariku—through the dead
Otonowa—through heaven
Elese ocha—through the orishas
Aye—through material prosperity
Loguo—through his own initiative
Eledda—through his own intelligence
Elese Oloddumare—through God
Elese eggun—through a dead person
Owo—through unexpected money
Ori yoco—through "making the saint"

The bad luck or *osogbo* may involve one of a variety of things as well, such as:

Ikú—death
Areyé—hatred and envy

Ofo—losses, suffering
Eyó—arguments
Ogo—witchcraft
Ano—illness
Ona—punishment
Fitivo—sudden death

If the person has osogbo in his oracle, a piece of bone is substituted for the stone.

Once the babalawo knows the good or the bad coming to a person, he must either cleanse the evil or reinforce the good promised by the oracle. To determine how, he asks Orúnla what is the best ritual that person should undergo, and to which of the orishas it should be dedicated, unless it is the eggun who control the oddu. The ebbó "marked" by Orúnla will ensure that the person will be rid of any evil influences surrounding him, so that good luck and prosperity will accompany him always. According to the babalawos, people who consult Orúnla often are able to solve their problems with ease and, as a result, live better and richer lives.

The second divination system used by the babalawo is the opón Ifá, the round wooden tray known in Santería as the Table of Ifá. The tray is usually carved along its rim with various African figures, often representations of Orúnla. It is a symbol of the world and is used only during difficult situations and to prescribe special ebbós. Over the surface of the tray the babalawo sprinkles some special powder known as *eyerosun*, which in Santería is prepared with powdered *ñame* (a kind of yam) and other ingredients. (In Nigeria the babalawos crush *ikin*—the nuts of the sacred palm tree of Ifá—to make the powder.) After sprinkling the powder on the tray, the babalawo proceeds with the divination procedure, which uses a deer horn known as *irofá*. With the tip of the horn the babalawo proceeds to draw on the powder the lines and zeroes which represent the oracle.

The most important of the oracles is that which uses the ikin, or sacred palm nuts. The Yorubas only use the palm nuts during crucial moments or during the crowning of a king. The system employs sixteen palm nuts for divination. In Santería, at least three babalawos are needed to use the ikin. One of them determines the oddus and the others decide which igbos are to be used. They also write down the oddus. The system is similar to that of the opelé in that it also requires igbo and the ceremony of moyubbar.

The babalawo who has the ikin takes them in both hands and shakes them. He then tries to take as many of the nuts as he can with his right hand. If he takes them all, the reading is not valid, and he must try again until either one or two nuts remain in his left hand, considered to be the hand of life. If only one nut remains, he marks two lines on the tray with his second and third fingers. If two remain, he marks one line on the tray with his middle finger. This operation is repeated eight times until the correct oddu is obtained. The ceremony is known in Santería as *tefar*, that is, "to write" or "mark" in Ifá.

As soon as the oddu has been obtained, all the babalawos present—beginning with the youngest—make their prognostications to the individual who is undergoing the ceremony. The predictions are usually written on a notebook that is later handed to the person so that he or she may remember what was said and what he or she must do to improve his or her life. This complex ceremony of divination and prediction where more than one priest participates and prognosticates is known as an *itá*.

The ceremony of itá is also used to determine who is the guardian orisha of an individual. It is the highlight of the twin ceremonies of initiation conferred by the babalawo and known as the *Abo-Facá* (Mano de Orúnla), given only to men, and the *Ico-Fá* (*Cofá de Orúnla*), given only to women. The babalawos give the two initiations at the same time and usually to several people, both male and female. The process is known colloquially by the babalawos as *plantar*. It is not necessary for an individual to be a santero to receive the Abo-Facá or the Ico-Fá, but he or she must have received the initiation known as Elegguá and the Warriors.

The ceremony lasts three days, during which the initiates are presented to Orúnla and the various ritual sacrifices are given to the orisha. The ceremony is immensely complex and enlightening. Its secrets are jealously guarded by the babalawos, who warn the initiates against revealing its details if they do not wish to be severely punished by Orúnla. I underwent the initiation of the *Ico-Fá* several years ago. During the itá, the head babalawo told me, "I understand you have written several books about Santería. The ceremony you have just undergone is both sacred and secret. It is not for the eyes or the ears of the uninitiated. Take care you do not divulge it. If you do, it is not going to be me or any of the other babalawos present who is going to punish you, but Orúnla himself who will tear your head off." This may or may not be true, but I have never revealed the details of that ceremony.

As we have already seen, the babalawo also confers the initiation known as Elegguá and the Warriors. There is considerably less secrecy attached to that ceremony, and the babalawo who gave me the Warriors gave me permission to divulge the details of the initiation.

Prior to the ceremony he consulted the opelé to determine how my particular Elegguá was to be made. He then asked me to go into the woods and find three otanes and bring them to him. He would then ask the opelé which of the stones was to be the foundation for my Elegguá.

"Are all Elegguás prepared this way?" I asked.

"No," he said. "There are many ways to prepare Elegguá, but yours must be made with a stone from the woods."

I knew that the type of stone the santeros and babalawos used for otanes was typically smooth and round. But the first stone I came across in the woods was pyramidal in shape, rough in texture, and grayish in tone. It was not a typical otán, but I felt myself irresistibly attracted to it. When I dislodged it from the ground where it was embedded, I saw that it was half covered with moss. It exuded a strong smell of fresh herbs. I pocketed it swiftly and continued looking for the other two stones, which turned out to be like the classical otanes.

A few days later I was back at the babalawo's house. Giving him the stones, I apologized for the unusual shape of the gray one and explained my great attraction to it.

"Let's find out right away if it is the right stone," he said immediately. "Often the stone you like best is the one Elegguá wants."

He threw the opelé, stared at it for some time, then shook his head in disbelief.

"This is phenomenal," he said after a while. "Not only is this the stone, but this particular letra, or pattern of the opelé, is my own special cipher as a babalawo."

"What does it mean?" I asked.

He looked at me with his wise old eyes and smiled gently. "Let's just say Elegguá has chosen this stone for you and me as your padrino," he said. But something in his voice made me feel he was not telling me everything he saw in the opelé.

I did not ask him any further questions. He told me to return after a week's time to receive Elegguá and the Warriors, as he needed seven days for the preparation of Elegguá. When I came back at the appointed time, he gave me the Warriors in a short but impressive ceremony.

After saluting Orúnla, his orisha, he told me to kneel down facing him and to extend my opened hands toward him. He then placed the sandstone head representing Elegguá on my palms, praying all the time in Yoruba. After a while, he lifted Elegguá off my hands and told me in a grave voice that I was never to kneel in front of Elegguá again. I could stand or crouch, but I could not kneel. He replaced Elegguá with a small cauldron containing Oggún's and Ochosi's implements, and continued praying. The last thing he placed on my hands was the small silvery cup, surrounded by small silver bells and topped by a rooster, that represents Osun. He asked me to shake the cup and ask for the orisha's protection. Finally he helped me stand up, and touched his cheeks to mine in the Santería embrace.

"You are now my godchild—my ahijada—and I'm your padrino," he said with an affectionate smile. "You must come to see me once in a while, especially on my saint's birthday. And remember I'll always be here any time you need help."

The price of the initiation also included the yellow and green bead necklace belonging to Orúnla and the orisha's beaded bracelet known as the *idé*. The bracelet was placed inside a hollow gold circlet to "avoid curious glances," as the babalawo told me.

The idé, or *ilde-fá*, must be worn always on the left hand, which is, as we have seen, a symbol of life. The right hand symbolizes death. Because the pact between Orúnla and Death, ratified by the idé, signifies life for the believer, he or she must wear the bracelet on the left hand.

Several years after I had received the Warriors and the idé from the babalawo, I had an opportunity to see how the idé works. My mother, who is not a believer in Santería, had a severe stroke that left her totally paralyzed. Her condition was so grave that her doctors did not believe she could be saved. Day after day we hoped in vain that she would improve, only to see her condition deteriorate. Finally her cardiologist told me it was a question of days, maybe only hours, before she died. In despair, I called the babalawo and asked him if there was anything he could do for my mother. He told me to come to see him at once. When I arrived at his house, he immediately threw the opelé and asked Orúnla if my mother could be saved. The orisha's answer was that she would survive and recover fully, but only if she would wear Orúnla's idé. My mother was unconscious and I had no way of asking her if she would agree to wear the bracelet, so I decided to take the responsibility of the decision upon myself, and agreed to put the idé on her wrist. The babalawo instructed me as to how to do this and gave me the bracelet to bring to the hospital.

During this time my mother was in intensive care, with IV

needles in both arms, so I had to ask her head doctor's permission to place the beads on her left wrist. Luckily, he is a very openminded person who believes in the psychological benefits of deep faith, and he allowed the use of the idé. Under the curious eyes of the nurses, I conducted the simple ritual prescribed by the babalawo, and tied the bracelet in place.

A few days later my mother's doctor called me to tell me that a minor miracle had happened. My mother was showing some improvement and she no longer needed a respirator. He gave orders that she be taken from intensive care and brought to her bedroom. Her condition was still critical, but now there was hope for some improvement. He nevertheless warned me against expecting too much, as the damage to her brain had been so severe he doubted she would ever recover in full.

The second day after my mother returned to her room, I came to see her with my son early in the afternoon. There was another woman sharing her room, and she was desperately ill. Her doctors were expecting her to die at any moment. When I walked into the room, the first thing I noticed was that my mother's idé had been taken off her wrist and placed on the windowsill. What I could not understand was how the bracelet had been removed without undoing the tiny double knots I had used to tie it, which were still intact. There was no way the bracelet could have been slid off her wrist without breaking it. I asked her private nurse if she had removed the idé, and she said she had not even noticed my mother was wearing it. I then questioned the doctors and all the nurses on the floor, and none of them knew who had taken the bracelet off my mother's wrist. I returned to the room and sat down, but almost immediately I felt so uncomfortable that I got up and began to pace up and down the room. My son asked what was troubling me, and I said I was not sure, but I had to have some air. I told him I would go downstairs to the coffee shop and return within the hour. About an hour later I went back to my mother's room. As soon as I came in, my son asked me if I noticed anything different in the room. I looked around and noticed that the bed next to my mother was empty. When I asked my son what had happened, he said that in the time I had been out of the room, the lady who had the bed next to my mother's had died, her body had been removed, and the bed linen had been changed. When I told this story to the babalawo, he said that the idé had been removed from my mother's wrist because, according to the pact made between Orúnla and Death, no one can die in a room where someone is wearing the idé. Since I was also wearing an idé, I had to leave the room so that Death could enter it and claim the woman whose time had come.

Several years have passed since this incident. My mother is alive and well. She can walk and speak, and her doctors cannot understand how she survived at all.

The babalawos can do a vast number of cleansings and ebbós specifically designed to save a person's life or rid him or her of negative vibrations, especially of evil spirits. One of the best known of these rituals is the *panaldo*, a type of exorcism through which a negative entity can be dislodged from a person's aura. There are many types of panaldos. In a typical ritual of this type, the person who is to undergo the cleansing is asked to bring to the babalawo a rooster, some cloths, flowers, candles, and other substances. All persons who are to participate in the ceremony have to be marked on the forehead with a cross made with cascarilla. This is designed to protect them against the spirit that is going to be expelled from the person's life.

The ceremony is conducted in a special room where only those who are going to take part in the exorcism are allowed to enter. In the center of the room is drawn a semicircle at the base of which is placed the ritual *palo* with which the eggun are invoked. The babalawos call this staff the *ikú achán* or *igüi eggun*. On the four cardinal points of the room the babalawo draws one or more of Orúnla's oddus, appropriate to the type of panaldo that is being used.

The subject of the exorcism is asked to stand opposite the palo, outside the semicircle. The babalawo and his assistants begin the prayers or suyeres belonging to the oddus. As the prayers continue, the babalawo keeps tapping the palo lightly on the floor. The person to be exorcised is then asked to enter the semicircle. The babalawo follows him, carrying the rooster, which is presented to his forehead to ask his orisha's permission to conduct the cleansing. The rooster is then killed by hitting it hard against the floor, after which the animal is passed all over the person's body in order to trap within it the negative entity that is troubling him. Later the rooster's body is placed inside one of the cloths with several other ingredients and tied in a knot. This is known as a *macuto,* and is usually brought to the cemetery or buried in the ground, depending on what Orúnla decides.

I had an experience with a babalawo recently that I feel I should relate here. One of my dearest friends was very ill, suffering from AIDS. I went to see the babalawo on his behalf, although his doctors had given him only a few more days to live. The babalawo threw the opelé and told me that Orúnla said that the grave had already been dug for this man. This is a special saying in Santería that indicates that a person is about to die. Nevertheless, the babalawo continued, Orúnla said that there was a special ebbó that could be made during which the "earth" could be "fed," thereby saving the man's life. "What this means," said the babalawo, "is that Orúnla will prolong his life until a cure can be found for the disease. And whether it takes one year or ten, he will not die if he does the ebbó." I brought this answer to my friend in the hospital. He thought it over for a few minutes, then he said he was too tired of fighting for his life. He would not do the ebbó. Two days later he was dead. I will always wonder what would have happened if he had done as the babalawo suggested. Would he still be alive? I will never know.

Every year, on December 30, a group of the most important babalawos in a community start the ceremony known as the "Opening of the New Year." The two most important of these ceremonies are those celebrated in Nigeria and in Cuba. Most babalawos in the United States tend to ignore all other ceremonies and guide themselves by the Cuban one.

During this ceremony, Orúnla tells the babalawos, through the ikin, all the major events of the coming year, as well as the names of the orishas who will rule it. The ceremony lasts three days. The first day, the babalawos make offerings to Elegguá, the Warriors, and Orúnla. Offerings are also given to the four cardinal points of the opón Ifá, to the river, to the sea, and to the earth. The type of offering is determined through a special divination rite. On the second day, nothing is done; the offerings just rests in front of the orishas. On the third day, January 1, the babalawos "give coconut" to Orúnla (that is, read the coconut rinds) to determine whether he and the other orishas are satisfied with the offerings. If he says no, other offerings are made until he is satisfied. If he says yes, all the various offerings are placed on seventeen plates and placed in the room where the major divination ceremony, or itá, is to take place. This room is divided into two sections. In the center are placed the seats of the babalawos. On one side are placed the seats for the public, who are allowed to witness the ceremony.

When the spectators are seated, the ceremony begins with a parade of the babalawos, one of whom carries a bowl with the ikins and other divination implements. Another babalawo carries the opón Ifá, which is placed on the floor, facing Orúnla. The babalawos kneel in front of their orisha, touching their foreheads to the floor. Afterwards, one of the elders begins the divination procedure with the *ikin*. At this point it is ascertained whether the year brings iré or osogbo, as well as which of the orishas governs the year. Once the oddus are written down, the babalawos begin to interpret the oracle, beginning, as always, with the youngest, that is, the one who was initiated most recently. The interpretation of the oracle by the babalawo is the itá, and what is known in Santería as the *letra del año*, what is to happen during that year.

A babalawo of my acquaintance, Carlos Collazo of New York

City, kindly made available to me the itá or letra for the year 1987, as ascertained in Havana, Cuba.

		+	
0 0	0 0	0 0	
0 0	1 1	0 0	Iré Arikú Oyale
0 1	1 0	1 0	
1 0	0 0	0 0	

The oddu to the left was the first to be designated by Orúnla. It speaks to the dead as controlling the oracle. The other two oddus modify the first, and determine whether it comes with iré or osogbo. Because the middle or second oddu is "senior," that is, "greater" than the first, the oddu is said to come with iré. The last oddu ratifies the other two. Its name is Oyale.

The prognostication for this sign was to beware of problems with the law or legal matters, as the year would bring much political turmoil. But these problems could be surmounted if the persons involved were wise. The less said, the better. Everyone was advised to strengthen his relationships with his brothers and sisters, and with people at a distance. The eggun had to be cared for, either with food offerings or with prayers and candles. The ocean waters were not very safe that year. Care had to be taken when bathing in the sea. Family life must be protected and arguments avoided at all costs. In general, the oddu did not speak of a particularly difficult year. Many things could be accomplished because the dead were benevolently inclined toward mankind. But nothing could be taken for granted because that was a year in which a lot of effort was required to accomplish what was desired.

The Nigerian oddu for the year is undoubtedly different from the Cuban one, but the Cuban oddu is the one accepted by the babalawos in the United States.

There are many restrictions for the babalawo initiation. Very often, santeros are initiated into Orúnla's mysteries, but only if their ruling orisha has never possessed them, and if they have not initiated many people as santeros. Once a person becomes a practicing santero, he cannot "make Ifá," that is, he cannot become a babalawo. Another important restriction forbids homosexuals from becoming babalawos. Women are also forbidden Orúnla's mysteries, as we have already seen. But several enterprising women have decided to challenge this ancient tradition, as we will see in the following chapter.

I do not want to close this chapter without expressing my gratitude and deep affection for the babalawo from whom I received Elegguá, the Warriors, and the *Ico-Fá*, and thanks to whom my mother is still with me, even though he is not. His name is Pancho Mora, and he died on March 19, 1986. *Iboru-Iboya.*

7.

Iyanifá━━━━━━━━━━━━━━━━━━━━━━━
Mother of the Secrets

On January 22, 1985, one of the most jealously guarded traditions in Santería was shattered. A woman was initiated in the
Americas into the mysteries of Ifá. These initiation, which up to
that day had only been conferred upon men, created such shock
and consternation among the elders that its repercussions are still
being felt among the practitioners of Santería. Condemnation of
the initiation was universal. The Latin American babalawos—
who are the repositories of Ifá's mysteries, and are Orúnla's
priests in the West—were the most vociferous in expressing their
indignation at what they called an abuse and an outrage. But
they were not alone in the denunciation of the initiation. Most
santeros and santeras, and other practitioners of the religion,
joined the babalawos in their condemnation of the ceremony,
which they rejected publicly as false and meaningless.

The subject of this fury and controversy was an American Jew
named Patri Dhaifa, who had been a member in good standing of
the Santería community since 1979, when she was initiated as a
santera. I first heard about her controversial initiation through a
Venezuelan magazine called *Africanías*, which published a detailed article on the ceremony, as well as photographs taken

during the rituals—another taboo in Santería. I called Patri Dhaifa in New York, where she lives, and asked her for an interview, explaining that I was working on a new book on Santería and I wanted to write about her initiation in some detail. She was very interested in being interviewed, as she wanted to make public her experiences and the reasons she had undergone the controversial ceremony. What follows is her personal account of her initiation into Ifá, and of her involvement with Santería, as she related it to me during that interview.

My name is Patri Dhaifa, but in Santería I am known as Dhaifa Odufora Ifatogún. I was born in the United States of Jewish parentage, but I have lived in many countries and most of my education has taken place abroad. I am at present residing in New York City, where I work with a major airline as a supervisor and trainer of reservation agents.

I first learned about Santería in the early 1960s, immediately after the Cuban revolution, when many Cuban refugees came to New York in search of asylum. Many of the Cubans who moved into my neighborhood were santeros or practitioners of Santería. It was through them that I learned about the Religion.

One day I was brought by a friend to the house of a well-known santero called Benigno (Rudy) Domínguez, an initiate of the orisha Obatalá. At the time I did not speak Spanish, but through my friend—who translated for me—Rudy told me that before I left this earth I would be initiated as a santera into the mysteries of Obatalá. I did not know who Obatalá was, and I thought Rudy was telling me I had to put a piece of bacalá (salted codfish) on my head. I laughed and told him I did not believe he was right. Shortly after that I began to work with the famous Cuban composer, Eduardo Davidson, who was not a santero, but who had much faith in the Religion. Through Eduardo I learned a great deal about the orishas and the importance of the eggun. I became in-

creasingly interested in Santería, but the santeros were very
reticent with me and quite reluctant to accept me in their midst
because I was Jewish and the practices of Catholicism—
especially that of baptism—are very important to them. They
were very insistent that I should become baptized before I
underwent any of the lesser initiations of Santería, but I was
quite as adamant in refusing. I simply did not see the need
to be baptized to practice an African-based religion.

In 1977 I received a very grave injury to my spine and was
confined to my bed for a year. One vertebra had healed out
of place and I was nearly paralyzed. I felt quite lost and did
not know what to do about my life. I had heard about the
great stabilizing and beneficial influence of the Santería initiation of Olokun, the orisha who represents the depths of
the seas. I decided to take the initiation, which was of great
help to me in dealing with my illness. Shortly after that, during a consultation with the seashells, Obatalá said that he
would take care of my complete rehabilitation if I received
him during the initiation of the asiento. I was still moving
around with crutches, with a very dim view of the future,
so I decided to undergo the initiation. On May 12, 1979, I
became *asentada in ocha*, that is, I received the initiation
of the asiento and became a santera. As Rudy had predicted
so many years before, the saint I received was Obatalá. Rudy
was my padrino. And as Obatalá had promised me, my back
was totally healed, to the amazement of all my doctors.
(Obatalá rules all the bone structure of the human body.)

Rudy respected my resistance to baptism and did not insist
on my being baptized before my initiation. Because the first
ritual to be undergone by the initiate is to be bathed in the
river, he felt that this part of the initiation would act as a
baptism for me.

On the third day of the ceremony, known as the *itá*, when
the initiate is told what is to take place during the rest of
his or her life, the santeros also determine—through the

seashells—the person's private oddu or letra, which is to
become her insignia while she lives. The oddu has taboos and
ordinances attached to it: things the initiate must and must
not do. On this day one also finds out the true name of his
or her ruling orisha and of the second orisha who compli-
ments this divine protection. The orishas are always male and
female, father and mother. If the ruling orisha is male, he
is the father. The other orisha is the mother. In my case, my
oddu was Ofun Mewa. This is the oddu of kings and of
people with extraordinary life-styles. These people are surrounded by phenomenal occurrences, and whatever happens to them in this world is brought by them here from
previous lives. This was the opening oddu of the ceremony,
which I threw myself as prescribed by tradition. The closing
oddu, necessary to ascertain the name of the second orisha,
was Yroso, with a value of four. This oddu indicated that
my second orisha was Yemayá, in her aspect of Okutti (really
Oggun-ti, indicating her close relationship with Oggún).
That meant Yemayá Okutti was my mother, while my father and ruling orisha was Obatalá in his aspect of Obbamoro.
My new name was to be Odufora.

My initiation as a santera revealed to me for the first time
strong links with the orisha Oggún, of which I would have
further proof later on in my life. One of the strongest indica-
tions of my connection with Oggún was the fact that my
mother "in the saint" was Yemayá, who comes from the
Abeokuta region of Nigeria, in the state of Oggún. The river
that crosses Abeokuta is the Ogun River.

As soon as I became initiated as a santera, I felt obligated
to investigate the Religion. I felt the need to know more
about its practices and traditions. As I delved into its mysteries, I was overawed by its wisdom, its profundity, and its
power. I had never expected to find so much that was pure
and original in Santería. Suddenly many doors and avenues
of exploration opened before me. I had been a world trav-

eler for many years and was often engaged in distributing food
to needy people in Thailand and Cambodia. But now I felt
I could not do this anymore. I thought, "If I were to stand in
the middle of these starving people and hand out bowl after bowl of rice to them, I could never hope to feed them all,
even if I stood here all my life. But if I could only feed their
spirits, they would then be able to feed their bodies." I understood then the wisdom of Jesus, who taught twelve men,
who in turn taught twelve more, and so on, until the whole
world had his message and could feed on his words.

After this, I began to visit many orisha houses, *casas de
santo*, where the santeros did not congregate, that is, meet
with other santeros. They were not elitist, but they seemed
to me to be on a higher level than the santeros who were
very involved with initiations. I learned very much from these
people, most of whom practiced the Religion in the privacy
of their homes. Around this time I met someone who was to
be very important in my life. He was a renowned *oriaté*—a
santero who is the master of ceremonies during the asiento.
He was introduced to me by my padrino, Rudy. His name
is Alberto León, and he is also an initiate of Obatalá.

Alberto and I soon became close friends. I started to accompany him to the asientos where he acted as oriaté. Soon
I learned so well the secrets of his trade that he allowed me
to carry the initiate's libreta, the notebook in which all the
taboos and ordinances are inscribed and which was given to
him one year after his initiation. By this time I spoke Spanish fluently, and the santeros had accepted me fully as one of
them. I also began to study Yoruba.

One day Alberto told me that my initiation oddu spoke of
being initiated into the mysteries of Ifá. I knew that Santería
tradition forbade women to undergo this ceremony, whereby
men become babalawos. I told Alberto that such an initiation carried a terrible stigma, and that if I were to receive it I
would be totally ostracized by the santeros as well as the

babalawos. Alberto shrugged. "The decision is up to you," he said. "I'm only telling you what the oddu says."

Alberto's words remained embedded in my mind and I could not forget them. I decided that my best course of action was to go to Nigeria, where Santería had come from, and learn the basis for the tradition that denies women the right to receive Ifá. During a conference in New York on the Orisha Tradition, I had met Professor Wande Abimbola, Vice-Chancellor of the University at Ile-Ife. He had told me that the university taught courses on the orishas. So I decided to attend one of those courses.

The first time I went to Nigeria, I spent three months at the University of Ile-Ife, using a translator all the time, as I did not speak fluent Yoruba. I found that the secrecy that surrounds Santería does not exist in Nigeria. The Yorubas are very protective of the orisha religion, but they do not attempt to hide it. Their greatest fear is that their natural religion may be dying due to the Christian and Muslim influence in Nigeria. At present about forty percent of Yorubas practice Christianity, forty percent practice Islam, and the remaining twenty percent observe the Orisha Tradition. This is alarming to the elders of the natural religion.

Some of my teachers at the University asked me why I was not studying the oddu Ifá, the oracle known in Santería as the Table of Ifá, which only babalawos can read. I was surprised by the question and asked them if they would allow me to study the oracle. Their answer was "Why not?" When I told them of the prohibition banning women from receiving Ifá in the New World, they said that no such taboos existed in Nigeria. One of the *arabas*—chiefs of the major towns—told me that there was no oddu that denied women the right to Ifá. Such a prohibition, according to him, was probably started by mistake in the New World.

After speaking with several of the priests and arabas, I made the decision to study the oracle. I found the studies so fas-

cinating that I decided to speak to one of Nigeria's best-
known babalawos, Ifayemi Elebuibon, chief priest of Oshogbo,
and ask if he would agree to initiate me into the mysteries of
Ifá. Without hesitation, Ifayemi agreed. But I was still not
sure. I needed the confirmation and approval of my padrino.
I therefore returned to New York and called on Rudy.

In April of 1984, my padrino, Benigno (Rudy) Domínguez,
known as Ifáfumike in Santería, brought Obatalá "down to
the *estera*," that is, he read the special seashells belonging
to my "crown orisha," Obatalá, directly on a straw mat on
the ground. This is an especially solemn ceremony conducted
when a santero wants to speak directly with his own orisha.
The santero cannot speak to his orisha himself; that is why I
needed Rudy to do the ceremony on my behalf.

During that consultation, my future was cast. The reason
for the inquiry was to find out from Obatalá if he allowed
me to receive Ifá. Obatalá responded with the oddu Ofún-
Mewa, which was the same oddu I had received when I
made Obatalá. To Rudy, this answer was an affirmation from
Obatalá that he gave me his blessing to receive Ifá. Rudy
himself pledged his total support to me during this undertaking. Many years before, Rudy had taken part in the first
initiation of a santero in the United States, when the Changó
initiate Mercedes Noble, known as Obañoko in Santería,
had initiated another woman into the mysteries of Changó.
With his direct participation in the first initiation of a woman
in the mysteries of Ifá in the United States, Rudy had once
more been instrumental in forging the history of the orishas
in the western world.

As soon as the consultation was over, I returned to Nigeria to discuss the arrangements of my initiation with Ifayemi.
He told me that Ifá had directed him to come to America to
perform my initiation, but with much caution, owing to the
enormous opposition to a woman breaking the traditions of
more than four hundred years of orisha in the West. My

planned initiation received the approval and blessings of the babalawos, arabas, chief priests of the orisha shrines, and even the Ooni of Ife, King Okunade Sijuwade, by the power invested in him through Oddudúa. (Oddudúa is to the Yoruba people what Abraham is to the Jewish people.)

The date for the initiation was set for January 1, 1985, but Ifayemi was delayed nearly two weeks in leaving Nigeria. Communication with him was nearly impossible, so I went to an elderly Cuban psychic to investigate the reasons for the delay. She revealed that the underlying obstacles were in fact my own spiritual guides, which she described as a rabbinical council that were obstructing the proceedings in their quest for recognition. I summoned a rabbi, very well versed in the Jewish occult tradition of the Kabbalah, and we prepared a token offering to placate their clamor and to ask for their continued guidance. People unfamiliar with either of these two tribal customs are amazed by the similarities in their rationale. Comparing the orisha rituals with those taught by the Kabbalah helped me to assimilate and interrelate both teachings in perfect harmony.

Life, Rudy, and myself were at a standstill for three weeks while we waited for the arrival of the African priest. He finally arrived in New York and set the new date for my initiation as January 22.

As soon as Ifayemi arrived, he summoned several of his godchildren, whom he had initiated into Ifá in Oshogbo, to assist him with my initiation. Among them was another American woman, whom he had also initiated in Nigeria.

On the first day of the ceremony, which lasted seven days, I was blindfolded and introduced to the sixteen *ikin Ifá*, the palm nuts used in the oracle of Ifá, which are a symbol of Orúnla's powers as diviner. Each ikin is a representative of a historical person and bears the name of an ancient prince. Immediately afterwards, I underwent the ritualistic physical punishment that is a test of endurance and a necessary discipline.

In Nigeria, Ifá initiates are bathed in boiling oil and made to walk through fire without burning themselves. They are sometimes beaten severely with sticks. Because of my spinal injury, Baba 'Yemi, as I was now supposed to call him, was very lenient and kept the punishment to a minimum. After this, my head was shaved and painted with the elements *osun* (red pigment) and *efun* (white pigment), in a design particular to Ifá.

After my sixteen *ikin Ifá* were consecrated, Baba 'Yemi consulted them at great length to determine my *oddu* in Ifá. This was Oggúndabedé. In the possible 256 positions of the oracle, this oddu occupies the thirty-ninth. It denotes a great affinity with Oggún, the orisha of war and iron, as the oddus I received during my initiation as a santera. Because Oggúndabedé is also the personal oddu of a senior Ifá priest, Chief Babalola Ifatogún, a mentor of Ifayemi and a lecturer of oral tradition at the University of Ile-Ife, it was decided that my Ifá name should be Ifatogún as well. Its meaning in Yoruba is "Ifá is stronger than oogun"; oogun is an herbal or talismanic preparation. That is why my name in Santería is Dhaifa Odufora Ifatogún. (Odufora is my name as a santera.)

Throughout the initiation week I wore a sheet wrapped around my body and tied over my left shoulder. Over this I wore a massive necklace of brown and green beads sacred to Orúnla. A string of green and brown beads was tied around my head, with a red parrot feather (*ikoide*) attached on the center of my forehead.

There were continuous sacrifices the entire week, starting with a male goat sacrificed to Elegguá (Eshu) on the first day and a female goat to Ifá on the third. In addition to Eshu and Ifá, I also received Orisha-Ori, the deity who protects the head. To him Ifayemi sacrificed a guinea hen, which is believed to nurture the human aura. On the fifth day, we made a major ebbó or offering called *Itán*, in which one fills twenty-one small gourds with pounded yams and other ingredients. These are placed outside the house and left to be absorbed by the elements. That same day, the parrot feather and the beads were removed from my head and pulverized with a sacred stone. This powder was mixed with *ashé Orúnmila*, a yellowish powder used in Ifá divination, which is made from the ikin, or palm nut. The combined powders were then rubbed into sixteen incisions that were cut on top of my shaven head.

One of the most interesting parts of the initiation was the offer to the *ajé*—the witches—which I had to bring in the dead of night to a public place. The chosen place was one of the corners of 125th Street and Broadway. The offering was placed inside a small gourd that was left on the street.

Because of the great opposition to my initiation, we were forced to conduct the ceremony in the greatest secrecy. I rented a vacant building in Harlem at 137th Street and Adam Clayton Powell Boulevard, and I spent the entire week there under the protection of Ifayemi and the other babalawos who were assisting him.

I calculate my total expenses to have been about $9,000. My title after the initiation was not that of a babalawo, because that word means "father of the secrets." Since I am a woman, my title is *iyanifá*, which means "mother of Ifá."

Patri Dhaifa's initiation into Ifá may have been conducted in secret, but it did not remain secret for long. Within days of the ceremony, the news spread like wildfire in New York, Miami, Chicago, Latin America, and everywhere Santería communities exist in the New World. Patri Dhaifa herself ensured that the news spread fast by sending photos of the initiation and information about it to a great number of people. It was her intention to show that she did not believe in the need for secrecy in Santería. Accounts of the initiation appeared in newspapers and magazines in the United States, Latin America, and Nigeria. The *National Concord*, a newspaper based in Lagos, published two articles about the initiation, extolling Ms. Dhaifa's courage in undertaking the ceremony. Even New York's Mayor Edward Koch, with whom Ms. Dhaifa corresponds from time to time, wrote her a letter congratulating her on her Ifá initiation. Her new padrino, Ifayemi Elebuibon, proudly announced in a Nigerian circular that he had initiated Ms. Dhaifa into the "Ifá cult" and given her "ikin Ifá." Both the Araba and the Ooni (king) of Ile-Ife extended their congratulations.

But this rosy state of affairs did not last very long. Ifayemi, who traveled often to the United States on lecture tours, found a very cool reception among the American and Cuban babalawos, who deeply resented and unanimously condemned the initiation. A Cuban babalawo who was initiated in Nigeria told me the Nigerian babalawos were scandalized by the ceremony and had publicly chastised Ifayemi for performing it. According to this babalawo, there are no "female babalawos" in Nigeria. He claims Ifayemi told Cuban babalawos he never gave Patri Dhaifa the babalawo initiation, but a lesser ceremony. As of this writing, Ms. Dhaifa and Ifayemi Elebuibon are estranged from each other.

What about the santeros and babalawos? Will they ever relent and accept Dhaifa Odufora Ifatogún as one of them? Only the future can tell, but at present Patri Dhaifa is not an active member of the Santería community.

8.

Obi ⁄⁄
The Divining Coconut

According to Yoruba legend, at one time, Obi ("the coconut") was well loved and admired by Olofi, the father and creator of the gods. Obi was just and sincere, with a pure soul and a loving heart. As a reward for Obi's good qualities, Olofi made him shining white all over, and placed him on top of the highest palm tree. But as soon as he found himself in such a high position, Obi became very vain and arrogant. One day he decided to have a party and asked Elegguá, who was one of his closest friends, to invite all their mutual friends to this feast. Elegguá, who had noticed Obi's radical change and had noticed how proud and arrogant his friend had become, decided to test Obi's goodwill and invited to the party all the beggars and derelicts he could find. When Obi saw his beautiful house full of poor, ragged people dressed in dirty, smelly rags, miserable and unkempt, he almost choked with rage. Sputtering with indignation, he threw them all out of his house and told them never to darken his door again. The unwelcome guests left the party full of shame, and Elegguá, now convinced of Obi's sad change, left with them.

A few days later, Olofi asked Elegguá to go to Obi's house to bring him a message. Elegguá refused to go, and when Olofi pressed him for a reason, he told the Creator what had happened at Obi's party. Deeply saddened by this news, Olofi transformed himself into a beggar and went to knock on Obi's door. When Obi opened the door and saw a ragged mendicant standing there, he told the disguised Olofi to leave immediately and promptly slammed the door in his face. Olofi walked a few steps away from the door, and turning his back on the house, he called Obi in a loud voice, saying, *"Obi meye lori emi ofé."* ("Obi, look who I really am.") When Obi saw that the beggar was really Olofi, he was very frightened, and shaking with fear, he pleaded with Olofi to forgive him. But Olofi refused to forgive the offense and condemned Obi to fall from the palm tree and roll on the ground at the mercy of whoever might want to pick him up. He also changed Obi's color, and although his inside remained white, his shell became black and his outer cortex green. The color black symbolized Obi's sin of pride and arrogance, and the color green symbolized the hope that someday Obi would change his ways and become pure again. Olofi also condemned Obi to predict the future. The dry coconut is called *obi güi güi.* From this legend stems the tradition of placing a dry coconut at the feet of Elegguá's image.

In Santería, the coconut is used in all major ceremonies, and some of the most famous spells of the Religion are prepared with this fruit. It is also highly valued as a cure for several diseases, especially renal disorders.

The coconut divination is conducted by means of four coconut rinds. The coconut is used to determine an orisha's decisions and wishes. During the various ceremonies, santeros use this form of divination to determine whether the orishas are satisfied with the offerings received, and what must be done with them after the ceremony. The coconut is never used by santeros for a registro, or read in the same way as the cowrie shells.

Any of the orishas, as well as the eggun, can be consulted by means of the coconut rinds. But Elegguá is most frequently consulted.

The coconut rinds are brown on one side and white on the other. As the rinds are thrown on the floor, the four pieces will fall either on the white or the brown side. There are five patterns in which the rinds can fall. They are called *Alafia, Itagua, Ellife, Okana Sode,* and *Oyekun.*

Alafia—A pattern in which all four rinds fall on their white sides. Changó and Orúnla speak through this pattern and the answer is yes, although it is not a firm answer. When Alafia appears, santeros kiss the floor as an indication that the orishas give their blessings to the ceremony. If two of the rinds fall on top of each other, it means Alafia comes with iré—good luck—and to gather that special blessing, the santeros pour some water on the top coconut and drink it. If they are reading the coconut for someone else, that person drinks the water.

Itagua—A pattern that shows three white sides and one brown. The answer is uncertain, and the santero must throw the coconut again. if the pattern repeats itself, or if it is Alafia or Ellife, the answer is yes. It also usually means that there is something missing in the ceremony. Changó, Yemayá, Oggún, and Ochosi speak in Itagua.

Ellife—A pattern that shows two white and two brown sides. It is the strongest of the answers, and it means yes, without a doubt. Elegguá, Oggún, Ochosi, and Osun speak in this pattern.

Okana Sode—A pattern that shows three brown sides and one white. This "letter" means no, but it can also speak of death. Changó, Babalú-Ayé, and the eggun speak in this pattern.

Oyekun—A pattern in which all four pieces fall on their brown sides. It means no and predicts death. It is an evil pattern, and the orishas must be consulted immediately to determine what is wrong.

The coconut divination is simpler than the cowrie shells, but is just as delicate and must never be undertaken lightly or by someone who is not experienced in the method. To do so is to ask for trouble. If a pattern such as Oyekun falls, and the diviner doesn't know how to "clean" the evil influence of the "letter," he can become the recipient of harmful, negative energy. For that reason, santeros recommend that only santeros or people who really know the coconut should read the rinds. It is also said that the orishas speak only to initiated santeros through the coconut, and that the answers obtained by aleyos come not from the orishas but from the dead.

The ritual for reading the coconut begins by pouring three drops of water in front of the orisha who is being consulted, while saying, *"Omi tutu, ana tutu, tutu Laroye, tutu ilé."* Next, the diviner proceeds to moyubbar, that is, to remember all the dead elders of the religion, asking them for their blessing: *"Oloddumare ayuba. Bogwo ikú oluwo embelese Oloddumare ayuba, Igbae baye tonu."* Then he dispels evil influences: *"Cosi ikú, cosi ano, cosi eyé, cosi ofó, ariku babagwa."* Next he asks the saints for their blessing and for the protection of his padrinos: *"Kinkamaché Iyaremí. Kinkamaché Oyubbonami."* Finally he greets the santeros who may be present: *"Aché bogwo igworo. Afaché semilenu."*

After the initial prayers, the diviner tears several pieces off of each coconut rind and drops them over the stones of the orisha being consulted. If the orisha is Elegguá, he tears off three bits of each rind; if it is Changó, six pieces; if it is Oshún, five pieces, and so on. As he tears off the coconut bits, he says, *"Obinu ikú, Obinu ano, Obinu eyó, Obinu ofó, arikú babagwa."*

Now the diviner places the rinds, which he has been holding in his left hand, in his right hand. He then touches the floor and the orisha with his left hand and says, *"Ile mokueo, mokueo. Akueyé."* He repeats this three times, then says, *"Akueyé owó, akueyé omá, ariku babagwa."* Those present answer, *"Apkwaná."* He brings his hands together on his chest, with the rinds within, and throws them on the floor. He then proceeds to interpret the oracle.

One of the cast members in the feature film *The Believers*, which dealt with the beneficent powers of Santería, told me that one of the scenes called for the use of the coconut divination. The actors involved in the scene rehearsed it several times and, for that purpose, kept throwing the four pieces of coconut on the floor. Each time they did so, the coconut came up in the pattern of Oyekun, all the dark sides up. The santero they had engaged as consultant to the film happened to come in at that moment. When he saw what the actors had been doing and the pattern that had fallen, his face blanched. He immediately grabbed the coconut rinds, asked for some cold water, and proceeded to conduct the divination procedure with the proper respect it requires. When he threw the coconut down to ask for the orishas' blessings, everyone present held their breaths. But the pattern that came down was Alafia, four white coconuts and the blessings of the saints.

All the ceremonies and initiations of Santería require the use of the coconut divination. It is the most commonly used of all the divination procedures, and the only one that both the santeros and the babalawos may share.

The coconut divination does not exist in Nigeria. As we have seen, *obi* is the name given by the Yoruba to the kola nut. The kola-nut divination is known in Nigeria as *Didá obi* (casting the kola nuts). The type of kola used is the species known as *obi abatá*, which has four lobes (*awe merin*). Two of the lobes are said to be male and the other two female.

To read the *Didá obi*, the diviner breaks the kola nut into its four natural parts and casts them on the floor. The pieces can fall either on their convex or concave sides. As in the coconut divination there are five patterns in the *Didá obi*, although the names and meanings of the patterns are radically different from those used in the coconut system.

9.

The Diloggún ━━━━━━━━
The Divining Cowrie Shells

Among the Yoruba, the divination of the cowrie shells is known as *Erindinlogún*, and it is used principally by the worshipers of Changó. These diviners are known as *Iransee Changó*.

In Santería the seashell divination is known as the *Diloggún* or *caracoles*. Only santeros and santeras read the cowrie shells. Aleyos, those who have not been initiated in Santería, should not attempt the cowrie shells and the other divination systems. The reason for this taboo is that sometimes, during a registro, a negative pattern, or letra, may appear. If the person conducting the reading does not know how to nullify the bad influences of that pattern, he or she can be faced with severe difficulties.

The cowrie shells used for divination in Santería are a type of small, elongated seashell with an opening on one side that resembles a tiny mouth. Through this "mouth" the orishas speak to the santeros. The shells are bought "closed," that is, one side has the opening described above, while the other has a smooth, rounded surface. Only an initiated santero has the power to "open" the shells. He does this by filing the closed side until the rounded part breaks off, revealing an open space that is built naturally in each shell. This is done so that the shells may fall on either the mouth side or the open side.

When the santero throws the cowries during a reading, he counts the shells that have fallen mouth side up. Each number of shells has a different meaning and represents the voice of one or more orishas.

There are usually eighteen seashells in a *mano*, or "hand," but only sixteen of these are used in the reading. Elegguá has twenty-one seashells, but again only sixteen are read. Each orisha has twenty-one seashells that are kept in the tureens with the otanes. The seashells read by the santero in his registros are those of Elegguá.

The shells that are removed from each hand—usually two—are called *addele*. The ones that are read are called *Diloggún*. The Diloggún, are the mouthpieces of the orishas and are therefore of tremendous importance to the santero. Those santeros who are extremely proficient in the reading of the cowries are called *italeros*.

As in the opelé, there are five divination aids added to the Diloggún, which are called *igbo*. They are a small black stone called an *ota*, a rather long seashell called an *aye*, the head of a tiny doll called an *eriaworan*, a ball of powdered eggshell (cascarilla) called *efun*, and a piece of animal vertebra, *eggun*.

The santero begins the registro by dipping his middle finger in water and sprinkling some on the floor to refresh the house and the Diloggún. He begins to pray in Yoruba, asking for the blessings of the elder santeros who are dead and the blessings of the orishas, whom he names one by one, with their respective Yoruba prayers. These prayers are known as *moyubbar*. He then touches the shells to the forehead, hands, and knees of the consultant, and proceeds to throw the shells on the straw mat used for the reading. The cost of the reading is known as the *derecho*, and is usually between five and ten dollars. First the money is wrapped tightly and dropped on the mat with the cowrie shells; then it is put aside and the reading begins. At this point it is important to clarify the matter of the derecho in Santería. Every initiation, ceremony, and divination has a derecho or fee, which is sacred to the orishas. This money does not belong to the santero but to his personal orisha, and it is used for candles, fruits, and other offerings. The santero may use this money for his personal needs only if the orisha gives him permission.

There are sixteen patterns in the Diloggún. As in the opelé divination, each pattern is called an *oddu* or *ordún* and has a name and a refrain, as well as several legends, accompanying it. The oddu that falls on the mat tells the santero which igbo or divination aids to use in deciphering the oracle. Each oddu has its own set of igbo. The igbo are used two at a time, one in each hand. The person takes the igbo offered by the santero, shakes them between the hands, and separates them, presenting his closed fists to the santero. The santero then chooses the hand indicated by the oddu or pattern of cowrie shells. The igbo that is hidden in the hand answers yes or no to the question asked by the santero. The black stone invariably means no, while the shell and the ball of eggshell mean yes. The oddu also tells the santero which of the two hands presented to him by the consultant is to be chosen. Generally, the major oddus call for the left hand, while minor oddus call for the right. Based on the oddu of seashells and the igbo on the chosen hand, the santero interprets the oracle. He does this by adapting the refrain and the legends attached to each oddu to the particular problems of the consultant. To do this accurately, the santero must know by heart all of the refrains and legends attached to each oddu. The reading of the cowrie shells is highly complex; a santero therefore needs many years of careful study before he can master the oracle.

As in the opelé divination, one of the first things that the santero must determine during the reading is whether cowrie shells come with iré, good luck, for the consultant. This is done in the beginning of the reading. When the oddu gives the consultant iré, santeros call the pattern *ebodda*, that is, "good."

Otherwise the oddu is said to bring osogbo, which is not good.

There are several kinds of iré and several kinds of osogbo, describing the good or the bad situation facing the consultant. After he determines the nature of the problem and of the good fortune predicted by the shells, the santero finds out what is to be done. If the oddu gives iré, the santero asks if anything has to be done to bring that good luck to fruition. If the oddu presages osogbo, the santero finds out if there is *lariche*, a way out of the problem. There are several lariches, among which is *addimu*, a small offering to the orisha who protects the individual, that may range from coconut and water to special food offerings and cleansings. Another is the *ebbochure*, which calls for offering to the orisha a small part of everything the person eats for one or more days. Other types of lariche are the *ebbokun* and the *kilase*. The *ebbokun* says that the person must perform some sort of personal cleansing, such as special baths and rubbing rituals. The *kilase*, which is more complicated, may require a *rogación de cabeza*, or head purification.

The determination of the type of lariche to be used is of great importance, as it is the final answer to the person's problem. It is therefore vital that the santero be thoroughly competent in the interpretation of the oddu, so that he may give the consultant the correct solution to his problems.

It sometimes happens that a santero is very competent in the actual reading of the shells, but is unable to determine what must be done to better a person's life. Such santeros can be very impressive in describing a person's problems in great detail, giving him intimate descriptions of his personal life, and foretelling the future with great accuracy. But they are unable to give that person the answers to his problems, or the type of remedies necessary to make his wishes come true. This happens because these santeros are quite familiar with the meanings of the various oddu, but do not possess the ashé, the grace and power, to ask the orishas the right questions to determine how a person's life may be improved. Santeros who possess this ashé become very famous and sought-after, even by other santeros.

Because there are sixteen seashells in the Diloggún, there are also sixteen oddus in the oracle. Following is a list of the sixteen oddus and their accompanying proverbs.

1. **Okana Sode**—"If there is nothing good, there is nothing bad."
2. **Eyioko**—"An arrow between brothers."
3. **Oggundá**—"Arguments cause tragedies."
4. **Eyorosun**—"No one knows what lies at the bottom of the sea."
5. **Oche**—"Blood flows through the veins."
6. **Obbara**—"A king does not lie. From the lie, the truth is born."
7. **Oddi**—"Where the hole [grave] was first dug."
8. **Eyeunle**—"The head carries the body."
9. **Ossa**—"Your best friend is your worst enemy."
10. **Ofun**—"Where the curse was born."
11. **Ojuani**—"Water cannot be carried in a basket."
12. **Eyilá chebora**—"When there is war, the soldiers do not sleep."
13. **Metanlá**—"Where illness is born, blood is bad."
14. **Merinlá**—"A family that does not get along; envy surrounds you."
15. **Manunlá**—"The same way it moves you, it paralyzes you."
16. **Mediloggún**—"You were born to be wise, if you only listened to advice."

Of the above oddus, numbers 1, 2, 3, 4, 8, 12, 13, 14, 15, and 16 are major. The minor oddus are 5, 6, 7, 9, and 11. The smallest of the minors is 5 and the largest minor is 11. At least one orisha, and often several, speak in each oddu. Some of the oddus are said to "belong" to a particular orisha. When the specific oddu of an orisha appears, it means that orisha is speaking and desires to help the individual. For example, Obbara (6) is said to belong to Changó, Oche (5) to Oshún, and Ofun (10) to Obatalá.

The santero is empowered to read all sixteen patterns, but those numbering 13 to 16 really fall within the province of the babalawo. When one of these four oddus appears in the Diloggún, the santero must tell his client that he must visit a babalawo so that he may consult the opelé or the Table of Ifá on that person's behalf.

Sometimes when the santero casts the seashells, none of the oddus will appear. That is, all the shells fell facedown. The santeros say at such times, *"Se me fué el caracol de la mano,"* meaning the seashells "left his hand." This is an indication of forthcoming troubles and often death and tragedy to the person who is undergoing the registro. Shortly before my mother's stroke, a renowned santero read the Diloggún for me, and this "non-pattern" appeared. I still remember the shock in his eyes when he saw it. When I asked him what was wrong, he explained the meaning of the pattern and told me that someone very close to me, either my mother or father, was going to die suddenly unless something was done immediately to prevent it. He was fairly sure that my mother was the one who was going to die, so he told me she had to do several cleansings and ebbós, as well as receive the Necklaces. But my mother, who did not believe in Santería, refused to do any of the things he recommended. After her stroke, he reminded me of the oddu that had prognosticated her death, and told me to go to a babalawo for help. That is how she received the idé I described in Chapter 6.

As we have seen, the divination procedure followed in the Diloggún is similar to that of the opelé. Like the babalawo, the santero *moyubba*—that is, he prays to the dead and the saints. Then he asks permission of his client's ruling orisha to conduct the registro; he casts the seashells three times to get the principal oddu and two minor ones; and he uses five divinatory aids (igbo) to help in the divination. He also determines if the oddu comes with iré or osogbo, and what must be done to help the person. Like the Ifá oddu, those of the seashells also have a proverb and a legend attached to each. The combination of oddus add up to 256, like that of the opelé.

10.

Ewe ┃┃┃
Magical Herbs

The plants and parts of plants used in Santería are known collectively by the Yoruba term *ewe*. All santeros are botanical experts. One of the first lessons a yawó must learn is how to identify the trees, plants, roots, barks, and flowers used in Santería, and to which orisha each of them belongs. All of the ebbós of each orisha, as well as his initiation and rituals, must make use of their distinctive ewe. Santeros must therefore be thoroughly familiar with the ewe so that they will not make mistakes during the ceremonies. Although some herbs are shared by two or more orishas, some belong to only one, and those herbs can only be used in that particular orisha's rituals.

The herbs in the asiento and other major rituals must be fresh. They are usually imported to the United States from Puerto Rico and the Dominican Republic, although some can be found in Miami. Some of the ebbós and cleansing baths can be done with dried herbs, but santeros try to use green ewe whenever possible, in order to receive in full the ashé of the orishas.

The five-leaved silk-cotton tree, known in botany as *Ceiba pentandra*, is the sacred tree of Santería and the basis of some of the greatest magic of the Religion. No one in Latin America likes

133

to cut down one of these trees, which are considered by many to have great spiritual force. The santeros believe that even lightning respects the ceiba, and in reality, the tree is very seldom, if ever, struck by lightning.

At the foot of the ceiba are buried many of the bilongos and ebbós of Santería. The ground around the tree is always covered with fruit offerings, money, and sacrificed animals. The ceiba is so highly respected by the santeros that they never cross over its shadow without asking its permission beforehand, for the tree is supposed to be very sensitive and easily offended. When it is angered, it will not give its precious protection to the santero, whose spells will come to naught without it. With the help of the ceiba it is possible to cast great beneficial spells for love and increase, and also for death and destruction; the tree does not discriminate between good and evil as long as it is paid for its services, and full respect is shown during the transaction. In Cuba, when a santero wants to harm an enemy, he goes to the ceiba at midnight, and after taking off his clothes, he walks around the tree several times, brushing the trunk with the tips of his fingers and asking the ceiba to accomplish his will. All magical operations are conducted by means of words or songs. Thus, speaking softly and sweetly to the ceiba will compel it to do whatever one asks of it.

The santeros believe the ceiba is a saint. Its spirit is essentially maternal. It is a female tree. Its African name is Iroko, and it is one of the African aspects of the Conception of Mary. The Kongos call it *nkunia casa sami* (the tree house of God), *mamá Ungundu*, and *Iggi-Olorun*. The original Iroko is a gigantic species of African mahogany tree that is venerated by many African tribes along the coast of Guinea. Since this tree does not grow in the Caribbean, the African in the New World substituted the ceiba for it, which he rebaptized as Iroko, paying it homage ever since that time.

The santeros sacrifice a bull to the ceiba during some of their special ceremonies. They walk in a circle around the tree with the animal before killing it, while carrying lit candles in their hands. Every month, white chickens are sacrificed by its roots.

The roots and leaves of the ceiba are believed to be of great medicinal value, especially in treating cases of venereal disease and difficulties in the urinary tract. The leaves are also reputed to be excellent in the treatment of anemia. The bark of the tree is used in a special tea that is believed to make barren women conceive.

The santeros explain that they use the ceiba in six different ways for their magical work: (1) the tree trunk is used to cast evil spells; (2) the bark is used for teas and other medicinal purposes; (3) the shade of the tree attracts the spirits and gives its supernatural strength to all the spells buried underneath it; (4) the roots are used to place the offerings to the ceiba and to receive the blood of sacrificed animals; (5) the earth around the tree is often used in black magic; and (6) the leaves of the tree are used for medicinal purposes, to cast love spells, and to prepare the omiero used during the asiento.

The palm tree is almost as powerful as the ceiba in Latin American magic, and is believed to be the habitation of Changó. This belief is based on the fact that the palm tree is often the recipient of lightning bolts, which are the weapon of the orisha. Lightning is believed by many to be Changó coming home to the palm tree. One of the legends that explains why the palm tree is the constant victim of lightning tells that Changó, who is an incorrigible woman-chaser, asked a small lizard to bring a present to one of the Orisha's paramours. The lizard put the gift in its mouth and hurried to the lady's house. Unfortunately, in its haste to get to its destination, it stumbled and swallowed the present, which became stuck in its throat (this explains why the skin of the lizard's neck is distended). When Changó found out that the gift never reached the lady in question, he became enraged with the lizard and demanded of the terrified messenger why the present had not been delivered. Fire gushed out of Changó's mouth with every word. The lizard was unable to answer because of the pressure of the package on its vocal cords, and trembling with fear, it ran up the palm tree to seek refuge among the branches. Changó, believing himself mocked by the lizard, threw a lightning bolt at the tree, intending to scorch the lizard. Since then, the palm tree has been the target of Changó's anger because the lizard is still hiding there to protect itself against the orisha.

Some rituals use the palm tree to bring rain. During these rituals the santeros usually invoke Changó or Yemayá, after lighting twelve cotton wicks soaked in olive oil. Another rite for rain consists of making a cross on the ground under the palm tree. Over the cross the santeros build a small mound of earth, on top of which they place fruit offerings to Changó and sacrifice a rooster. They light two candles to the orisha, who answers shortly thereafter with heavy rain and peals of thunder and a bolt or two of lightning.

The elm tree also belongs to Changó, and it is used by the santeros to cast their spells when the ceiba or the palm tree is not available, especially in the northern United States, where the palm tree and the ceiba cannot grow because of the colder climate.

In the United States the ewe and all the various ingredients needed for the rites and the magic spells of Santería can be found at the botánicas. The salespeople in these stores are usually well versed in the lore and traditions of Santería and are also herbal experts. Botánicas specialize in herbs of Santería, most of which they sell fresh.

The following list gives the herbs most commonly associated with the major orishas. The herbs are listed in Spanish because that is how they are known in the botánicas. Most of them are tropical plants, not readily available or known in the United States.

Elegguá

grama de caballo
lengua de vaca
espartillo
abre camino
pastillo
yerba fina
hedionda

itamo real
meloncillo
albahaca
piñón criollo
pata de gallina
llamao

Oggún and Ochosi

caña santa
pata de gallina
yerba de sangre
yerba mora
pegojo
hueso de gallo
adormidera
siempreviva

anamú
romerillo
amanza guapo
albahaca morada
palo manaju
ebano
quita maldición
salvadera

Changó and Aganyú

bledo punzó
moco de pavo
zarzaparrilla
paraíso
álamo
jobo

almácigo
granada
mamey
rompe zaragüey
ruda

Obatalá

bledo de clavo
saúco
campana
algodón
aguinaldo blanco

higuereta
almendro
guanábana
jagua blanca
malva

Babalú-Ayé

cundiamor	apasote
zalgazo	piñón botijo
zazafrán	caisimón
alacrancillo	tapa camino
escoba amarga	salvia

Yemayá and Oshún

malva té	guásima
lechuga	botón de oro
lechuguilla	yerba de la niña
yerba añil	colonia
verbena	marilope
prodigiosa	panetela
helecho	huevo de gallo
flor de agua	guacamaya
berro	yerba mora
yerba buena	diez del día
albahaca morada	palo canela
guamá	

Oyá

yerba garro	caimitillo
baria	caimito
mazorquilla	flamboyán
yuca	geranio
ciruela	guara
palo caja	maravilla
cabo de hacha	

The special herbal baths called despojos are said to have the special ashé of the various orishas. The combination of herbs brings about the "chemical reaction" necessary to improve an individual's life. Santeros believe that herbs are divided into two groups, the sweet and the bitter. These denominations do not have anything to do with taste, but with spiritual vibrations. Sweet herbs are used for attracting good luck, love, money, and prosperity. Bitter herbs are used to dispel evil and negative energies. Sweet and bitter herbs should not be mixed, as they nullify each other's vibrations. Following is a small list of sweet and bitter herbs.

Sweet Herbs	Bitter Herbs
manzanilla	rompezaragüey
colonia	abre camino
yerba buena	apasote
mejorana	anamú
yerba luisa	escoba amarga
altamisa	jobo
maravilla	álamo
berro	tártago
albahaca	ruda
salvia	arrasa con todo
siempreviva	yerba bruja
menta	hedionda
verbena	cortadera
mirto	pata de gallina
prodigiosa	espartillo
botón de oro	lengua de vaca
paraiso	romerillo
llamao	zarzaparrilla
	salvadera
	quita maldición

Any combination of three, five, seven, or nine bitter herbs boiled in several quarts of water make an excellent bath to destroy evil. At least three baths should be taken (on three consecutive nights). It is advisable to add some holy water to each bath every night after the herbal decoction has been boiled, strained, and cooled. Santeros recommend lighting a white candle in the honor of the person's guardian angel after taking the bath.

The sweet herbs should only be used after the bitter herbs. Again, three, five, seven, or nine herbs are recommended, and an equal number of baths, although in some instances only one bath is necessary. The sweet baths are also prepared with holy water, and santeros recommend the addition of honey, cinnamon, and some perfume—either the person's favorite fragrance or Loción Pompeya or Kolonia 1800, the staple perfumes of Santería. It is always better to consult a santero to determine which are the best baths for each person, as there are people who do not need the bitter herbs and others who should avoid the sweet herbs until their bodies are thoroughly cleansed of negative vibrations.

Following are some of the specific baths of the most popular orishas.

Elegguá

⬙ Escoba amarga, guairo, altamisa, canutillo blanco, yerba-buena, cimmarrona, abrajo (This powerful bath combines both bitter and sweet herbs to underline Elegguá's dual force.)

Obatalá

⬙ Cascarilla, campana blanca, algodón
⬙ White flowers, anon, guanábana, prodigiosa, higuereta blanca, bledo blanco, colonia, verdolaga, yagruma, paraiso, vergonzoza, jagüey, caracolillo blanco

Changó

⬙ Piñón, almácigo, ponasí, palma, tres marías, algodón, álamo, malva, hinojo de monte
⬙ Ruda, apasote, peonía, granada

Oggún

◪ Salvadera
◪ Amanza guapo, guaco, yerba quimbisa, pata de gallina, malva cochinera

Aganyú

◪ Iroko (ceiba), algarrobo, lino de monte, guairo, santo jagüey

Babalú-Ayé

◪ Pata de gallina, escoba amarga, yerba sangre, güano real, cordovan, guira, malva té, albahaca morada, cundiamor

Yemayá

◪ Canutillo blanco, lechuguín, mejorana, altamisa, mazorquilla, flor de agua, malanguilla, yerbabuena

Oshún

◪ Sauco amarillo, botón de oro, girasol, guacamaya, guano del rio, paraiso, ciruela, canitel, helecho, caracolillo

Oyá

◪ Malanguilla, caimito, llagruma, hoja de palo ramón, algarrobo de mar, higuereta morada, cordovan, flamboyán, maravilla

THE OMIERO

All of the major ceremonies of Santería, including that of the Necklaces and the asiento, require the use of the omiero, the sacred elixir of the religion. The omiero for the asiento is prepared with the blood of the sacrificial animals and other ingredients. This liquid is used to wash the stones consecrated to the orishas, to bathe the iyawó, and to drink. During the seven days that he spends at his ayugbona's house, the yawó drinks a glass of the omiero several times a day. (The ayugbona is the priest or priestess who assists the officiating santero or padrino.) In spite of the mixture of herbs, blood, and other substances, the omiero is not unpalatable. It is not the most pleasant of drinks, but it does not taste as bad as one might think. It has a pungent smell that is easily recognizable. Some casas de santo, especially those of babalawos, seem to be steeped in the smell of the omiero. It is a strange smell, bitter and yet fragrant, that conjures images of things not quite of this world.

The herbs of the omiero must be quite fresh, as their juices are vital for the success of the ceremonies, especially the asiento. For that reason, santeros order these tropical plants from Puerto Rico, the Dominican Republic, and sometimes from Miami a few days before the asiento. Each orisha is represented by at least one of his or her initiates, who is in charge of the various herbs. Each group of herbs pertaining to an individual orisha is placed in a white basin to which some water is added. The herbs are then crushed by hand by a santera initiated in the mysteries of the orisha who owns that group of herbs. Another santera, usually younger, goes from basin to basin, adding more water as the herbs are being crushed. The basins are usually placed on the floor in a row, and the santeras sit or kneel behind them. As the santeras work, they sing the ritualistic chants of each orisha in the original Yoruba. The order of the chants is always the same, starting with Elegguá and ending with Ibeyi, the sacred twins who have access to all the ewe of the other orishas.

After the herbs are crushed, the resulting liquid is mixed with other ingredients, among which are rainwater, sea water, river water, holy water, rum, honey, manteca de corojo, cocoa butter, cascarilla, pepper, kola nuts, and some of the blood of the sacrificial animals.

The omiero is said to have great medicinal properties, and everyone present at an asiento will eagerly drink a few mouthfuls for good luck and better health.

The following table lists twenty-one of the most common plants used in the preparation of the omiero, with the names of the orishas who claim them, and some of their medicinal and/or magical properties.

PLANTS USED FOR THE OMIERO

Plant	English or Latin Name	Owner(s)	Uses
Hedionda	*Cassia occidentalis*	Elegguá	against colitis
Yerba mora	Solanium nigrum	Oggún, Yemayá	throat infections, nerves, skin trouble
Rompe-zaragüey	*Eupatorium odatorum*	Changó	against evil (in baths)
Albahaca morada	Basil	Oggún, Yemayá	stomach troubles
Zarza-parrilla	Sarsaparilla	Changó	rheumatism, nerves, syphilis
Paraiso	*Melia azederach*	Changó	against evil (in baths)
Añil	Indigo plant	Yemayá, Oshún	tumors, epilepsy
Verbena	Vervain	Yemayá, Oshún	liver, care of the hair

PLANTS USED FOR THE OMIERO

Plant	English or Latin Name	Owner(s)	Uses
Lechuga	Lettuce	Yemayá, Oshún	against evil
Yerba buena	Spearmint	Yemayá	skin troubles, for luck
Canela	Cinnamon	Oshún	intestinal trouble, love
Campana	Elecampane	Obatalá	bronchitis
Higuereta	*Ricinus communis*	Obatalá	diphtheria, headaches, cancer
Algodón	Cotton (plant)	Obatalá	bronchitis, asthma, tumors
Verdolaga	Purslane	Yemayá	good luck
Malva té	*Corchorus siliquosus*	Oshún	purifying baths
Berro	Watercress	Yemayá, Oshún	stomach irritations
Anis	Aniseed	Oshún	indigestion, hysteria
Helecho	River fern	Yemayá, Oshún	against evil
Calabaza	Pumpkin	Oshún	burns, skin diseases, whooping cough
Espartillo	Sporobolus	Elegguá, Ochosi	against evil

☑ This hill shrine (*Oke Tase*) in Ile-Ife, Nigeria, was constructed in honor of Orúnmila, the holy diviner and patron of babalawos, the high priests of Santería.

☑ The twenty-one cowrie shells make up the seashell divination known as the caracoles. The system uses sixteen cowries, while the other five are set aside by the reader. The cowries are the mouthpieces of the orishas and the most important divination system of Santería.

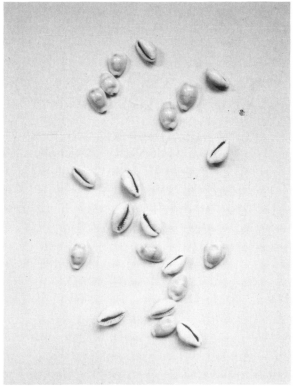

◼ A carved Eshu (Elegguá) figure from Nigeria. Elegguá is in the center, bearded and flanked by two female figures, a subtle hint of the orisha's great phallic powers in the Yoruba tradition. The many cowrie shells around the figures represent Elegguá's ability to gather riches.

◼ In Santería, Elegguá is represented by a cement or clay head with eyes, mouth, nose, and ears formed by cowrie shells.

☑ The top of a staff of Changó (*oshé Changó*) usually depicts a woman with a double-edged ax (*edun ara*) balanced on her head. The figure is kneeling with uplifted breasts, the traditional posture Changó's priestesses use to worship the orisha.

☑ Three Eleggúa heads appear in clay vessels. Very often santeros have more than one Eleggúa because this saint is said to have twenty-one paths, each path governing a different place. For example, one path may rule the four corners, while others may rule the forest, the sea, the jails, the hospitals, and so forth.

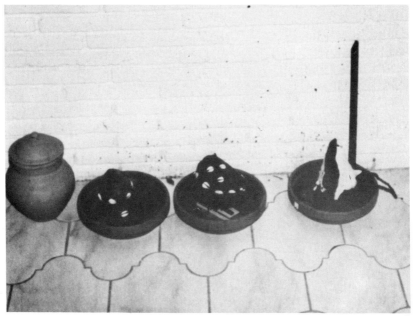

An image of Saint Barbara, syncretized as Changó, stands over the table that houses Elegguá and the Warriors. The toy truck is an offering to Elegguá, a childish, impish deity.

Several of the bead necklaces of Santería sit next to the small tureen that houses the mysteries of the Cofá de Orúnla, the only initiation conferred upon women by babalawos.

☑ This black rag doll dressed in gingham is a representation of an African eggun, a spirit believed to guide the santero who owns it. The doll wears blue and white, the colors of Yemayá, who was the ruling orisha of the eggun when he or she was alive. Gingham in the colors of the orishas is very often used by santeras to make skirts with ruffles and lace.

☑ A figure of Oggún, surrounded by a string of *mariwó* (his favorite clothing) in a Nigerian grove. Oggún's groves are usually located near the Oshún River to symbolize Oggún's hopeless love for the beautiful Oshún.

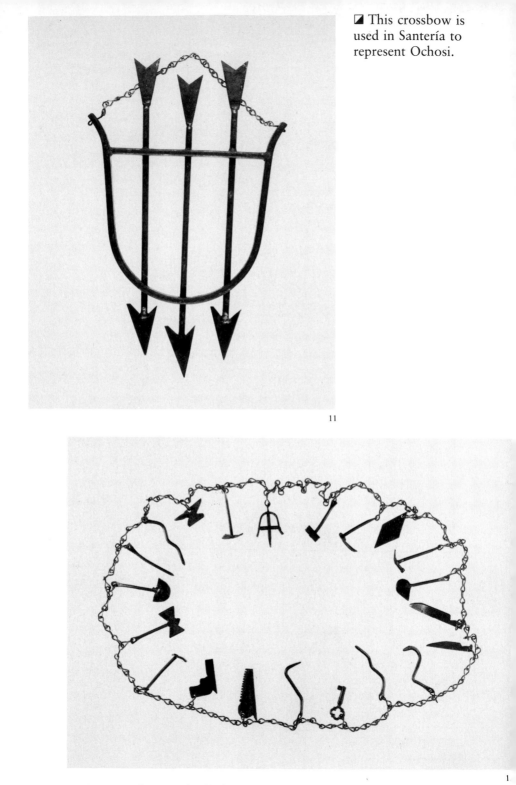

◪ This crossbow is used in Santería to represent Ochosi.

11

1

◪ An iron chain with all the work implements of Oggún is commonly used in Santería to represent the orisha.

13

◢ The Oshún River in Oshogbo, Nigeria, is the manifestation of Oshún in nature. A figure representing Oggún—her forlorn lover—stands in front of the tree, arms extended, as if wishing to embrace the rushing waters.

14

◢ The Catholic representations of Oshún (Our Lady of Charity, patron of Cuba), Obatalá (Our Lady of Mercy), and Yemayá (Our Lady of Regla). Oshún's Catholic image shows a boat with three men at her feet. The three men—all of them called Juan—were shipwrecked sailors who saw the Virgin for the first time outside Havana, while praying during a violent storm.

■ This tureen contains Oba's secrets. Draped over it is the large necklace (*collar de mazo*) of blue and pink beads worn by her initiates.

■ This small metal rooster represents Osun, companion to the Warriors. When Osun falls down, danger is near.

■ This altar for the eggun, Elegguá, Oggún, and Ochosi is known as a *bóveda*. There is a basin at its foot containing blue-colored water upon which five yellow plastic ducks float. This indicates that either the eggun who protect the bóveda or the santero who owns it is a child of Oshún, whose number is five and whose color is yellow.

■ A beribboned *palo,* used to call the dead, hidden behind a kitchen cabinet. There are several food offerings on the floor, including black coffee and a glass of rum tied with a red ribbon. The chalk marks on the wall are a representation of the earth and the four cardinal points.

☑ Fernando Sierra, O-Yeya-I, an initiate of Obatalá for twenty-five years, is one of my godfathers and a very knowledgeable babalocha. Against the walls behind the lace curtains are the shelves where the tureens are kept. A plate on the floor, just visible at right, holds a food offering. The Christmas gifts are for Elegguá.

☑ Eduardo Pastoriza Changó-Larí, an initiate of Changó for more than forty years, is also one of my godfathers. He stands below a statue of Saint Barbara (Changó). The image holds her sword with the point up, in a warrior's attitude of defense. Usually Saint Barbara's image holds the sword with the tip down. Here the santero has reversed the sword's position to invoke Changó's protection against evil.

◢ Constantine Bailly—an initiate of Oshún—and her husband Gene—an initiate of Yemayá—with their daughter Marie Alexandra, who has already received the initiations of the Necklaces and the Warriors.

21

22

◢ Margot Torres, a well-known New York santera and initiate of Oyá, visits the Nigerian town of Ode Omu, where she is seen receiving the title of *iyalode,* or chieftain. The title is honorary but has religious connotations. Lately, many santeros are traveling to Nigeria to rediscover the roots of their religion.

23

◪ This is an offering to Yemayá, who is the ruler of the ocean. The large seashell is one of her attributes.

◪ A cake is part of the offering to Changó during an orisha's anniversary. The fruit and other food are all attributes of the orisha. The offerings are placed on the floor in front of Changó's batea and are known as the plaza.

24

◪ The inside of Yemayá's tureen, showing her ritual stones (*otanes*) and some of her symbols. Among them is a sun, a moon, an anchor, a key, and a ship's steering wheel.

◪ The tureen holding the *Abo-Faca*, or *Mano de Orúnla*, an initiation conferred only upon men by the babalawo. The sixteen kola nuts (*ikin Ifá*) are clearly visible inside the tureen. To the right are some of the ritual necklaces, including the yellow and green one that belongs to Orúnla.

◪ The inside of the *Ico-Fa*, or *Cofá de Orúnla*, conferred only upon women by the babalawo during a lengthy three-day initiation. A small crocodile—a symbol of Orúnla—is poised in front of the tureen.

☑ This sea of coconuts and ñames are the *derechos* (rights) brought to a babalawo's house by his godchildren on October 4, the day ascribed to Orúnla as Saint Francis of Assisi. In the background, a statue of Saint Francis sits on a table that covers Orúnla's secrets. The draperies are green and yellow, the colors of Orúnla in Santería.

☑ The late babalawo Pancho Mora received the *Abo-Faca* initiation. Mora was one of the first to bring Santería to the United States in the 1930s. He was known as the dean of babalawos. The cap he wears in the photo is similar to the ones worn by both santeros and babalawos during all major ceremonies. Sometimes the cap is made of gingham in the color of the orisha who rules the santero or babalawo. Pancho Mora died in 1986. *Iboru-Iboya.*

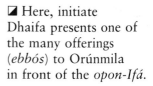
☑ Here, initiate Dhaifa presents one of the many offerings (*ebbós*) to Orúnmila in front of the *opon-Ifá*.

30

☑ Ifayemi makes sixteen cuts on Dhaifa's shaven head with a razor blade. Later the cuts were smeared with Orúnla's sacred powder, made with crushed kola nuts. Through the powder rubbed into the incisions, Dhaifa receives Orúnla's mysteries.

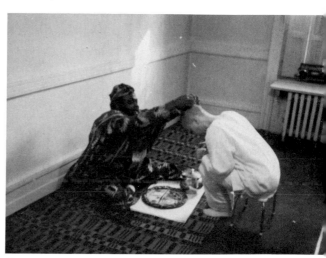

31

☑ Ifayemi offers an animal sacrifice to Eshu (Elegguá) as Dhaifa looks on. On her forehead she is wearing the *ekodide*, the red parrot feather that is a symbol of the initiate.

32

33

◪ At midnight, Dhaifa places a propitiatory offering to the witches (*ajé*) on the corner of 125th Street and Broadway, so that they will not interfere with her initiation.

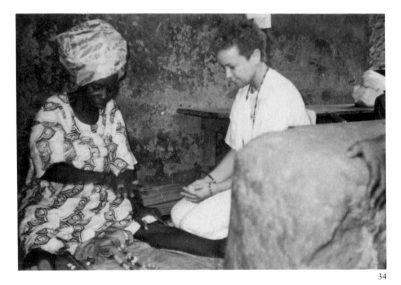

34

◪ Patri Dhaifa watches attentively as the iyanifá Mopelola Fawenda Amoke reads the opelé for her while she visits in Oyo, Nigeria.

II.

Ebbó ///
The Offering

The ebbó, as we have seen, is an offering to an orisha for the purpose of acquiring ashé. This ashé, which is raw cosmic energy, can be manifested in many ways, depending on the santero's needs or desires. The basic difference between an ebbó and an ordinary spell is that the ebbó is always directed to an orisha to enlist his aid in the solution of our human problems, while the spell is usually cast only with the intention of channeling the will of the individual. When an ebbó is used, something must be given to an orisha in order for him or her to work for us. This is not necessary for spells, which do not usually require the help of an orisha, although some spells are conducted with the help of a supernatural agency, especially the guardian angel—*Eledáa*—of an individual.

The concept of Eledáa in Santería is very complicated. It generally indicates the head of a person, as well as his guardian angel. Some santeros believe that the Eledáa and the person's ruling orisha are one and the same. Others contend that they are separate entities. The consensus is that the Eledáa is the mind or mental processes of a person. The best way, say the santeros, to influence an individual for either good or evil is by attempting to distract his Eledáa or guardian angel by invoking it and offering it candles or a *plaza* (an offering of fruits and candies). Sometimes a glass of water with honey and some perfume is sufficient to divert the attention of the Eledáa from the person it protects. While the Eledáa is entertained, anyone can attack its protégé, who is helpless against such an attack. For that reason, santeros believe that the Eledáa should always be refreshed and well fed so that it will be alert and will not let any harm come to the person it guards. If the Eledáa is not cared for, it becomes restless and thirsty and may cause an injury to the head so that it may drink its own blood.

THE ROGACIÓN

According to santeros, the best way to refresh the Eledáa is through a *rogación de cabeza*, which is a combination of prayers and coconut plaster applied directly to the head. The basic rogación is made with coconut, cascarilla, and coconut butter, although sometimes other ingredients are added.

The rogación is the most important of all the cleansing ebbós in Santería, and is undertaken before each of the initiations. Santeros recommend extreme caution in the choice of the person who is to do a rogación. One must trust that person implicitly and be sure that he or she has been initiated as a santero or santera. People with known bad habits, who are irascible or of changeable character, should not be allowed to do a rogación. The reason for these precautions is that the Eledáa can receive negative vibrations from the person who is doing the rogación, which can bring about many disturbances for the one who receives it. Also, it is possible that while a person is doing a rogación, he may try to influence the Eledáa of the individual for whom he performs it, in order to bring that person under his will. The best person to do a rogación is one's padrino or madrina, or another santero who is serious and responsible. Then one can be sure that the ceremony will be done properly.

The term *rogación de cabeza* means, literally, "prayers for the head." The santero who conducts the ceremony begins by grating half of a coconut and mixing it with cascarilla, cocoa butter, and any other ingredients that may be required. The other half of the coconut is divided into four parts, to be used in divination. He puts the coconut mixture and the four coconut sections on a white plate with a large piece of cotton and a gourd filled with water, and asks the recipient to sit on a chair, barefoot and with both hands resting on his knees, palms up. The santero faces the recipient and presents the plate with the coconut to his forehead, the back of his neck, the shoulders, the hands, and the feet. As he does this, the santero prays to the Eledáa: *"Emi kobo ori. Cosi ikú, cosi ano, cosi eyo, cosi ofo, arikubabagwa."* With this prayer he greets the Eledáa and asks for the orishas' blessings in banishing death, crime, bloodshed, illness, and all evil from the recipient.

After completing the prayer, the santero places the plate on the floor, dips his finger in the gourd, and makes the sign of the cross on the person's forehead, the back of the neck, the temples, the base of the throat, the inner sides of the elbows, the palms of the hands, and the feet. He then chews a bit of the cocoa butter and divides it among those same points. This is done because the saliva of a person is said to have great ashé, and is considered helpful in the rogación.

Now the santero takes the largest part of the coconut mixture and puts it on top of the person's head, covering it with some of the cotton. He divides the rest of the coconut mixture among the various body points he has already blessed. He covers the coconut mixture with cotton, and asks the person to pray to his orisha and to Obatalá—who owns both the head and the coconut—requesting good health and *desenvolvimiento*, that is, spiritual and material evolution. The santeros always advise against asking for riches of material wealth. "The saints know what you need," they are fond of saying. "What you must ask for is desenvolvimiento. That way you'll get everything you want and need."

After the recipient finishes his prayers, the santero asks him to rub the cotton with the coconut between both hands and let it fall on the ground. The santero picks it up and places it on the plate. He then lights two white candles on the floor in front of the recipient, and picks up the four pieces of coconut to be used for divination. First he throws the coconut behind the recipient, asking him not to look back. He does this because he is asking the eggun if they are pleased with the rogación. When the coconut falls on the floor he immediately informs the recipient which of the oddu patterns has been formed. If the pattern is positive, he does nothing. If it is negative, he must ask the eggun what they want to cleanse the bad "letter."

After consulting with the eggun, the santero throws the coconut once more. This time he faces the recipient, as he is now consulting the orishas to learn if everything has been done correctly. The last thing he does with the coconut is to ask the orishas where the rogación must be taken after the ceremony. Once all this has been ascertained, the santero removes the coconut mixture and the cotton from the various places he has put them, with the exception of the head. The rest is put on the plate. The santero then covers the person's head with a white handkerchief, which, together with the coconut mixture, must remain in place until the next day, when it is removed and taken to the place indicated by the orishas through the coconut. The plate with the rest of the rogación is placed under the recipient's bed, where it must stay until the next day. The contents of the plate and the head mixture must be disposed of at the same time.

As mentioned above, there are several types of rogaciónes. Sometimes the orishas indicate that bread and milk must be added to the coconut; at other times the added ingredient is ground meat or the blood of two white doves. The type of rogación depends upon the specific needs of an individual, but santeros say that there are ways to refresh the Eledáa without a rogación. The most common way is to open a coconut and pour the milk over the head, either alone or mixed with other ingredients, such as rainwater, river water, and water in which rice has been steeped overnight. This is said to clear the mind and bring great prosperity to an individual.

There are twenty-one ingredients that keep recurring in the ebbós of Santería. All are of vital importance in the magic of santeros, and include the following:

cascarilla (powdered eggshell)
cacao (cocoa butter)
manteca de corojo (palm oil)
coco (coconut)
maiz tostado (toasted corn)
pescado ahumado y jutía (smoked fish and opossum)
miel (honey)
melao (sugar cane syrup)
pimienta de guinea (guinea pepper)
harina de maiz (corn meal)
canela (cinnamon, stick or powder)
tabacos (cigars)
ron (rum)
alcanfor (camphor)
quimbombó (okra)
ñame (a type of yam)
agua Florida (Florida Water)
Kolonia 1800 (cologne)
Loción or Esencia Pompeya (cologne)
agua (water)
agua bendita (holy water)

As stated above, ebbós are offerings to the saints and include both food and animal sacrifices. Each orisha has his own special ebbós, which are linked to the oddus of the Diloggún. The libreta, or notebook, that the santero receives at the end of his year of initiation lists all of the ebbós of the orishas and the corresponding oddus.

Sometimes, during a registro with the seashells, the orishas ask for a simple ebbó or offering that requires only some fruits, candies, or one of the foods preferred by the orishas. As we have seen, this type of offering is known as an addimú. Each orisha has many favorite foods, and the officiating santero must ask the saint which of these foods he or she desires to be given. Elegguá, for example, is often propitiated with three balls of cornmeal and guava paste. Obatalá is offered "towers" of mashed ñame sprinkled with cascarilla and cocoa butter and covered with cotton. Changó loves an offering of his favorite, okra, sliced and mixed with cornmeal and water. The resulting paste is known as *amalá*. Yemayá is sometimes propitiated with *mariquitas*, fried plantain chips and fried pork rinds. Oshún's favorite dish is a pumpkin filled with *ochinchín*, scrambled eggs with shrimp and watercress. All the orishas are partial to baskets of fruits and cakes, but some fruits are sacred to certain of the deities. Apples and bananas belong to Changó, pumpkins and oranges to Oshún, watermelon to Yemayá, white grapes and pears to Obatalá. Both Oggún and Aganyú accept green plantains covered with manteca de corojo as a suitable offering, and Oyá will do miracles with an eggplant sliced in nine parts.

After the orisha has chosen the addimú it wants, the santero must find out how many days the offering must remain at the feet of the deity. Sometimes the orisha does not indicate any days, and then the offering remains by the orisha's sopera until the fruit rots or dries out. If the individual who is making the offering does not have the orisha in his house, he often brings the addimú to the house of the santero and leaves it there.

The rubbing rituals that use meat, bones, and other ingredients such as eggs, fruits, and plants, are known as sarayeyeos, and generally serve to rid an individual of negative influences.

The larger and more complicated ebbós invariably require an animal sacrifice. These will be discussed in detail in the following chapter.

12.

Sacrificial
Ceremonies ///////////////////////////

In the spring of 1980 the ASPCA, apparently acting on a neighbor's tip, raided an apartment in the Bronx where an asiento was about to take place. According to an article in *The New York Times*,* ASPCA agents came upon "a scene of blood-spattered confusion." Several chickens and hamsters and a goat had already been sacrificed, and the raiders confiscated eighteen chickens, three goats, and several hamsters.

This report gave Santería a few months of adverse and much sensationalized publicity, and a great deal of speculation took place as to the purpose of the sacrifices. The press, obviously unfamiliar with Santería, commonly used terms like "satanic cults" and "bizarre ritualistic activities."† This near-hysteria was quite understandable. Ritualistic killings and "blood sacrifices" are supposed to be the exclusive realm of horror stories and B-grade films and are not supposed to happen in real life. It compounded the santeros' plight when a young boy was found hanging upside down from a tree in a Bronx park, with his

---

The New York Times, May 24, 1980.
†*New York Post*, April 9, 1980.

152

throat cut and a bottle filled with his blood at the roots of the tree. When two bodies showed up in Manhattan, completely drained of blood and showing all the signs of ritualistic murder, again Santería was momentarily suspect.

The santeros withstood all these suspicions with their proverbial equanimity. "It will be all right," an iyalocha commented. "It's all in the hands of God and the orishas. This religion did not come all the way from Africa to fall prey to religious discrimination."

Oddly, this statement found echoes in the attitudes of the ASPCA, who publicly expressed the sentiment that there was a "great deal of good in this religion,"* and that they were not trying to persecute people for their religious beliefs. A high official of the ASPCA went so far as to say in the same newspaper interview that he only wished that "we could get together with the babalawos and talk. Maybe we could straighten this thing out."†

The New York Police Department is no stranger to ritual sacrifice or ritual murder. There are so many new cults, sects, religions, and occult groups and subgroups sprouting all over the city on a regular basis that the police have been forced to create a task force just to deal with them. Detectives work hand in hand with psychologists, psychiatrists, sociologists, anthropologists, and a host of other specialists in human behavior and cult-related aberrations to try to understand the motivations of each group and to determine how dangerous they may be to public safety. It did not take the police very long to learn the essential practices of the santeros and their strict moral codes.

Recently I had the opportunity to speak with one of the officers in the Public Relations Division of the NYPD. When I asked him what the police thought about the santeros, he said that as far as the police department was concerned, the santeros were

*(New York) *Sunday News Magazine*, August 10, 1980.
†Ibid.

among the most respectable members of the Latin communities. "We have no problems with them," he said. "The ones who are constantly harassing the santeros are the officers of the ASPCA because of the occasional animal sacrifices the santeros conduct during their initiations. When the ASPCA learns of an initiation, they invariably raid the house where it is to take place in order to confiscate the sacrificial animals. They call us to help them enforce the raid, and we have to do it because it is the law. Neither the NYPD nor the ASPCA have any complaints about the sacrifice itself, because this is a question of civil liberties. The problem is that in order to slaughter animals within the city limits, a person or group needs special permits from both the ASPCA and the New York Health Department. The santeros do not have such permits. This is why they are having problems with the ASPCA. But other than that, they are pretty decent people and seem to be of great help with the problems of the community. In many ways, Santería is like an extension of the Catholic Church. The two religions have a lot in common."

The reason why the santeros are having difficulties with the ASPCA and the Department of Health is that there are many different *casas de santo*, and the various members of these houses have so far failed to unify themselves. Until they do so, and take legal procedures to legalize their ceremonies and get the proper licenses, they will undoubtedly continue to be harassed by the city departments involved.

There are three basic types of animal sacrifices in Santería.

1. Ritual cleansings, in which the animals are believed to take on the negative vibrations surrounding an individual, and therefore cannot be eaten. During a ritual cleansing, the blood of the animal is offered to God through the saints or orishas. The remains of the animal are disposed of in accordance with the wishes of the orisha.
2. Offerings to the eggun or to the orishas. These are generally known as ebbós. Some are eaten and some are not.

3. Initiation offerings, in which the blood is given to the saints and the meat is always eaten. The meat of the animals sacrificed during an initiation is believed to be full of the ashé of the orishas.

As we have already seen, an orisha sometimes ordains an ebbó requiring an animal sacrifice to cleanse a person's aura. This is usually undertaken when a person's life is in danger or when he or she is surrounded by insurmountable obstacles.

To be on the receiving end of this type of cleansing is quite an unforgettable experience, and one that is likely to reshape the most skeptical mind. I witnessed such a ceremony in New York City a few years ago. A friend of mine had told me she knew of a santera who worked wonders, and I decided to pay the woman a visit. At the time, I was contemplating a trip to Europe, and I was curious about the outcome of my traveling plans.

The santera consulted Elegguá by means of four pieces of coconut rind. Elegguá's answer was that I would do better to remain in New York, as I would not be able to carry out my plans the way I wanted. Furthermore, the trip posed a very grave danger to my personal safety, and the only way I could overcome this threat was through the sacrifice of a chicken and an offering of fresh fruits.

I agreed to bring both offerings to the saint as soon as possible, and the very next day I returned to the house of the santera with a young rooster and a basket full of fresh fruit. The santera conducted the cleansing ceremony, tearing off the head of the chicken in front of Elegguá's image and guiding my hand while I spread the blood over the floor with a handful of feathers. The fruit basket was placed on the canastillero, the small cabinet in which the santera kept the saint's image. After the cleansing was over, she used the coconut rinds again, to ask Elegguá if he was satisfied with the sacrifice. The orisha expressed his approval of the ceremony and told the santera that I would be protected against physical harm during my travels, but otherwise the trip would be a total disappointment.

Undaunted by this prediction, a few days later I left for Europe as scheduled, only to find out that Elegguá's prophecy came true sooner than expected, and I was unable to accomplish anything worthwhile.

The second part of the oracle, predicting personal danger, became evident during the flight between Copenhagen and Frankfurt, when the plane in which I was traveling developed technical difficulties and had to return to Denmark. Already disappointed with my lack of success and badly shaken with the plane incident, I decided to return to New York immediately. The plane in which I made the return flight also developed technical difficulties. It circled the airport for two hours with faulty landing gear, but it finally landed without any trouble. When I stepped out of the plane, I saw that the landing strip was covered with foam and that there were fire engines near the landing area, anticipating the possibility of a major disaster.

Most of the animals used in a ritual sacrifice are fowl. They include male and female chickens, roosters, ducks, guinea hens, and pigeons. They are known collectively as *plumas*, "feathers." On special occasions, such as the asiento, the orishas may require four-legged animals. Among these are goats and rams. Other animals that are offered, though not as often, are fish, turtles, quail, and opossum. These last are better known as *jutías* among the santeros. One of the most popular of the magic powders prepared by the santero is known as *polvo de jutía* or *pescado y jutía*, a mixture of powdered fish and opossum meat.

The sacrifice of a chicken during a cleansing ritual is not very lengthy. The chicken's feet and beak are first rinsed with cool water, as the animal must be clean before it may be offered to an orisha. Then the officiating santero asks the person making the offering to kneel in front of the vessel that holds the orisha's otanes, and pray for good health, material and spiritual evolution, and whatever else he may need or desire. As he prays, the person holds the sacrificial animal in front of the orisha and asks the deity to accept the sacrifice.

Before he begins the sacrifice, the santero must "give coconut" to the saint to determine whether he or she is satisfied with the offering. Only when the orisha expresses his or her gratitude for the offering and agrees to help the individual does the sacrifice take place.

As soon as the prayers are over, the person stands up and the santero passes the animal all over the supplicant's body, praying all the time to the orisha that the cleansing may bring good luck and many blessings to him. As the santero prays, the person must turn slowly around, first to the left and then to the right. The santero then removes some of the chicken's chest feathers and proceeds with the sacrifice.

A fowl may be sacrificed by tearing off the head with a swift wrist movement or by cutting off the head with a sacrificial knife. Doves or pigeons must be killed by tearing off the head. During the sacrifice, the one making the offering must hold the animal by the legs and the wings.

As the santero plucks the feathers, he sings, *"Ñaquiña, ñaquiña loro."*

At these words, those present pull on the skin of their throats to evince their empathy with the sacrificial animal and to protect themselves against harm. The santero then chants, *"Oggún shoro shoro, Oggún dekun."* This means that it is Oggún who is doing the killing, not the santero. *Shoro* means "work," so the chant implies that Oggún (symbolized by the sacrificial knife) is doing his rightful work.

The blood is allowed to drip onto the orisha's stones, or, if it is Elegguá, over the cement head that represents him. A circle of blood is also made around the vessel holding the saint's emblem. The santero then opens a jar of honey (*oñi*) and pours a thin stream of it over the stones, again in a circular motion. He then takes a large mouthful of rum (*oti*) and sprays the orisha and the bird with it. All during the ceremony, the santero chants special prayers honoring the orisha who is receiving the offering. The carcass of the dead bird is placed respectfully in front of the orisha.

The santero takes the coconut rinds once more to ask the saint where the dead bird is to be disposed of. The first place he asks for is the garbage pail, as this is the easiest form of disposal. If the orisha says no, he continues to ask for different places that may be more agreeable to the saint. There are many possibilities, among which are the *nigua* (the woods), a crossroads, a railroad, or a cemetery. The animal cannot be disposed of in any other way than the one prescribed by the saint.

As soon as the ritual is over, the santero instructs the person to tear off as many feathers as he can from the bird's body and use them to cover the orisha. This is believed to "cover up" all the negative influences around the individual, as well as illness, envy, enemies, and other evils. The person is then directed to rub the floor with some of the feathers, picking up all the blood, honey, water, and bits of coconut that may remain. The mound of wet feathers is then squeezed in front of the orisha and placed on the floor facing the vessel. The santero lights two white candles on a white plate, and the ceremony is ended.

The body of the animal is then opened and stuffed with candies, bits of coconut, manteca de corojo, and toasted corn. It is aspersed with rum, honey, and the smoke of a large cigar, which is then placed inside the animal. Pennies in the number allotted to the orisha are also placed inside the carcass, which is then wrapped in a paper bag and taken to the place indicated by the saint.

It is of vital importance that the animal offered be of the kind "eaten" by that particular orisha. To sacrifice the wrong animal to a saint can result in grave difficulties for a person. The animal's gender is also important, as some orishas only eat animals of their own sex. For example, it would be unthinkable for a santero to offer a hen to Changó or Elegguá or a rooster to Oshún. Both Oshún and Babalú-Ayé enjoy an occasional offering of a gelded goat, and in some old Cuban households it was the custom to castrate many of the male goats at birth. These animals, known as *chivos capones*, were sacred to Babalú-Ayé. Since this orisha is the patron of illness, especially smallpox and other epidemics, it was believed that castrating the goats would stop the "reproduction" of any illness.

Following is a list of the animals "eaten" by the most popular orishas.

Elegguá—he-goat, opossum, rooster, and young male chickens (He also favors turtles, but only an experienced santero or a babalawo can conduct this ritual.)

Changó—ram, rooster, turtle, guinea hen, quail

Oggún—he-goat, rooster, pigeon, guinea hen, opossum

Obatalá—she-goat, white hen, white dove, guinea hen

Ochosi—he-goat, rooster, pigeon, guinea hen, opossum, bird

Babalú-Ayé—gelded goat, rooster, pigeon, guinea hen, quail

Yemayá—ram, rooster, duck, guinea hen

Oyá—she-goat, pigeon, hen, guinea hen (all black)

Oshún—gelded goat, yellow hen, guinea hen, quail (Quail are only eaten by Oshún in her aspect of Oshún Ibo Acuaro).

The sacrificial ceremonies of Santería are very similar to those still observed by the Yoruba. Like the santeros, the Yoruba believe that there is an intrinsic link between divination and sacrifice. The link exists because only through divination can the priests ascertain the type of ebbó required by an orisha. And invariably, every divination ends with a prescription for an ebbó or sacrifice. This is particularly true of Ifá divination. That is why the Yoruba say, *"A ki ndífa kámá yan ebó,"* that is, "One cannot consult Ifá without prescribing a sacrifice."

There are two types of sacrifice among the Yoruba: those that are offered to avert dangers and calamities, and those that are given in a spirit of thanks to the orishas and are shared by the community as a whole.

Like the santeros, the Yoruba believe it is an offense to offer an orisha a food he or she does not like. The food and animal offering are similar, but with some very distinct variations. A list of Yoruba sacrifices or offerings to the orishas follows.

Eṣu (Elegguá)— black fowl, palm oil (*epó*), cowrie shells
Ṣangó (Changó)—ram, bitter kola (*orogbo*)
Ogún (Oggún)—dog, snail, turtle, palm wine, roasted yam, and sometimes ram
Obatalá—snails fried in shea butter, white maize, white kola nut, bitter kola
Osun (Oshún)—goat, fowl
Ṣonponno (Babalú-Ayé)—rooster, palm wine, palm oil, corn meal

A comparison between the animals offered to the orishas by the santero and those offered by the Yoruba shows some similarities but also discrepancies. The santeros do not offer rams to Oggún, who lost this right to Changó during one of their battles. On the other hand, the Yoruba list does not include gelded goats, opossum or quail, which are popular offerings in Santería.

The custom in Santería of plucking feathers from a fowl's body before sacrificing it to an orisha is also found among the Yoruba. The feathers are believed to give protection to the one making the offering. The Yoruba say, in this regard, *"Bí adìe bá sokún iyé, ihùrìhù a bò ó; àyà ni adìe fi ḿbo omo,"* meaning, "If a hen lacks [long] feathers, the young feathers will cover it up; a hen protects her chicks with her chest feathers." The saying implies that the hen is both protected by and protective with her feathers. That is why the feathers are part of the animal sacrifice.

The practice of moyubbar, which is so important to the santeros, and during which they invoke and honor the eggun and the orishas, is also traced to the Yoruba. In Nigeria it is known as *Ijúbà*, which means "to pay homage." *Mo júbà* means "I pay homage."

The priest begins the ceremony by shaking a rattle and pouring a bit of water, gin (otí) or palm wine on the ground. He then starts to pray:

Olójó oni, mo júbà	Owner of this day I pay homage
Ilà oorùn, mo júbà	To the East I pay homage
Iwò oorùn, mo júbà	To the West I pay homage
Aríwá, mo júbà	To the North I pay homage
Gúusù, mo júbà	To the South I pay homage
Akódá, mo júbà	To the First Created I pay homage
Asèdá, mo júbà	To man's Creator I pay homage
Ilè, mo júbà	To the Earth I pay homage
Esù Odàrà, mo júbà	To Esu, the trickster, I pay homage
[Ancestors], mo júbà	To my ancestors [names] I pay homage
Bí ekòlò ba júbà ilè, ilè a lanu.	If the worm pays homage to the earth, the earth will heed it.
Omodé ki ijúbà, kí ibà pà á.	Because small children never pay homage, they are often destroyed.

To each utterance of the priest, those present answer, "Ibà á se," that is, "May it be so." Like the santeros, the Yoruba conduct the *Ijúbà* (moyubbar) ceremony before each divination ritual and before each sacrifice or ebbó.

Many books and treatises have been written on the subject of sacrifice. E. B. Tylor, the English anthropologist, saw it as a way of "bribing" the gods or paying them homage. Sir William Robertson Smith, the English theologian, defined it as a means of consolidating a communion between the gods and man. The Dutch theologian Gerardus van der Leeuw saw it as an offering that enables the gods to give something in return. But by far the best definition was given by Edwin Oliver James, who said that sacrifice is "a means of giving life to have life."

Sacrifice is a universal panacea to cure the ills of mankind and to redeem its sins. Every human society has practiced it at one time or another. Sometimes the sacrifice is minimal, like a candle lit in church. Sometimes it is apotheosic, like Christ's death on the cross. But the sacrifice is always there, an intrinsic part of man's soul, a primeval need to give of his essence to the creative force of the universe. Sacrifice is irrevocably linked to mankind's awareness of his own inadequacies and perennial follies. Mankind sins more through weakness and ignorance than through evil intent. Sacrifice is the means by which human beings acknowledge their inabilities to cope with the challenges of life, and ask for help in meeting that challenge.

Traditionally, blood is the ultimate sacrifice because it is the source of life. That is why it is the quintessential offer to God. All major religions acknowledge the importance of blood sacrifices to the Deity. Jews still observe the Mosaic laws during their koshering ceremonies, when the blood of the slaughtered animals is given to God and the meat is eaten by the congregation. During Yom Kippur, Hassidic Jews conduct cleansing rituals similar to those conducted by the santeros. In rubbing ceremonies they use chickens that are later sacrificed in communal rituals. The chickens are believed to take on the sins and the evil influences surrounding the object of the cleansing. Only the words and other minor details of the ritual differ from those of the santero.

In India and Nepal, thousands of animals are slaughtered every year during ritual sacrifices. And the Catholic Church sacrifices a lamb during the opening of each Holy Year. Furthermore, the Catholic mass is seen as a sacrifice during which the Host and the wine are transformed into the body and blood of Jesus Christ, which are then consumed by the priest and the congregation.

Blood sacrifices were conducted by the Babylonians, the Hebrews, the Egyptians, the Greeks, the Romans, the Aztecs, and the American Indians. All the ancient cultures of the Middle East, the Far East, Europe, and Africa have had religions with sacrificial rituals. Sacrifice continues to take place because of mankind's fears and his need for guidance. In essence, a sacrifice is a transmutation of energies whereby that which is given to a deity is transformed into that which is desired or needed by the supplicant.

13.

The Initiations ////////////////////////

Santería is a religion based on an initiation system. That is, the scale of knowledge within Santería's ranks increases with each progressive initiation. The knowledge is sometimes directly imparted by the initiate's teacher or initiator, but most often the initiate is encouraged to learn through careful observation of the leaders' actions and through direct participation in the ceremonies and rites. Only experienced santeros should initiate outsiders or aleyos into the religion.

When a santero dies, his ahijados mourn him rigorously during a three-month period. After this time, the ahijados must "remove the orisha's tears," that is, they must "feed" all the orishas and the implements that they receive from their padrino. The same is true of the death of a babalawo. This means that each object received from that dead priest or priestess must be "given" the blood of an animal, usually a chicken or a pigeon.

Each of the major initiations of Santería requires both a padrino or madrina and an ayugbona or assistant. Both must be initiated santeros. The initiate should treat his ayugbona, who can be either a man or a woman, with as much respect as his padrino or madrina. Only the initiation of the Warriors, when given by the babalawo, does not require the assistance of an ayugbona. But both the Cofá de Orúnla and Mano de Orúnla, initiations given only by the babalawo, require the presence of an ayugbona.

THE NECKLACES (ELEKES)

The initiation of the necklaces, known in Yoruba as *elekes*, is the first of the initiations given in Santería. The necklaces given in the initiation are five and belong to Elegguá, Obatalá, Changó, Yemayá, and Oshún. There are various color combinations ascribed to each orisha, depending on the particular path represented by the necklace. Generally, Elegguá's necklace is made of three black beads alternating with three red beads for the entire length of the eleke. Obatalá's necklace is usually all white, although sometimes it alternates with green, violet, or red beads, depending on the path. Changó's basic necklace is made of a pattern of six red beads alternating with six white ones. Yemayá's is made of seven crystal or white beads alternating with seven blue ones. Oshún's is basically all yellow or amber beads, although it sometimes has one red bead alternating with five yellow.

Santeros say that the necklaces are the banners of the saints, with which they protect their followers. Each necklace confers upon its wearers the blessing of the orisha it represents and helps him in those areas controlled by the orisha.

After the first five necklaces have been received, the initiate may get other necklaces from other orishas, as he needs them. The most popular necklaces after the first five are those of Oyá, Babalú-Ayé, Aganyú, and Oggún.

Not everyone is called to receive the initiations of Santería. Sometimes, when a person goes to a santero or a babalawo for a reading, the first thing the orisha will tell him is that he should never take any of the Santería initiations, as he does not require them. At other times, the orishas will say that the person needs only one necklace from his protecting orisha. This solitary necklace is given without any special ceremony, as it is not part of the necklace initiation. But generally, most people are allowed to undergo at least the first initiation for elekes.

Before the initiation is given to an individual, the necklaces must be washed in the omiero of the asiento. Most santeros string the colored beads and prepare the necklaces in large quantities and wash them in the lustral waters of the omiero during an asiento. Then they consecrate and "baptize" the necklaces with the blood of the sacrificial animals. This is known as "feeding the necklaces."

The person who is going to receive the Necklaces must abstain from sexual activities for at least twenty-four hours prior to the ceremony. He or she must bring a complete change of new white clothes, including a hat or a handkerchief, to his new padrino or madrina's house. Before the investiture of the Necklaces, the neophyte is given a cleansing bath in the liquid of the omiero. He is dressed in his new white clothes, and his padrino or ayugbona proceeds to conduct a rogación de cabeza. The coconut is read to ascertain whether the orishas are satisfied with the ceremony. Only then does the santero give the necklaces to the initiate.

If the santero does not know who is the ruling orisha of the person, he conducts the ceremony through Obatalá, who is the owner of all the heads. If he knows the name of the ruling orisha, he invests the necklaces in the name of that deity.

The necklaces must not be worn while taking a bath, during sexual intercourse, or by women during their menstrual periods. If one of the necklaces breaks, the beads must be brought back to the padrino, if possible, so that he may mend it and reconsecrate it. A broken necklace is said to have saved its wearer from a severe danger.

The necklaces are not given to acquire money or for personal aggrandisement. They are given for protection against evil. People who have received the necklaces are expected to respect the orishas and to observe decent and moral behavior.

THE WARRIORS (LOS GUERREROS)

The initiation of the Warriors—Los Guerreros—includes, as we have seen, three of the most powerful orishas in Santería: Elegguá, Oggún, and Ochosi, as well as Osun, who is equated with the individual's self. Elegguá is usually received in the form of a cement head with eyes, mouth, nose, and ears formed from cowrie shells. The head is hollow, and inside it the santero or babalawo places several secret ingredients, as well as the person's name. Among the ingredients are bits of gold and silver and various types of earth. On top of the head there is always a tiny blade, sometimes accompanied by a small feather. The babalawos embed a few green and yellow beads—the colors of Orúnla—in the top of the head, at the base of the blade. This clearly distinguishes that particular Elegguá as having been given by a babalawo.

As mentioned earlier, santeros and babalawos prepare Elegguá in entirely different ways. Babalawos generally ask the person who is going to receive the initiation to bring three small stones that have to be taken from the path walked by the aspect of Elegguá that walks with that person. The stones are taken from the woods, the river, the seaside, or a large field. The babalawo then asks Elegguá, by means of the opelé, which of the three stones should be used in the preparation of Elegguá's head. When the orisha gives his answer, the babalawo proceeds to construct the head over the chosen stone.

Oggún and Ochosi are received inside a black cauldron. Oggún is represented by his seven work implements, already described, and Ochosi by his crossbow. Osun is represented by a small rooster atop a cup fringed by tiny bells. Osun must never be allowed to fall over, for when this occurs it predicts all sorts of misfortunes for its owner. Most babalawos give Orúnla's necklace and his bracelet—idé—together with the Warriors. The necklace and idé are made of green and yellow beads, the colors of Orúnla.

Santeros cannot give this necklace and bracelet, as only babalawos are empowered to work with Orúnla, but the Elegguá given by the santero is the one that must be used if the person goes on to undergo the ceremony of the asiento. Some santeros believe that it is wiser to receive the Warriors from the babalawo and then get another Elegguá if the recipient decides to make the saint. A person can get more than one Elegguá because the orisha has twenty-one paths, but it is important that the paths chosen for the initiate are compatible with him, as not all Elegguás work well with every person.

Santeras are not supposed to give Elegguá and the Warriors, as they are male orishas of a pronounced virility, but those who dare give the initiation must do so with the help of a male santero, who has to lend some of his own "maleness" to the initiation by crouching for a few minutes over the Warriors.

Elegguá is sometimes given in a seashell, a coconut, or a variety of stones. One particular Elegguá has two faces, to protect his owner against deceit and treason. Oggún, Ochosi, and Osun, however, are always given in the same fashion.

The cost of the Warriors is between $150 and $200. The initiation is said to gain for the initiate the protection of the three orishas against danger, enemies, accidents, and physical attacks. It is also helpful in the acquisition of material goods. Elegguá is particularly useful in worldly matters. There are a number of ebbós or "works" that can be done to ensure his help, which the padrino or madrina will teach the initiate. Every Monday, Elegguá must be presented with a small offering of candies or fruits, and he must be sprayed with rum and have some cigar smoke blown on his head. Three drops of water are poured on the floor in front of his image, and a small prayer—preferably in Yoruba—is then said in his honor. The last offering is a white candle, which is also placed at his feet.

The two initiations of the Necklaces and the Warriors are known as "half the asiento" and are considered to be the foundation of Santería. Most people who receive these two initiations eventually make the saint and become santeros.

Twenty-one days after having received the Warriors, they must receive "entry" into the house of the initiate. The babalawo or santero who gave the initiation must go to the house of his ahijado and "feed" the Warriors a rooster. This ceremony is accompanied by the appropriate prayers. The Warriors are asperged with honey, rum, and cigar smoke during the rite, and later the officiating priest uses the coconut divination to be sure the orishas are happy in their new home. This concludes the initiation. The padrino instructs his godchild on the proper care of the orishas and warns him or her against indulging in sexual dalliances in the room where the Warriors are kept. The person cannot appear in front of the orishas in the nude or scantily clothed. Women must abstain from touching the orishas' implements during menstruation. After these instructions, the padrino leaves and the initiate begins his lifelong relationship with the Warriors.

The Warriors are received for protection against evil and to dominate and overcome enemies and difficulties. The names of those persons who are causing trouble to the initiate are placed on strips of unlined paper and placed under Elegguá's image. The orisha then makes sure that those people are controlled and are unable to harm his protégé. If the individual has a lawsuit pending, or any type of legal difficulty that is not his fault, he can then appeal to the other two Warriors, Oggún and Ochosi, for help in his ordeal. But before a person can reap any benefits from the Warriors, he must remember to take care of them properly, especially on Mondays. This means providing them with candies, rum, water, *manteca de corojo*, cigars, and a white candle. When the initiate wants something special from the Warriors, he asks for the favor and promises to give something in return. Offerings may vary from toys for Elegguá, to fruit baskets, fancy cakes, and candies. Only in severe cases, and when the orisha himself demands it, does the individual make an animal offering. This is undertaken by the person's padrino or by an initiated santero.

The initiation of the Warriors is indispensable for the asiento, as Elegguá is the most important of the orishas during that ceremony. Without him, the asiento cannot take place. That is why the santeros say that the initiations of the Necklaces and the Warriors are equal to half the asiento.

OLOKUN

Olokun is an aspect of Yemayá, generally associated with the ocean floors. She is sometimes visualized as a beautiful siren and other times as a hermaphrodite. In the beginning of Creation, according to one of the legends, Olokun's watery domain extended throughout the entire planet. But then Obatalá, who hated to see all that gray expanse empty of life and movement, took away some of Olokun's territory and created the first land, which became known as the holy city of Ife.

Olokun is one of the most powerful of the orishas, and her initiation gives great stability and control over life. She is also very sensitive and must never be offended, as her punishment is both swift and terrible.

Olokun's initiation requires the presence of several santeros, besides the padrino and ayugbona, as it is very lengthy and complicated. Again, like most of Santería's ceremonies, it is very secret and its details cannot be revealed by the initiate.

Olokun's secrets are placed inside a great urn, which is usually blue or blue and white, and often depicts upon its surface a maritime landscape. Some santeros place a lead image of a woman with extended arms inside the urn. The image, which holds a snake in one hand and a mask in the other, is a representation of Olokun. Seven lead implements are also placed inside the urn, among which are a sun and a moon, symbolizing that Yemayá-Olokun is the queen of the world.

Some santeros give a special necklace of Olokun with her initiation. The necklace is made of crystal and turquoise beads, with beads of coral in between. An Eleggúa called Eshu Ayé is usually given with the initiation. This Eleggúa, which is prepared inside a large seashell, is said to "walk" with Yemayá-Olokun. The initiation is costly, approximately five hundred dollars.

THE CUCHILLO

After the asiento, the santero will have to receive many other initiations. Chief among these is the ceremony of the *cuchillo* or the Knife. Only santeros can receive this initiation, which is almost as costly as that of the asiento. Prior to receiving the Knife, the santero is not considered to be fully competent in his duties. The Knife is an initiation that brings prestige and self-assurance to the santero. Many of the elders have received the Knife. Without it, the santero is unable to take part in many ceremonies and cannot conduct animal sacrifices in which the animal offering has four legs. Receiving the Knife is the result of peer pressure. It is something that must be done for the asiento to be complete.

The initiation of the Knife is known as the Pinaldo and simply confers upon the santero the right to use the sacrificial knife during the major ceremonies. It costs around four thousand dollars.

BABALÚ-AYÉ

The initiation of Babalú-Ayé is not an asiento, as this saint does not "go to the head"—that is, he is not "crowned" on a person's head. But is still lengthy and complicated and has an itá, like all major initiations, in which the santeros make predictions for the future of the initiate. After the initiation is complete, the santeros conduct a beautiful ceremony that is open to aleyos. During this ritual, which is known as *aguán*, the center of the initiation room is covered by dozens of *minestras*, or different types of grains and fruits that are placed in many dishes arranged in a circle. All of those present enter the room and cleanse themselves with the minestras, which are sacred to Babalú-Ayé and are replete with his blessings. At the doorway leading to the room are two santeras. One is holding two eggs in her hands, the other is holding a guinea hen. As each person walks in, the santeras cleanse him or her with the eggs and the guinea hen. The eggs are rubbed over the eyes and the hen over the entire body. These rubbing rituals are said to transfer the person's problems and illnesses onto the objects used.

During the aguán, the santeros constantly pray and sing to Babalú-Ayé, calling him with a peculiar sound, not unlike an Indian war cry. Very often the orisha descends during the aguán and takes possession of one of the santeros. He then cleanses each person individually with his own special powers.

The initiation of Babalú-Ayé can be received by anyone, even if a person is not a santero. It is an expensive ritual that costs around two thousand dollars.

There are many other initiations in Santería, most of which can be received only by initiated santeros. Among these are the initiations of Orisha-Oko, Oba, and Inle.

The major initiation of Santería, in which a person becomes a santero, will be discussed in the following chapter.

14.

Asiento /////////////////////////////////////
Making the Saint

When a person "makes the saint," he or she becomes known as a
iyawó or *yaguó*. During the year following the initiation, that is
how he or she is addressed by santeros and the practitioners of
Santería. During the ceremony of the asiento when he "makes the
saint," the iyawó "dies" a mystical death and is reborn in Ocha,
the African name for Santería. A year later, when the madrina or
padrino gives the iyawó the libreta, or notebook, in which his
future life is revealed, the iyawó sees a notation on the libreta's
first page that says, "Today was born in Ocha a child which was
named . . ." Here is written the iyawó's new African name,
followed by the date of the initiation. The libreta, which must
never be seen by anyone except its owner, lists all the other
orishas that the initiate must also receive and how he can protect
himself from any dangers or difficulties that may arise.

I am not a santera, since I have never received the initiation of
the asiento. What I know about this ceremony I have learned
from initiated santeros. Some of the information I received was
purposely vague, as the ceremony is secret and should never be
revealed. But several years ago, one of my closest friends was
initiated as a santera, and she revealed to me most details of the

ceremony, although she still kept some secrets about which she dared not speak.

If I were an initiated santera, I would be breaking an oath of secrecy to reveal the details of this awesome ceremony, but since I am not, I will be simply repeating what was told to me by someone who received the initiation. Therefore I will not be breaking any oaths. Since I cannot use the real name of the santera who underwent the initiation, I will call her Laura.

Several weeks before the date of the asiento, Laura went to her madrina's house with the $3,500 she had saved for the cost of the initiation. Some initiations are more costly, especially those of Elegguá, which could easily have doubled the cost of Laura's asiento; but she received the mysteries of Obatalá, whose initiation is among the least expensive, perhaps because it is one of the most popular. The reason for Obatalá's popularity is that he is the owner of all heads, and when there is doubt as to who is the true guardian angel of the iyawó, it is always safe to initiate him into Obatalá's mysteries. Also, when a person makes the saint to recuperate from a serious illness, santeros sometimes crown Obatalá on the person's head, to ensure that he will escape from death. But a babalawo I know always jokes about the high incidence of Obatalá initiations in Santería and blames them on the incompetence of some santeros who do not know or do not dare undertake some of the more complicated initiations, such as those of Elegguá, Changó, and Oyá.

Laura remained in her madrina's house until the day of the asiento, the African name of which is *karioriocha* (*ka*, "to place"; *ri*, "on top"; *ori*, "head"; *Ocha*, "gods"). The day of the asiento was carefully chosen to make sure Laura would not be menstruating, as during this time a woman must abstain from touching anything pertaining to the orishas or even approaching the room where the otanes are kept. The necklaces are not to be worn during this time, either.

The money Laura gave to her madrina had many uses. Some of it was used to pay the derechos of the babalawo, the oriaté, the ayugbona, and the sixteen iyalochas who attend the ceremony, all of whom had to receive the sacred stipend demanded by tradition. (Sixteen is a number sacred to Obatalá; other orishas require their own number of iyalochas or babalochas.) The madrina received $800; the ayugbona $120; the babalawo $150; the oriaté $100; the iyalochas $30 each. Of the rest of the money, the madrina spent $450 for the sacrificial animals; $150 for the various implements and weapons of the orishas; $300 for food; and $700 for Laura's clothes, including the beautiful dress and crown she wore after the asiento. What was left was spent on other needs, such as soperas in which the otanes are kept, several dozen white plates, Changó's batea, the beads for the collares de mazo, and the metal bracelets of the female orishas.

Among the clothes the madrina bought for Laura were seven different outfits (skirts, blouses, dresses, no slacks), as the iyawó has to change clothes every day to preserve the meticulous cleanliness the orishas demand. The madrina also bought seven sets of underwear and sleepwear, to be changed at least once daily, preferably twice; seven pairs of white stockings; seven bed sheets; seven pillow cases; seven large and seven small towels; a robe; and a pair of shoes and slippers. All of these clothes were white, as the iyawó has to dress in this color for a whole year. The skirts, blouses, dresses, and initiation gown were all sewn by a santera who specialized in designing and sewing initiation clothes. (Men buy their clothes ready-made.)

Laura is married, but her husband—a strong believer in Santería—did not object to her spending the sixteen days before the asiento at her madrina's house. He knew Laura had to abstain from sexual intercourse for at least seventy-two hours before the initiation and considered himself lucky that the santeros had relaxed the ancient rules that used to demand a whole year's sexual abstinence. Sixteen days is the usual time spent at the madrina's or padrino's house, or ilé-orisha (house of the saints), because there are sixteen orishas worshiped in Ocha, and sixteen cowrie shells in that divination system. After the initiation is over, the iyawó must remain seven more days in the madrina's house, after which time he or she is allowed to leave. And if married, as in Laura's case, he or she is then allowed to resume normal marital relations.

The first of many steps in the asiento is the *ebbó de entrada*—the ebbó of entry. As already discussed, the ebbó is a remedy, a cleansing, and any of a thousand ways in which an individual propitiates an orisha to help him. In the ebbó de entrada, at which the babalawo should officiate, the iyawó asks the orishas' forgiveness for all his past sins and all the impure acts he has committed in his life.

During Laura's ebbó de entrada, her madrina and ayugbona were present with her. The babalawo asked Orúnla what type of cleansing Laura needed to purify herself of her past faults so that she could receive the karioriocha. The orisha responded that besides the usual components of the ebbó, such as coconut, water, Orúnla's yefá, smoked fish and opossum, and certain herbs, several chickens and doves were required.

Laura was cleansed in accordance with Orúnla's instructions. The animals were passed ritualistically over her body and then sacrificed by the babalawo. As they had taken upon themselves all of Laura's sins, these animals were not eaten.

After the first ritual cleansing came the second cleansing, this one with river water. Some santeros insist on bringing the iyawó to a river and cleansing him there, but sometimes the river water is brought in pails to the ilé-orisha, where the initiate is bathed. This procedure was followed in Laura's case, since the river water surrounding New York can hardly be considered suitable for purification. The water for Laura's purification was therefore brought in pails from upstate New York, but Laura still had to go to the river with her madrina and ayugbona and ask Oshún's blessing and deposit at the riverside the ritual offerings to the orisha—a shrimp stew, Oshún's favorite fruits, and special honey cakes. Next to the food were left five pennies, as Oshún's derecho.

Upon returning to the ilé-orisha, the ayugbona and two other

☑ This is the typical dress worn by a santero when initiated into the mysteries of Changó. The colors are red and white, and the crown is shaped like a tower—reminiscent of the tower at Saint Barbara's feet and a clear example of syncretism between Changó and the virgin martyr of the Middle Ages.

☑ A food offering (ebbó) to Obatalá rests on top of this white tureen. The silver agogo used to call the orisha faces the vessel.

This ebbó consists of a beef tongue pierced with needles and tied with a red ribbon, obviously an offering to Changó to control an enemy's tongue. This is a typical case of sympathetic magic.

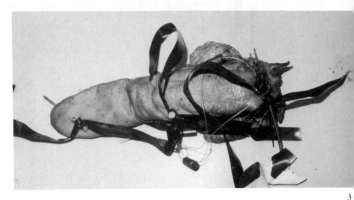

3

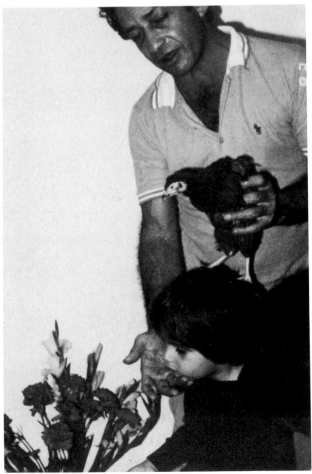

Here a santero performs a cleansing ritual on a young boy with a live chicken.

■ The orishas "reside" inside this small cabinet, which houses two sets of the Warriors (Elegguá on his clay vessel and Oggún and Ochosi in their cauldron), probably the property of husband and wife. Some of Elegguá's toys rest near his vessels and a half-smoked cigar lies on the floor, all offerings to Elegguá.

■ Changó's wooden batea, or vessel, sits on its pilón, a short wooden column, with Changó's collar de mazo (red and white initiation necklace) and beaded ax draped over it. To the left are the implements of Aganyú, who is Changó's father in Santería.

◪ In Cuba, an iyawó waits during the asiento, his head and face covered with spots in the colors of his orisha. His shaven skull has been painted in concentric circles in the four major colors of the orishas: white, yellow, red, and blue. On his cheeks he wears Yoruba tribal marks in the main color of his orisha.

◪ In the background, an iyawó sits under the canopy of the throne after the asiento initiation.

A covered tureen with a food offering to Oshún. The pumpkin in the foreground is ~c of Oshún's attributes. The image next to the tureen represents Our Lady of ~ercy—syncretized with Obatalá.

Drum music for the Batá toque. Courtesy of Milton Cardona.

☑ Batáa rhythms (toques) for Changó and Elegguá.

☑ A *plaza* in honor of Oshún. Various tureens of the orishas, draped in bright colors and heavy beaded necklaces, surround the fruit and food offerings. On the lower left-hand side is a white cake trimmed in yellow frosting, dedicated to Oshún.

☑ (Facing page) The three phases of possession. This unusual possession took place on stage at the American Museum of Natural History in New York during a series of conferences on Santería. In the first photo, the lead singer (akpwón) uses a *canto de puya* to needle Elegguá into taking possession of the dancer. In the second photo, the akpwón's teasing of Elegguá succeeds and possession begins to take place. In the last photo, the now possessed santero proceeds to dance Elegguá's complicated *zapateado*. In the background is the throne with its fruit offerings.

46a

46b

46c

▨ A statue of Saint Lazarus (Babalú-Ayé) wearing a sackcloth cape trimmed with gold braid. The loincloth is purple, one of the saint's colors.

47

▨ A *loa* (Voodoo deity) possesses an initiate, who feeds on the blood of a dove in a trance similar to an orisha possession.

48

◪ The inside of Changó's wooden vessel (*batea*) with the thunderstones (*piedras de rayo*) that represent him.

◪ Chango's double-edged ax (*edun ara*), beaded in white and red, with six cowrie shells in the center. His maraca lies at its side.

◪ Several *ngangas* (paleros' cauldrons) holding the *kiyumba* (skulls and bones of the dead), and the herbs and *palos* (wooden sticks) that make their foundations.

◪ A "Christian" nganga with the palos and the kiyumba inside. A Christian nganga has been asperged with holy water.

◪ The kiyumba covered with the blood of sacrificial animals.

◪ A palo ritual animal sacrifice. The horn next to the sacrificial animal is used by the palero to invoke the spirit of the nganga.

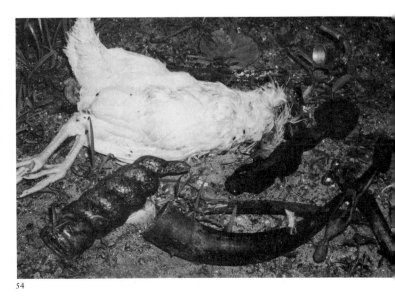

55

56

■ The dessicated head of a cobra, still covered with the feathers of sacrificial animals. This ferocious entity is probably part of the array of noxious animals of the "unbaptized" nganga, the most evil of the cauldrons.

■ Various *filhas de santo* (the Brazilian term for santeras) surround an iyalocha possessed by Oshún, who wears the crown and costume of the orisha. Notice that the ritual necklaces worn in Candomblé are twice as long and numerous as those used in Santería.

57

◪ Several filhas de santo, laden with many necklaces and flower vases, ready themselves for a major ceremony.

58

◪ An open sopera, or tureen, belonging to Oshún contains her sacred otanes (stones) and implements. This rare photograph was taken during a raid by the Miami police on a santero's home. Ordinarily, photographing the saints is forbidden.

◪ A clear example of syncretism in action. Our Lady of Charity (Oshún) in her niche, surrounded by her *otanes* (sacred stones), a pumpkin, and money, all of which she rules. A Puerto Rican lottery ticket is also in the background.

◪ The Seven African Powers. The images are those of Catholic saints, but the names are those of the orishas.

No. 472 Siete Potencias Africanas

◪ Allan Kardec, who wrote the basic texts of Spiritism, which are the basis of the spiritist beliefs of many Latin Americans.

◪ A modern séance in England, where Spiritualism is very popular.

◪ Milton Benezra and Jack Mizrahi, the owners of Original Products. On the wall behind them hang many of the dried herbs used in Santería for baths, teas, and magic spells.

◪ Otto Chicas-Rendón, in his botánica in New York at 116th Street between Park and Madison avenues. This was the first botánica established in New York.

iyalochas took Laura to the bathroom for the purification bath. The three women tore Laura's clothes in shreds, until she stood naked on the bathroom floor. This action represents the destruction of the iyawó's links with the past and her willingness to be born anew. The waters that will cleanse her are a symbol of the amniotic fluid in which she floated in her mother's womb before she was born.

Naked, Laura was helped by the iyalochas into the bathtub filled with river water. With a brand-new bar of Castile soap— the only soap the santeros accept for ritual cleansing—the ayugbona scrubbed Laura vigorously from head to foot, chanting all the time in Yoruba, invoking the orishas to be present at the cleansing. The soap was wrapped in harsh vegetable fibers that left Laura's skin tingling. When the bath was finished, Laura was wrapped in a new white towel, dried, and dressed in new white clothes. The ayugbona then sat Laura on the toilet seat and proceeded to comb and braid her hair. At no time during the bathing, dressing, or grooming was Laura allowed to do anything, since a newborn child is unable to care for itself and must depend on others for every need.

After she was dressed and her hair was combed, Laura was brought out into the room where her madrina's canastillero was kept, and she was asked to sit on the floor on an *estera*, or straw mat. The ayugbona then brought her a plate of food and sat by her side to watch her eat.

That evening the ayugbona cleansed Laura's head with coconut. This rogación de cabeza completed her final purification as an iyawó. The corners, windows, and doors of the ilé-orisha were then ritually sealed. Late in the evening, as Laura sat by herself on a low stool, her madrina approached her from behind and, taking her completely by surprise, slipped Obatalá's collar de mazo around her neck. This ceremony, called *la prendición* (the pinning), is the true beginning of the initiation. The *inafa*, or collar de mazo, is a symbol of the orisha's laying claim on the iyawó's head. La prendición is the iyawó's final commitment.

Anytime before the inafa is slipped around his neck, the iyawó can change his mind about making the saint and walk out of the ilé-orisha. But the moment the prendición is over and the inafa rests upon his chest, the iyawó is committed for life to the worship and care of his orisha. There is no going back.

Immediately after the prendición, Laura was taken to a sort of cubicle formed in a corner of the room, with several white sheets for walls. She was told to sit on a low stool facing the wall and was warned not to speak unless told to do so. For several hours she sat in her cubicle, listening to the sounds of the iyalochas as they got ready for the asiento.

During the time she spent facing the wall, Laura learned what it was like to be in the clutches of acute paranoia. Very slowly, a horrible sense of doom began to take hold of her. The most outrageous fears started to infiltrate her mind. What if these people were going to kill her in some kind of hideous human sacrifice? After all, how long had she known her madrina? Three years was hardly any time at all.

As her fears grew, Laura began thinking of how to escape from the ilé-orisha. She tried to remember the positions of the doors and windows and began to put together a plan of escape. Sweat was pouring in rivers down her face and back. She placed her hands on her chest to feel the hammering of her heart, and her fingers came to rest lightly upon Obatalá's collar de mazo.

The sudden contact with the bead necklace immediately brought Laura out of her blind panic. Great waves of relief came rushing down upon her, and her fears receded. Clutching her necklace with trembling fingers, she began praying to Obatalá, asking forgiveness for her doubts and beseeching his help during the coming ordeal. The orisha seemed to hear her prayer, because a great sense of peace extended over her, and she was able to relax while she continued her long wait.

Minutes grew into hours, and Laura's mind began the inward voyage that was to take her into inner dimensions that she never dreamed existed. Her first feeling, one of drowsiness, was soon replaced by an awareness that she was outside her body looking at herself and all the activity that was taking place in the ilé-orisha.

While Laura was beginning her long descent into the depths of her unconscious, the iyalochas were preparing the omiero, the basis of the initiations in Santería.

The preparation of the omiero is known as "making Osain," who is the owner of all ewe. All the herbs used in the omiero are usually—though not always—provided by the babalawo, who gets them from a santero who specializes in the knowledge of herbs and who is known as a *yerbero* or *Osainista*. In Cuba and Puerto Rico, the yerbero goes to the woods to gather fresh herbs for the omiero, but in the United States, where some of the required tropical plants do not grow, the yerbero gets the ewe from selected botánicas, which import the herbs from the tropics and keep them refrigerated to ensure their freshness. Sometimes he orders them directly from the Caribbean or from Miami.

The babalawo places the herbs in several large baskets and brings them to the house of the iyawó's madrina. The iyalocha receives the ewe at the door of her house in a short ceremony and gives the babalawo a derecho, usually $5.25. She brings the ewe inside the igbodu, or sanctuary, where the asiento will take place, puts them on an estera on the floor, and purifies them with water and coconut. The babalawo then spits on them to confer on them his ashé, which is concentrated in his saliva.

Seven iyalochas, all dressed in white, with handkerchiefs tied around their heads, barefoot, and wearing their necklaces and ceremonial bracelets, sit in front of the estera, each holding a clay vessel painted with the color of her orisha. One of the elders, who knows by heart which herbs pertain to which orisha, divides the 101 herbs among the seven iyalochas so that each receives her orisha's ewe. Kneeling on the estera, each iyalocha receives the ewe of her saint and intones an invocation to her deity in Yoruba.

When all the ewe has been distributed, the oriaté arrives in the igbodu and begins the chanting that consecrates the herbs to the orisha. After the ritual prayers to the eggun, Olofi, and the orishas, including Osain, the oriaté chants the sixteen suyeres or ceremonial invocations to the orishas, starting as usual with Elegguá. As each suyere ends, the oriaté marks the floor with a vertical line in chalk, and two of the younger iyalochas—who are not among the traditional seven—pour water over each clay vessel.

In the meantime, the seven iyalochas crush the ewe with their hands and answer in chorus each of the oriaté's chants. When this long and tedious process is completed, each orisha's otanes, necklaces, corresponding cowrie shells, and implements are washed in the light green liquid resulting from the crushing of the herbs in water. These are the otanes that the iyawó will receive during the asiento.

During the ritual washing, the stones receive the blessing of each orisha and are consecrated in their names. Afterward, the liquid that is left is gathered together in a large vessel. At this time, holy water, coconut milk, river water and sea water, rainwater, honey, rum, cocoa butter, crushed eggshell (cascarilla), opossum, smoked fish, toasted corn, pepper, and several seeds— erú tuché and obí kolá, which are untranslatable as well as indispensable to the mixture—are added to the omiero. When all these ingredients are mixed, one of the iyalochas dips a hot coal into the liquid and brings it immediately out again, saying that "it is better to drown than to burn to death." The last two ingredients of the omiero are some of the blood of the sacrificial animals and the yefá or ritual powder of Orúnla.

The light touch of the ayugbona's hand on her shoulder brought Laura out of her reverie. As if in a trance, she felt the ayugbona's hands help her stand up, and then wrap her in a white sheet. During this second part of the ceremony, known as the "second prendición," the ayugbona instructed Laura to close her eyes.

Guided by the ayugbona's hand, she left the cubicle and was led to knock on the igbodu's door. A voice from within told her to identify herself and asked what she wanted. "Santo," she answered. "Which saint?" the voice asked. "Elegguá," Laura answered. As if she had not spoken, the voice repeated the same question: "Which saint?" This time, Laura answered, "Aganyú." The same question was asked a third time, and Laura answered, "Changó."

On and on went the voice, demanding the names of each of the orishas to be received in the initiation, and Laura named them all. The last orisha she mentioned was Obatalá, in whose mysteries she was going to be initiated. Only when Obatalá's name was said did the door open for Laura.

Still with her eyes closed, Laura entered into the igbodu, where the iyalochas stripped her of her clothing and carefully washed her in some of the omiero. All during the washing, the iyalochas chanted in Yoruba, asking the orishas to bless and protect Laura and watch over the asiento. By this time, Laura was in such a dazed state that she was hardly aware of what was going on around her. She heard the voices and felt the iyalochas' hands as they washed, dried, and dressed her. But part of her seemed to be missing, and what was left was slowly sinking within a deep, dark pool.

Still with closed eyes, Laura was brought to the *apotí*, or throne, which is a round low stool shaped like a drum. Only those orishas who are "kings" and "queens," such as Changó, Obatalá, Oshún, and Yemayá, may sit on the apotí. All the others sit on chairs. The apotí is also washed in the omiero. Painted on the floor in a corner of the igbodu are four concentric circles of white, red, blue, and yellow. Over the circles, wrapped with some herbs on a white handkerchief and covered with a large *malanga* leaf, is placed the orisha's derecho. The apotí is placed over all this.

As soon as Laura sat on the apotí, she was immediately surrounded by the iyalochas, who, led by Laura's madrina, began to cut her hair. As each iyalocha snipped a lock of Laura's hair, she expressed a wish for Laura's health, happiness, and general welfare. Through the payment of a derecho, it is possible in some houses to "buy" the iyawó's head from an orisha, thereby avoiding the total loss of the initiate's hair. But Laura had been very ill immediately before the asiento, and Obatalá had demanded the sacrifice of her hair. Laura's madrina had advised shaving her head completely, in full accord with tradition.

While the oriaté shaved her head, he and the iyalochas chanted in Yoruba, invoking the orishas in their traditional order. When Laura's head was completely shaved, the oriaté painted on it six concentric circles in the colors of the four main orishas: white for Obatalá, red for Changó, yellow for Oshún, and blue for Yemayá. On the center of her head the oriaté painted a white circle to symbolize Obatalá, Laura's deity. All over the head, forehead, and temples, each iyalocha painted a dot in the color of her orisha. On each of Laura's cheeks the madrina painted three vertical white lines to symbolize the *yeza*, the tribal marks of the Yoruba.

Then the central part of the asiento, the actual "crowning" of the saint, took place. This ceremony is known as *la parada*, "the parade," and when it is completed, the iyawó has been initiated in Ocha.

The iyalochas prepared a paste of crushed herbs and other ingredients—the "secret" of the saint—and placed it on top of Laura's head. At this point, eight of the iyalochas—symbolizing Obatalá's number—suspended four pieces of cloth in the colors of the main orishas—white, red, yellow, and blue—over Laura's head. The various otanes of the orishas, starting with those pertaining to Elegguá, were then placed on the cloth as a "crown." All the chants and invocations of each orisha were intoned by those present. The last otanes to be placed over Laura's head were those of Obatalá.

As the chanting continued, Laura seemed to lose her last vestiges of consciousness. She felt herself falling forward and knew no more. Later her madrina told her that she had stood up from the apotí and walked around the igbodu, completely possessed by Obatalá, whose presence had been so strong that it had required several santeros to overcome the orisha and talk him into leaving.

When an orisha takes possession of the initiate during the asiento, he or she is said to "come with ashé." The madrina had sacrificed a chicken and fed the orisha some of its blood. The sacrifice had been followed by a bit of opossum and smoked fish, honey, and some of the omiero.

With a razor blade, eight cuts were made on Laura's tongue to ensure that her orisha would have the gift of speech. Eight cuts were made because that is Obatalá's number. At this point, Obatalá smiled and saluted all those present, thanking them for all their devotion and hard work.

When the orisha finally left and Laura opened her eyes, she could not remember anything of what had transpired. She was asked to sit once more on the apotí, and the last part of the ceremony, the sacrifice of the animals sacred to the orisha, then took place.

The four-legged animals were all kept outside the igbodu and brought inside one by one, each with a piece of white silk embroidered in gold braid draped on its back. While Laura sat on the apotí during most of the ceremony, she was asked to kneel each time the babalawo immolated one of the animals.

Before each animal was sacrificed, Laura chewed a few bits of coconut and some grains of pepper, which were placed on the animal's eyes, ears, and forehead. She was then instructed to touch the forehead of the animal three times with her forehead, breasts, and legs. The sacrificial victim was then tied by the legs and placed sideways on the floor over a bed of ritual herbs.

As each animal was sacrificed, its blood was gathered in a clay vessel while everyone chanted in Yoruba. Later, this blood was poured into the various vessels where the otanes were resting in front of the apotí. The head was then cut off and offered to Laura, who tasted some of the blood and then spat it toward the ceiling. The babalawo danced a ritual dance with the head in his hands and then placed it in front of the otanes representing the orishas. The animal was immediately removed from the igbodu,

legs first, like all the dead. Each animal would later be ritualistically dismembered and each piece of meat presented to the orishas
before removal for the private consumption of the santeros and
their community.

The several four-legged animals included in Laura's asiento
were followed by a variety of fowl, such as roosters, hens, doves,
and ducks. The head of each animal was offered to Laura, who
tasted the blood and repeated the action of spitting upward. Each
part of the animals was carefully named in Yoruba as it was
presented to the orishas, and the chants and invocations never
ceased during the sacrifice.

The ritual sacrifice lasted more than four hours. When it was
finally over, the babalawo, his face streaming sweat, his clothes
and body spattered with blood, humbly lowered his head in front
of the orishas and uttered the final words of the sacrifice and of
the asiento: *"Eroko ashé."* "It is done, with your blessings." (In
those houses that do not work with babalawos the sacrifice is
conducted by a santero, who is an experienced elder.)

But not all asientos end with the orishas' blessings. Sometimes
a mistake is made somewhere in the preparation of the ceremony.
Then terrible things can happen.

Several years ago a woman whom I will call Eva became
impatient because her madrina did not hurry to give her the
asiento. She left her madrina's house and went to another santero
to make the saint. Although her madrina had told Eva that she
was a daughter of Oyá, the new santera to whom she went
insisted that Oshún was Eva's orisha. Without consulting a
babalawo to be sure of the truth, this santera proceeded to
initiate Eva into Oshún's mysteries.

The first sign that something was amiss took place during the
asiento, when the iyalochas tried to cut Eva's hair. Normally very
fine and soft, it suddenly became rough and stiff like wire and
projected outward like the snakes on Medusa's head. No matter
how hard the iyalochas tried, none of the ritual scissors would
cut through the hair. Eva's eyes, which were supposed to be

closed, suddenly opened and she stared at the terrified iyalochas as if her eyes were about to fall from their sockets. Her body began to convulse uncontrollably, until she fell from the apotí.

The ayugbona and the other iyalochas, trembling almost as much as Eva, told her new madrina that they did not dare cut Eva's hair. It was obvious, they said, that a mistake had been made in deciding which orisha should be crowned on Eva's head; she was clearly not Oshún's daughter. In their opinion, it was foolhardy to go ahead with the initiation as originally planned.

Eva's new madrina, however, was undaunted by the iyalochas' words, and she quickly dismissed Eva's reaction as hysterical and melodramatic. Taking the scissors from the ayugbona's hands, she told the frightened women that she alone would cut Eva's hair and accept Oyá's punishment if the initiation went wrong. She firmly seized a handful of Eva's hair and, after many struggles, finally managed to cut it off. Standing next to her was her husband, who was the oriaté in charge of overseeing the ceremony. No sooner had the scissors cut through the reluctant hair than the oriaté stumbled, clutching his throat, and fell dead at his wife's feet.

The santera dropped the scissors and knelt by his side to see what was wrong. Seconds later, her screams turned the initiation into a nightmare. Oyá had extracted her punishment.

This story is one of many I have heard on the dangers of making a mistake during the asiento. The orishas, who can be infinitely generous and loving to their children, can also be terribly unforgiving when offended.

The night of her asiento, Laura slept on the estera at the feet of the orishas. Her madrina slept on a cot by Laura's side. The next day, known as *el día del medio*, Laura was dressed in her coronation clothes, a beautiful gown made of white peau de soie embroidered in tiny pearls, with a wide skirt, fluffy sleeves, and a high neckline. A wide crown, made of the same material as her dress, completely encircled her forehead, covering her shaved head.

Barefoot, she wore the collar de mazo, the necklaces, and the bracelets of the orishas: seven silver for Yemayá, five golden for Oshún, nine copper for Oyá, and a solitary silver one for Obatalá, her orisha. She stood by the apotí, with the soperas containing her otanes by the side of her throne. The walls and ceiling over her were draped with white lace and silver brocade. There were white flowers all around her, and she looked breathtakingly beautiful, like all initiate omo-orishas. For, as she stood by her throne, she was no longer Laura, but Obatalá himself, in all his unearthly beauty.

Shortly after twelve noon, her husband, family, and friends, and all the friends of her madrina came to visit Laura and pay their respects to her orisha. Her visitors used the estera placed in front of her throne to prostrate themselves and thus pay foribale to Obatalá. A small basket by the side gathered the offerings— one dollar each—the people gave to Obatalá.

After six in the evening, the last visitor was politely escorted out the door, and the doors of the igbodu were again closed to outsiders. They remained closed for seven days, during which time Laura ate and slept in the igbodu, leaving it only to go to the bathroom. Her madrina and ayugbona never left her side, feeding her by hand, accompanying her to the bathroom, washing her, and watching her every mood, as if she were a small child—which was indeed what she was, as an initiate in Ocha.

Three days after the asiento, the itá took place. All the santeros got together to read the seashells and determine what would happen in Laura's future life, which further initiations she had to undergo, and how she might protect herself against enemies and other dangers. Her ritual name was also determined at this time. The extensive information was gathered together in Laura's libreta, which her madrina kept and gave to her a year later, at the end of her initiation period. Seven days after the asiento came the day of *la plaza*, the marketplace. Laura and her madrina went to the market to purchase a large offering of varied fruits for the orishas.

On each of the four street corners outside the marketplace, Laura deposited, under the madrina's instructions, a few bits of coconut, smoked fish, opossum, corn, and three cents, tightly wrapped in a piece of brown paper. These were Elegguá's derecho, so that he would bless her quest and protect her against all evil.

Inside the marketplace, Laura and her madrina purchased all the fruits that pertained to the orishas. When no one was looking, Laura stole a pear from a fruit stand; her madrina had explained that this ritual stealing was part of the initiation and would bring her luck. The token theft is a symbol of the orishas' ownership of all that exists, and their right to take anything they want from the material world. This right, which does not extend to the santeros, is exercised only once in the santero's life, on the day of la plaza. After Laura "stole" the fruit, the madrina paid the fruit vendor without Laura's noticing it.

After Laura and her madrina finished buying the fruit, they returned to the ilé-orisha. They were met at the door by the ayugbona with the ritual ringing of the *agogo*, the bells with which the orishas are called down to earth. Laura and her madrina placed the fruit in a large basket and carefully balanced it over Laura's head. Returning to the igbodu with the basket on her head, Laura presented the fruit ritualistically to each of the orishas.

That afternoon the fruit was divided among all the iyalochas and babalochas present during the asiento. A rooster and two coconuts were given to Elegguá. Laura paid a small derecho to her madrina, picked up her otanes, her soperas, her seashells, and all the implements of her saints, and returned home to her husband.

But this was not the end of the initiation, only the beginning. For three months after her return home, Laura was not allowed to sit at a table or use a knife and fork. She had to eat her meals sitting on an estera on the floor, using only a spoon. A vast array of foods were forbidden to her, among them coconut, corn in any form (which precluded even the drinking of most sodas), and anything colored red, such as tomatoes and apples; she could eat no hamburgers or pizzas, beans of any type, and most pastries. Also, she was not allowed to look at herself in a mirror.

When the three months were over, the "three-month ebbó" took place, with more ritual cleansing and chantings. Sometime after this, Laura was presented to the tambor, also known as the batáa, the ritual drums of Santería, in a beautiful ceremony for which she dressed in her coronation gown, necklaces, crown, and bracelets. She presented a deep dish to the batáa with two coconuts and two candles and the ritual derecho of $1.05. She was told to deposit her offering by the batáa and kiss each of the three drums while kneeling in front of them. Sometimes the presentation to the sacred drums does not take place until several years after the initiation. This depends on the availability of the drums, of which there are only two sets in the United States.

During the course of the year of initiation, Laura could not wear makeup or curl, cut, or dye her hair. During this period she was dressed in meticulous white, her head modestly covered by a white handkerchief tied in the African style. Except during menstruation, she had to wear her necklaces and bracelets whenever she went out into the street. Having to dress constantly in white and wear her initiation "jewels" did not bother Laura as much as the attention she received. Every day someone would stop her in the street and ask her if she was a nun, a Muslim, or a Moonie. She avoided going into the subway, where everyone in the car stared at her as if she had horns growing out of her head.

At times she felt the year would never end, but end it finally did. Her hair was several inches long. She had lost some weight and felt lighter. Her health had improved considerably; her eyes sparkled and her skin looked supple and smooth. Never had she felt or looked better.

At the end of the initiation year, Laura's madrina gave her the libreta, her coronation clothes, and the hair that had been cut from her head during the asiento. This hair was to be placed in her coffin upon her death, and the dress and "jewels" worn for that final voyage.

Laura has been a santera for ten years. She has attended innumerable asientos, tambors, and fiestas de santo. There is only one ceremony she has never attended and would prefer never to attend: the ceremony known as *itutu*, discussed in a later chapter, which is celebrated upon the death of a santero.

15.

Batáa
The Drums

The ritual drums of Santería are the *batáa*. They are played in special *fiestas de santo*, which are parties in honor of the orishas. The party is known commonly as a *tambor*, a word that means "drum" in Spanish, although it may also be called a bembé or a güemilere.

The tambor is always given in honor of a specific orisha. The reasons may vary. The most common occasion for a tambor is the asiento, although not every asiento offers a tambor. Another reason for this type of festivity is an act of gratitude to an orisha for a very special favor granted. When a santero "feeds" his saints or celebrates his anniversary, sometimes he offers a tambor to his "guardian angel" in recognition for his or her continued protection.

There are three batáa drums. They are called Iyá (the "mother" drum and the largest of the three), Itótele, and Okónkolo. The batáa are played together in an unusual drum rhythm that is known as a "conversation." Iyá always "speaks" to Itótele while Okónkolo marks the beat. But Iyá is the only one that "asks" for changes in the rhythm or *toque*.

Each rhythm has a meaning. For example, when someone

enters the room where the batáa are being played, the drums can "insult" the person with a rhythm. If the person does not know the language of the batáa, he will not get the message. There are also certain songs known as *cantos de puya*, which are sung to the beat of the drums. These are veiled insults to the saints, designed to anger them and make them come down and take possession of their initiates. In a canto de puya, the lead singer, or *akpwón*, can call Changó a fool and say he does not wear trousers but skirts. Changó, who is virility personified, will immediately take offense and descend in a fury to answer the challenge to his manhood. But as soon as he takes possession of one of his children, the akpwón changes his tune and begins to flatter the orisha. He has succeeded in bringing down the saint, as he had intended.

There are two types of batáa sets. Those that have not been consecrated are called *aberínkula*. The ones that have been consecrated and have *fundamento de santo* are called *ilú añá* (sacred drum). Both sets of drums are sacred, but the *ilú añá* are the ones used in the most important rituals of Santería, such as the presentation of the iyawó to the drums, described in the previous chapter. This is a very colorful ceremony during which several iyawós are dressed in the ritual clothes of their asiento and brought by two santeros in front of the drums. The iyawó carries a plate upon which rest a coconut and two white candles, the derecho of the batáa. Before him walks a santero asperging cool water to both sides of the room, so that the iyawó's life in Santería will be free from harm. Once in front of the drums, the iyawó dances to the rhythms and then leaves the room. Because there are only two sets of *ilú añá* in the United States, they have to travel all over the country to be present in the most solemn of the ceremonies. For this reason there are sometimes large groups of people waiting to be presented to the batáa, many of whom have been santeros for years. I once assisted in a ceremony at which eighteen persons were presented to the drums, only five of whom were iyawós.

When the *aberínkula* is playing, anyone can dance to the toques. But when the *ilú añá* is playing, only the santeros who have been presented to the drums can dance to their rhythms. In some casas de santo, the aleyos (the uninitiated) are allowed to dance to the *ilú añá*, but in others they are not even allowed in the room where the drums are playing.

The batáa are made of leather. Sometimes they are tied with leather thongs, but in some places, such as Matanzas, in Cuba, they are tied with ropes. The drums have two "heads" or sides. The larger head is known as *enu*, and the smaller is known as *tcha-tcha*. In Iyá and Itótele, the enu is smeared with a mixture of herbs and blood called *fadela* for greater resonance and deeper overtones.

Only the *aberínkula* can be played outside Santería, and then only certain rhythms can be played. Most *toques de santo* should not be played because the saint who answers to those calls can approach the drummer. Babalú's rhythms are particularly delicate because he is a very sensitive orisha. Although many drummers are initiated santeros, some are not. But all of them should have received at least the Necklaces and the Warriors.

The room in which the tambor is held always has a "throne" (*trono*) erected in one of its corners. The walls surrounding the throne are hung with silk and brocaded cloths in the color of the orisha being honored. In the center of the throne sits the sopera with the orisha's otanes. It is always perched on a high seat and draped with a fancy cloth in the orisha's color. The tureens of the other orishas are also in various places around the throne, also draped in their prescribed colors. All the attributes of the honored orisha are present, as well as a large *plaza* (offering) of fruits, cakes, pastries, and the orisha's favorite foods. The plaza is always spread on the floor, flanked by large vases of flowers. Facing the throne is a small basket in which the participants to the tambor place their money offerings to the saint. This is usually a small derecho ranging from one dollar to whatever the person may wish to give. Next to the basket is the instrument used to call the orisha. Each saint uses a different instrument. Changó uses a maraca, Oshún uses a bell, and Obatalá uses a *cencerro*, a square silver bell that is rung very slowly.

Each person who walks into the room must pay foribale in front of the throne; that is, he must lie facedown on the ground and shake the orisha's instrument. He then puts the derecho in the basket, kisses the floor, and stands up. There is always an estera, or straw mat, rolled up in front of the throne so that people may use it to lie on. At no time must anyone stand on the estera. If the occasion for the tambor is an asiento, the iyawó sits in the middle of the throne, surrounded by the tureens. Only initiated santeros can pay foribale in front of the iyawó; all others kneel, cross their arms as a sign of respect, then stand up. When a santero pays homage in front of the iyawó, the initiate must reciprocate and lie at the feet of the santero, his elder, who then blesses him in Yoruba, helps him to his feet, and embraces him in the traditional Santería custom.

The tambor begins with the *oru*, the rhythms or toques played on the batáa to honor the saints. Usually the oru is played without singing. Everyone present stands up to honor God and his saints. No one dances during the oru, which is played directly in front of the throne. There are twenty-four toques during the oru, each one for a different saint, although some orishas have more than one toque. The order of the saints honored by the oru never varies, with the exception of the saint to whom the tambor is dedicated. That particular orisha, as host of the tambor, is always honored last.

The order of the oru is as follows: first (as always), Elegguá, followed by Oggún, Ochosi, Obaloke, Inle, Babalú-Ayé, Osain, Osun, Obatalá, Dadá, Oggue, Aganyú, Orúnla, Ibeyi, Orisha-Oko, Changó, Yewá, Oyá, Oshún, Yemayá, Obba, and Oddúa. Some of the saints honored in the oru are less known, but they are all important parts of the ceremony.

When the batáa begin the toque for Babalú-Ayé, one of the santeras drops a few drops of water on the floor of the igbodu where the drums are playing. Everyone present moves forward to take some of the water with his fingertips and make the sign of the cross on his forehead. This is done to receive Babalú-Ayé's blessings.

After the oru, the batáa begins to play the *Eyá Aranla*, the music that is sung and danced by those present. The chorus that answers the akpwón is called the *ankorí*.

Each of the toques has a name. For example, Meta-Meta, Kan-Kan, and Tui-Tui are toques for Changó; Lalú Banché is a toque for Elegguá; Agüere is played for Ochosi; and Chén-ché Kurúru and Rumba Llesa are played for Oshún.

Sometimes, instead of a tambor, the santero may decide to offer a *güiro* to an orisha. During a güiro only one drum (a conga) is played, accompanied by three beaded gourds known as *shékeres*. The beads are loosely held around the gourd, and their sound is similar to maracas. The colors of the beads indicate the saint who owns them. The shékeres have their own toques, which are different from those of the batáa. Each shékere plays a different beat. In the güiro, the oru is almost always sung, in contrast with the tambor, where there is never any singing. Güiros are less expensive than a tambor and often more exciting.

Each of the orishas has his or her own special dance movements. The people dancing during the toques have that very much in mind, and always imitate the orishas' motions during the dance. Elegguá, for instance, often hops frantically on one foot or does a swift *zapateado*, not unlike a Flamenco dancer. During this complicated dance, the body is balanced on one foot, whose heel is tapped rapidly against the floor, while the other foot is swept backward off the floor, repeatedly, all in rhythm with the drums. Alternately, both feet may be flexed from right to left, one behind the other. The forefinger of each hand is often stretched out in a pointing gesture. Elegguá's dances are among the most exhausting and exciting of the toques. Changó always stretches out his legs in an exaggerated gesture, as if he were carefully measuring each step. Yemayá swirls very fast as she dances, bending her body sideways as if she were imitating the sea waves. Obatalá shuffles slowly, three steps to the front and three backward, his arms dangling at his sides, his body bent in the posture of a very old man. It is always interesting to watch the dancers during a toque, because even when the orisha's name is not mentioned, it is easy to recognize his toque by the motions of the dancers.

In Nigeria, the batáa are said to belong to Changó, who is the most graceful dancer among the orishas. Like the santeros, the Yoruba have special dances for each of the orishas. These ritual dances are not simply spontaneous movements in response to the music. They are carefully choreographed to represent sacred messages to and from the orishas. Each dance is an invocation to the orisha and a request for him or her to come down and manifest through one of the priests. To dance to an orisha in any manner but that prescribed by tradition is an offense to the deity. An ancient Yoruba saying expresses it best: *"Oní-Sangó tó jó tí kò tàpaá, abùkù ara rè ni."* "A Changó devotee who dances without flinging his arms and legs does discredit to himself." This refers to Changó's custom of stretching out his legs and arms in an exaggerated fashion during his ritual dances. The saying underscores the importance of adhering to the correct movements during each dance.

The importance of the batáa in modern percussion cannot be overemphasized. There is no drum rhythm in Latin music, jazz, or any type of music using percussion that does not exist in the batáa. Every possible combination of drum sounds can be found in them. They are the roots of all percussion, and those roots are deeply buried in West Africa, the country of origin of the drum.

Every drum that came from Africa, not just the batáa, carried inside it a kola nut that was believed to be the soul of the drum. For that reason each drum was believed to be "alive," speaking with a voice all its own. This tradition is still observed in Santería, in which the batáa are believed to be spiritual entities of great power.

16.

Spirit Possession⬛⬛⬛⬛⬛⬛⬛

On December 17, santeros celebrate the birthday of Babalú-Ayé, syncretized as Saint Lazarus. On and around this date, many festivities take place to honor this saint, much loved and revered in Santería because of his kindness and compassion.

Several years ago I attended a tambor in honor of Saint Lazarus in the house of one of New York's best-known babalochas, an omo-Changó known as Armandito. The santera who took me to the tambor was one of my madrinas in Santería.

When we arrived, Armandito's house was already full of people. My madrina went directly to a small room at the back of the basement, built to resemble a chapel, where Babalú's plaza had been set out. The room was empty of furniture except for some benches along the walls. In one corner, in the center of an exquisite altar, stood a large and ornate statue of Saint Lazarus, flanked by two heavy golden candlesticks upon which burned two tall white candles. On both sides of the altar, two large porcelain urns, laboriously embossed in gold and purple, overflowed with masses of flowers. Directly over the altar, and extending to the sides, was a pallium formed of intertwined flowers and masses of *cundiamor* (an herb used to cure diabetes, and

196

sacred to Babalú). Among the flowers one could distinguish irises, orchids, lavender, and other purple-hued blossoms, purple being Babalú's favored color. Purple silk handkerchiefs embroidered in gold were draped loosely around the altar, behind which hung a rich brocade curtain embroidered in the same colors.

A pair of crutches, a symbol of Babalú's infirmity, and several *alforjas* (shoulder bags) made of sackcloth trimmed with purple hung from the wall to the left of the altar. The alforja is one of Babalú's attributes; in it he keeps his favorite food, toasted corn, and it is usually made of sackcloth, as a reminder that Babalú-Saint Lazarus was a beggar during his life on earth.

It is important to remember that the scriptures speak of two different men called Lazarus. One was the brother of Martha and Mary, whom Jesus brought back from the dead. The other appears in a parable Jesus told the Pharisees in Luke 16. The story tells of a leprous beggar whose sores were licked by dogs and who barely sustained himself with the scraps from the rich man's table. When the beggar died, he went to heaven, while the rich man went to hell for not sharing his possessions with the beggar. It is this beggar Lazarus who has been syncretized as Babalú-Ayé.

Directly in front of the altar was the plaza with all the fruits, cakes, and other foods the orisha favors. The grass mat known as an estera was spread out on the floor facing the altar, for the comfort of those who wished to pay foribale to Babalú. A small basket next to the estera waited to receive the money offerings— usually of one dollar each—that devotees of the orisha would give.

When we came into the room, I stopped in front of the altar, overwhelmed by the brilliance and beauty of the arrangement.

"That is *el trono* of Babalú," said my madrina. "Inside that altar are hidden Babalú's secrets."

"What is the money for, madrina?" I asked.

"For candles, flowers, or whatever Babalú requires. It is his derecho," she said.

"Is there a derecho for everything?" I asked.

"Yes," said my madrina, "there is. With the derecho we buy candles, herbs, food, and many other things for the orishas. These things are energy in various forms. So what you're really doing with the derecho is giving the orisha an energy source, which he or she will give you back a thousandfold in the form of many blessings."

As we spoke, we left the room and crossed into the basement, where the tambor would be held. There were already several hundred people inside, all loosely clustered around the small kitchen built at one end. From this kitchen was issuing plate after plate of typically Cuban and Puerto Rican fare. Three pink-faced and harassed-looking young santeras were serving the food—rice with pigeon peas, roast pork, stewed potatoes, and a lettuce-and-avocado salad—on sturdy white china plates. Every santero's house has a closet where literally hundreds of these plates are kept, for tambors and other fiestas de santo.

I noticed that although all the three women were serving, they passed each plate to an elderly, slightly balding man standing next to the kitchen. He then passed the plates of food on to the guests. After my madrina and I had received our food from him, I asked her about the man.

"That's the omo-Babalú who will dance to the orisha," said my madrina. "He represents Babalú here today. That's why the food must pass through his hands."

"Does someone always dance to the orisha to whom a tambor is offered?" I asked.

"Yes," said my madrina, "but only a santero who has been initiated into the mysteries of that orisha." She looked up from her plate, and seeing the curiosity in my eyes, she smiled. "When someone wants to give a tambor to an orisha for whatever reason, he must first find a santero or santera who's a child of that orisha, and who knows how to dance to the batáa. If the omo-orisha agrees to dance in the tambor, then the person offering the tambor must pay him a derecho for the service and have a beautiful costume made, in the colors and style worn by the orisha, for the omo-orisha to wear. But he's not allowed to wear it until after he's danced to the orisha and been possessed by the saint. Then some of the other santeros take him to another room and dress him in the orisha's costume. When he returns to the main room, the orisha occupying his body blesses those present at the tambor."

"A tambor must be a very expensive proposition," I said. "Between the derechos, the plaza, the flowers, and the food to feed all these people, Armandito must have spent more than a thousand dollars."

"Yes," said my madrina, "tambors like this one cost much more, others a little less, but a thousand is the average cost."

When we finished eating, we returned our empty plates to the omo-Babalú. He passed them on to one of the santeras, who washed them swiftly and set them aside. The small kitchen was run so smoothly that there was little indication that hundreds of people were being fed. When I mentioned this to my madrina, she smiled. "Practice," she said. "We do this so often we can do it with our eyes closed. Incidentally, those santeras are also paid a derecho for cooking and serving."

At that precise moment, the three batáa at the other end of the room began to play, interrupting the conversation. Everyone began gravitating toward the players; my madrina and I found a place facing the drums. The sound made by the batáa is deafening and can be quite disturbing after a while, especially for a person unfamiliar with African rhythms.

At first the drummers did not sing but simply beat the batáa in a special rhythm, resembling a three-sided conversation. This drum music, I learned later, is called the *oru*, and is played to Olorún-Olofi and the saints. It is not danced.

After the oru, the drummers began to play to all the various orishas, starting naturally with the redoubtable Elegguá. The head drummer, who was also the akpwón (ritual singer and caller of the orishas), was a young Afro-Cuban who had recently flown in from Havana. He spoke Yoruba fluently and knew all the tribal songs traditionally associated with the orishas. He sang the songs while the other two drummers answered in chorus.

Next to the drummers stood a young man holding a large gourd painted in bright colors and covered by a net of large beads. The young man kept turning the beaded gourd in his hands, producing a sound similar to that of a pair of maracas. The gourd was used to accentuate the drumbeat and call the orishas down to earth. All the players were initiated santeros.

On the floor next to the drums was the small basket for the batáa's derecho. As the drummers played each orisha's favored songs, the omo-orishas of that particular saint moved forward and kissed a folded dollar bill, blessed themselves with it, and deposited it in the basket. Then they danced to their orisha using the special movements associated with the saint.

With the scrupulous courtesy of Santería, Babalú-Ayé, who was the true host of the tambor, was the last to be danced. Then there came an hour's intermission during which the drummers rested and everyone exchanged comments on the excellence of the tambor. Armandito circulated among his guests, dressed in sackcloth to honor Babalú and wearing a round sackcloth cap to which had been sewn four parrot feathers, similar to the ones worn by the iyalocha during my first tambor—a symbol of the initiated santero.

During the intermission, several iyalochas went through the room carrying large trays heaped with Cuban pastries, which they offered to the guests. My madrina urged me to partake of all the sweets offered, as they were full of ashé, the blessing of the saints.

After the refreshments had been eaten and the drummers were well rested, the playing of the batáa resumed. But this time no one came forward to dance to the orishas.

The omo-Babalú chosen to dance to the orisha now came forward. His air of authority and self-assurance immediately set him apart from those around him. When he started Babalú's dance, this dignified air added to the impact of his performance as the orisha's alter ego.

He limped and shuffled his feet, stamping with one foot, then with another, brandishing an invisible crutch in the air. As his dancing became more violent, I suddenly realized I was in the actual presence of the orisha. The possession was so gradual and yet so total that I was not aware at what point Babalú mounted the babalocha. The omo-Babalú began to tremble convulsively, his eyes rolling, his body weaving back and forth. But at no time did he miss the rhythm of the drumbeat or stop the ritual dancing.

The akpwón, seeing that Babalú was in complete possession of his omo-orisha, stood immediately and signaled to the man with the gourd to take his place behind the drum. Taking the gourd away from the man's hands, he approached the omo-Babalú. Face to face with the orisha, he began to taunt him in Yoruba, calling him to come forward and speak to the audience, shaking the gourd close to the omo's face.

A sudden movement behind me made me turn around. Another santero, also an omo-Babalú, became possessed by the orisha. Later on I asked my madrina how a saint could possess two people at the same time. She replied that the human body was too weak and imperfect to house an orisha's full energy. Only a small atom of that divine energy could enter in, which is why multiple possessions are possible.

The second omo-Babalú, a tall, slim man in his mid-twenties, was doubled up close to the floor, his body convulsing in the grip of possession. The akpwón approached him also and spoke to him in Yoruba. He was still teasing Babalú gently when another man, this time a son of Obatalá, became possessed on the other side of the room. That possession was followed by another and another, until seven persons were possessed. The orishas in possession were, in order of appearance, Babalú (twice), Obatalá, Aganyú, Yemayá, Oggún, and Oyá.

No one touched any of the omo-orishas as the possessions took place. The singer went from one to the other, singing and speaking in Yoruba, but always in rhythm with the tireless drums.

The omo-Obatalá, a good-looking man in his mid-thirties,

with very fair skin and prematurely gray hair, seemed reluctant to be possessed. (Later I learned it was Obatalá who was reluctant to come down to earth.) He kept turning away from the akoñrín, the ceremonial singer and caller of the orishas, who followed him relentlessly wherever he moved, always calling out to the orisha in Yoruba and shaking the gourd in his face. Finally, the batáa and the akpwón seemed to overpower the omo-orisha. He suddenly convulsed and became rigid, his face draining of color. Satisfied, the singer continued to move from one omo-orisha to the next, chanting all the time in Yoruba and shaking the gourd.

While the other possessions were taking place, Armandito and another santero steered the first omo-Babalú, still possessed, out of the room, gently coaxing the orisha in Yoruba, and asking him to come with them.

"They're going to dress him in his own sackcloth," my madrina whispered. "Then they'll bring him back to give the people his blessing."

While we waited for Babalú to return in full regalia, I watched the other omo-orishas complete their possessions. Yemayá had mounted one of her daughters, an iyalocha in her late thirties wearing a deep turquoise dress. The woman circled the room, pressing gently against the people, Yemayá's gentle smile illuminating her face. The powerful Oggún had taken possession of a very dark woman with coarse features and a heavyset figure. Her possession was most impressive, for she shed her personality completely to become a rough, virile man. She went through the room in Oggún's swaggering stride, picking up several of the small children present and tossing them up in the air. Someone handed the orisha a lighted cigar; he took it immediately and began to smoke it with relish. He continued lifting terrified children, throwing them up and catching them in one hand without even looking. The children's screams were drowned by the drums and ignored by Oggún, who at one time seemed to be juggling several children in midair. I expected a child to drop to the floor at any moment, but none did. The parents eyed Oggún's prowess with dismay, but no one dared ask the orisha to stop. After a while he seemed to become bored and moved away to play pranks on some of the older people.

In the meantime, the second omo-Babalú was cleansing one of the men present. He puffed on a cigar and blew the smoke in the man's ears and face and on the back of his neck. Several times he moved his hands swiftly over the man's body, from his chest down to his feet, then from his back down again to his feet. Then, quite unexpectedly, he grabbed the man by the waist with both hands and lifted him high over his head. For a few minutes he held the man aloft, shaking him all the while. Then he put the man roughly down on the floor and moved away, signifying that the healing was complete.

As the orishas descended, the santeros began to crowd around them in the hopes of getting a question answered or a problem solved. Suddenly there was a small commotion at the room's entrance. I craned my neck to see the cause of the excitement, but a sea of people obstructed my vision. Pressing forward through the circle, I saw the first omo-Babalú walking toward the batáa, dressed in the orisha's traditional costume—knee breeches and a close-fitting tunic reaching just to his hips. Both garments were of sackcloth, trimmed in purple braid with gold designs along the sleeves and legs. A wide purple band circled the omo-orisha's forehead and two purple alforjas were crisscrossed over his chest; in one shoulder bag he carried toasted corn and in the other he kept his beggar's alms. Bare-legged and barefoot, he carried a large sheaf of herbs tied with a purple ribbon in his right hand and a long staff in his left. The people offered him alms as he went by, and he humbly accepted them.

As the orisha made his way into the room, a wide path opened in front of him so he could walk easily. He shuffled slightly like an ailing old man who has preserved his dignity in the face of calamity.

Now several people came forward and paid their respects at the feet of the orisha. He then continued his laborious walk until he reached the batáa. The singer stood up immediately, as one does on an important guest's arrival, and began to sing one of Babalú's traditional songs. The other orishas, who had spread out during the early part of the tambor, came now to salute Babalú. For some time they stood in front of the batáa, embracing and greeting each other vociferously in Yoruba. There was much joyous laughter, and then they all joined arms and began to dance together in time with the drumbeat. Everyone present joined in the laughter and dance.

A few minutes later, Armandito came into the room carrying a large basket of fruits upon his head. On top of the fruits rested two dainty white doves, their legs tied securely with white satin ribbons. Armandito's wife, also an iyalocha, came right behind him, throwing fistfuls of toasted corn to both sides of the room in a cleansing ritual. When Armandito came to the batáa, the orishas stopped dancing and surrounded the babalocha, embracing him affectionately and thanking him for offering the tambor. Then most of them moved aside, and only the two omo-Babalús and the omo-Obatalá remained next to Armandito.

Then the three orishas began an extraordinary cleansing ritual. One omo-Babalú took the basket off Armandito's head and began a classical example of a purifying rite, or *despojo*, done by raining the fruits over Armandito's head and then rubbing them down over his body. As Armandito stood motionless, the second Babalú ripped open the pants legs and the sackcloth tunic that Armandito was wearing. Then all three orishas proceeded to lick every part of Armandito's body that was free of clothing—his face, neck, arms, legs. All during the cleansing, the batáa went on playing. The orishas kept on dancing in their peculiar jerking motion, eyes glazed, bodies tensed like wires.

Suddenly the omo-Obatalá bent down and in one swift motion picked up the two doves, which had been lying on the floor next to the batáa. With eager hands he untied the ribbons around the doves' legs and then, holding a bird in each hand, passed them all over Armandito's body. The doves fanned the air with their wings, which seemed to shimmer in the dim lights of the room. Their wings formed a momentary arch over Armandito's head before they dipped suddenly to his feet in the fast grip of the orisha.

Not wanting to miss any details of the ceremony, I leaned eagerly over the circle and saw the orisha switch both doves to his left hand. For one moment their wings fluttered over his clenched fist, then his right hand moved swiftly. Suddenly the two doves hung limp over his wrist, both heads torn neatly from their necks. From the severed necks spurted twin fountains of blood, spotting the immaculate white clothes of the omo-Obatalá. Fast as an eagle, his massive head bent sharply forward and caught the crimson stream in his mouth. For some minutes he drank thirstily, then lifted his head, lips bright red, eyes sparkling, and extended the doves in silent invitation to the other two orishas, who came forward willingly to partake of the blood offering.

For a while the three orishas joined their heads fraternally over the doves and consumed their sacrifice. Then once more they turned their attention to Armandito, who had stood in their midst all the time, waiting for them to finish. The omo-Obatalá dripped some of the blood over Armandito's head and body. All three orishas tore handfuls of feathers off the doves' bodies and rubbed them over the babalocha's body, spreading the blood over his skin. Then they placed the doves and crushed fruits on a large sackcloth handkerchief and tied it in a bundle, and marched Armandito out of the room to the incessant playing of the batáa.

I had often been present during animal sacrifices and had been the subject of innumerable despojos, but never had I witnessed a ritual in which the orishas actually drank the blood of the sacrifice. The ceremony had shaken me, perhaps because the actions were so instinctive, so far beyond the scope of anything human. Once, during an African safari, I had seen a lion pride feeding upon a felled zebra; the animals had huddled over their kill in the same close camaraderie the three orishas had displayed as they consumed the doves' blood. Somewhere deep within, I felt suddenly tormented and assailed in my most basic beliefs.

"For the blood is the life," say the scriptures. But they also say that blood is God's alone, and that man must never consume it or else risk the wrath of the Deity. How then did the santeros dare to drink blood? I expressed my doubts to my madrina.

"But the santeros don't drink blood," she said, "the orishas do. You'll never see a santero drink blood when he's not possessed by an orisha. The blood of sacrificed animals is either poured directly upon the otanes of the saints, who can drink it that way, or else it is drunk directly by the orishas when they are mounted upon their children. And remember," she added, "the orishas are manifestations of God. And as such, blood also belongs to them."

She took me affectionately by the arm and guided me out of the room. "What you need is to meet Obatalá in person," she told me as we walked toward the small chapel.

"What do you mean, madrina?" I asked.

"Obatalá," she answered cryptically, "the orisha who drank the doves' blood before. Doves belong to him, incidentally, so he was only partaking of his own food."

She directed me up the stairs leading to the small chapel. Entering the room, we saw that three orishas were holding consultations within. On a small bench, directly to the left of the altar, sat the first Babalú, surrounded by a small group of devotees. Obatalá, also surrounded by his followers, was seated at the far end of the room. In the center of the room stood the formidable Oggún, sturdy legs wide apart, a thick cigar in his mouth, rubbing his belly contentedly, totally oblivious of the fact that he was inhabiting the body of a female.

As soon as some of the people surrounding Obatalá left the room, my madrina pushed through until she was by the orisha's side. Obatalá greeted a little girl brought to him by her mother, blessed the child, and sent her away. As soon as the orisha was momentarily free, my madrina moved forward and lay down on the floor to pay him foribale.

Smiling, the orisha reached down to touch her shoulders and blessed her in Yoruba. He then helped her up again and stood up to embrace her. She motioned me to come closer and turned to address the orisha.

"Obatalá, my father," she said, "I want you to bless my godchild. She has not yet been initiated in Ocha, but she has the elekes, and loves the Religion." She moved a little aside and pushed me toward the orisha.

Obatalá turned his dark, luminous eyes upon me, opened his arms, and gently, with infinite tenderness, pressed me against his chest. Suddenly I was flooded with love. I leaned my head on his shoulder and his touch was bliss. I had never before known or felt such softness and warmth. I wanted to remain in his embrace forever. But the very next moment I was back in the small chapel and the orisha was smiling down at me.

"Omo-mi," he said, speaking to my madrina, but still looking at me, "I want you to make a new eleke for my child, the eleke of Eshu Alabwanna, who's the master of all roads. He'll see that she's always protected wherever she goes."

"Yes, my father," said my madrina, bowing her head respectfully. "I'll do so as soon as possible."

"Good," he said with a sigh, and pushed me toward her gently.

I moved away from him reluctantly. The tenderness of his smile told me he understood my feelings. A little hurriedly now, my madrina rushed me out of the room, as many other people were waiting to speak to the orisha. But when I turned to look back at him from the door, he was still smiling at me.

A year later, when I received Elegguá and the Warriors from a babalawo, I learned from my padrino that the path of my Elegguá was Eshu Alabwanna. The santero possessed by Obatalá and the babalawo who gave me Elegguá did not know each other. How could the santero know the true name of my Elegguá, especially considering that there are twenty-one paths of Elegguá in Santería?

17.

Spells and Magic —◿◿◿◿◿◿◿◿◿

Not all the santeros use the Diloggún to conduct a registro. Some use Spanish playing cards, while others divine with a cigar or with a glass of water. But most use the seashells as a divination system.

Regardless of the method of divination used, it is always the eggun or the orishas who determine the ebbó or "cure" for the ills besetting the santero's clients. But in order for either the dead or the saints to be able to work with the santero, he must be familiar with the never-ending list of magical solutions that exist for each specific human problem.

Most consulting santeros have recourse to an impressive roster of ebbós and magic spells for every conceivable ill that may afflict mankind. Many of these solutions are written in the libreta that the santero receives after the asiento. Each herb, root, or powder has an infinity of uses for a variety of purposes. The santero's memory is like a complex index file where they are listed by class and category.

A santero once told me how he had used his magical expertise to help a young woman with a love problem. It seems the girl had just met a very nice and highly eligible young man and was very interested in finding out what were her chances of capturing his interest on a permanent basis. The santero consulted Oshún, the patroness of love and marriage, and learned through her intercession that the young man liked the santero's client but that there were several other girls vying for his attention. This of course called for strong protective measures and the santero was ready with a whole arsenal of magical weapons. The first thing he advised his client was to buy a small image of Oshún in her Catholic aspect of Our Lady of La Caridad del Cobre. The image was to be bought with the intention of always remaining faithful and grateful to Oshún for her help in securing the undivided affections of the man in question. It was to be placed on a small table or shelf in the girl's bedroom. The girl was also instructed to buy a yellow nine-day candle, of the type that comes encased in glass. She was to ascertain that the candle could be taken out of its glass enclosure, as she was to inscribe her lover's name on the candle five times with her own name written across it, also five times. The candle was then to be dressed with five different types of oil: *sígueme, vente commigo, yo puedo y tu no, amor,* and *dominante.* (All these ingredients are readily available at any *botánica.*) After the candle was fully anointed, it was to be replaced inside the glass. Before the girl could light the candle, however, she had to complete the second part of the spell, which consisted of a small dish of honey at the bottom of which she had previously placed a photograph of her lover. Over the photograph she was to place five small fishhooks. The allegory was simple. The honey is a symbol of love, of everything that is soft and sweet. It is also one of the main attributes of Oshún. The fishhooks are also the property of Oshún, who is the patroness of all river waters. With the hooks Oshún would be able to capture the young man, and with the honey she would soften him and fill him with great love for her petitioner. The santero cautioned his client to taste some of the honey in the dish before offering it to Oshún. The reason for this precaution was that according to the Yoruba legend, one of Oshún's enemies, aware of the orisha's great predilection for honey, tried to poison the saint by introducing some very powerful venom in this substance. Ever since that time, Oshún will not accept any offerings of honey unless they are tasted in her presence. After the honey was tested, the girl could go ahead and light the candle in Oshún's name, asking the goddess to so inveigle the five senses of the girl's lover that he would think only about her and forget all his other interests for her sake. (The reason for the repetitive use of the number five in this spell is that it is the number attributed to Oshún in Santería.) After the candle was lit, the girl was not to call or contact her lover in any way, as he would be coming to her before the candle was spent. The santero did not hear from his client for nearly a year after this first consultation, and he assumed all was going well with her. He was not far from the truth, as he found out during her second visit. This time the girl told her adviser that the spell had worked wonderfully, that her boyfriend loved her madly, that they were very happy, but that in spite of all his promises and complete devotion, she could not get him to marry her. The thought of matrimony was totally alien to his nature, and every time she mentioned it he threatened to leave her. What could she do? Much, said the santero. This necessitated Oshún's attention again. Only this time the situation called for more drastic measures. The best spell to use would be that of the lily bulb and the man's sperm. This spell is one of the most powerful and best-known spells of Santería. The main ingredient is the onionlike root of the lily, which is hollowed and filled with several oils and other ingredients. Over the oil is affixed a floating wick made of a cotton wad soaked in the sperm of the victim. This original and personalized oil lamp is lit every day for an hour, preferably at nine in the evening, making sure that no one knows of its existence. The man who is the subject of this spell is unable to resist it. He must submit himself to the will of whoever is burning the lamp. For, together with the oil, the very essence of his being, in the form of his sperm, is also burning. The santeros believe that a man's sperm is a symbol of his manhood. Whenever his manhood is diminished or affected in any way, his will weakens. At this point he can easily be prevailed upon without being able to defend himself. By the time he realizes what has happened, it is usually too late to take any preventive measures. The santero's client was elated and full of praise for the santero's powers when her boyfriend, unable to resist such a magical fusillade, surrendered his bastion and acceded to marry her. The santero was pleased that the spell had succeeded but was very quick in reminding his client that it was Oshún's power and not his that brought about the miracle. He reminded the happy prospective bride that she owed her coming marriage to Oshún and that she should never fail to show her gratitude to the saint, one of the most gracious and also one of the most sensitive of the Yoruba pantheon. The girl assured the santero that she would not forget his admonitions, and gave him a handsome present for all his help. She was married soon after that, and all seemed to indicate that she and her bridegroom would live happily ever after. This, however, was not the case. Although she did not forget her promise to the santero and was careful to honor Oshún in the prescribed manner, her husband did not share her beliefs. One thing led to another, and in the course of a violent argument he swept Oshún's image off its niche and threw it on the floor, where it was shattered. Aghast at this reckless action, his wife picked up all the various fragments and desperately tried to paste them together, but was unable to do so. Convinced that something dreadful was going to happen, she threw the useless pieces away and hurried to the santero's house at the first opportunity. When he heard the whole story, the santero shrugged his shoulders. He told his client that since Oshún had made the marriage, she was entitled to finish it whenever she pleased. The saint had obviously been displeased by the husband's actions and had guided his hands in destroying her own image. In the santero's opinion, the marriage was finished and there was no one who could help, himself included. And indeed, before the year was over, the couple were separated and a divorce followed a few years later.

According to a legend, Oshún made the first lamp with a pumpkin. She always keeps her gold and all her implements for witchcraft inside one of these vegetables. Many of the ebbós prepared under her influence are made with a pumpkin. A popular spell of this type is made to bring back a lover. The santero hollows a pumpkin and puts inside it five toenails from a rooster, along with an egg, pepper, marjoram, Florida Water, a personal article of the person, and his name written on a piece of paper. He spits three times inside the pumpkin and places it in front of Oshún's image, where it remains for ten days. At the end of this period he throws the pumpkin into the river. According to the santeros, this ebbó guarantees the return of the most reluctant lover.

Great evil can also be done with a pumpkin, asserts a santero of my acquaintance, who has told me of a black spell that uses the leaves of this vegetable. Whenever the santero wants to hurt somebody, he gathers three different types of ashes and wraps them in a pumpkin leaf, together with a personal article of the intended victim, and the latter's name written on a piece of paper. He asks Oshún to turn the life of the person into ashes, and buries the leaf in the ground. Soon after this, his enemy dies or is overcome by some terrible fate. The same santero says a spell prepared with seven pumpkin leaves and twenty-one grains of ground pepper can demolish a building with great ease. Maybe this was the spell used against a well-known iyalocha from Delancey Street in New York City, known only as Doña Catalina, who had an argument with another santera, and very shortly afterwards had the unhappy experience to see a car hit the side of her four-story building, which promptly crumbled to the ground. Fortunately, no one was hurt in the accident and the iyalocha was able, with the help of Oshún, to buy another building in the vicinity.

The pumpkin is a symbol of money and belongs exclusively to Oshún. The santeros believe that to give away or to eat pumpkin is an offense to Oshún, who will immediately withdraw her favors from the one who dared partake of the fruit. Once this most important tenet is observed, the santeros can use any of their large array of money spells to ask Oshún for money in more explicit terms. A favorite spell for money involves a small bread roll that is soaked in milk and honey for several days in front of Oshún's image. When the bread has soaked up all the liquid, the santero makes a small hole in the center of the roll and places a yellow candle in the opening. He lights the candle in the name of Oshún and invokes the saint to give him the money he needs.

Also very popular in Santería are lodestones, which are kept in pairs (a male and a female stone) for good luck and to attract money. The santero puts the two stones in a glass or earthenware vessel and fills this container with iron scrapings. He adds several coins of different denominations and a bit of fake silver and gold powders. These powders are sold in small bottles and are used very frequently in all types of money spells. Every Friday the lodestones are removed from their container, washed in dry wine, and replaced in the vessel. Many santeros also recommend several needles attached to the lodestones. Whenever the santero wants to attract the love or the good will of somebody, he surreptitiously places one of these needles on the clothing of the person he wants to influence. Dress hems and trouser cuffs are favorite hiding places. The needle is believed to be loaded with the strong magnetism of the lodestone, and since the lodestone belongs to the santero, this powerful attraction reverts to him. Lodestones are believed to be such powerful good-luck and money charms that they are one of the most popular items in the santero's list.

I think it is fitting at this point to state that, although I am not a santera, I have great respect for the beliefs of Santería. I have witnessed too many unexplainable phenomena to have many doubts as to the validity of the magical claims of the santeros. I believe the saints are just so many points of contact with the subconscious mind, each one controlling an aspect of human endeavor. Unshakable faith and strongly concentrated will could tap the vast reservoir of power which is the unconscious mind, at exactly the point desired, by using a simple key word: the name of the orisha that controls that particular area. I believe this is exactly what the santero does when he invokes an orisha. The spells and the magical rituals he uses are simply additional fuel for his already unwavering faith and determination.

I would like to digress at this point and relate a personal experience that gives some validity to this theory. Several years ago I was living in Vienna, while I was under contract with the United Nations as an associate English editor. At the time I was having a romance with a young Viennese aristocrat whose mother could not become used to the idea that her son had long outgrown her lap. The situation was hardly an ideal one, and arguments succeeded each other to the point of ennui. It was during the course of one of these arguments that I completely lost my Latin temper and told my paramour that the affair was kaput. I regretted this rash action the moment the words had left my lips, but the damage was already done. The young lord's regal pride was vitally wounded and I knew apologies would be of no avail. Being the victim of a satanic pride myself, I felt this was indeed the death of a beautiful romance. We parted with a cold handshake and some polite remarks on the state of the weather. We did not see each other again after this final argument, but I could not forget him. I thought of countless ways to meet him and show him my repentance in the most abject manner, but I knew I would never carry out my plans and also that he would never return of his own accord. Several months went by and the situation did not change. One evening I went to bed very exhausted, after a particularly trying day, and fell asleep in that very light slumber that is like a semi-twilight of the senses, where one seems to be suspended between the conscious and the subconscious worlds. I do not know how long I slept or what awakened me. But suddenly I opened my eyes, and to my utter amazement, I heard myself muttering frantically: "Changó, bring Peter back to me on Sunday. Changó, bring Peter back to me on Sunday,"

over and over, through tightly clenched teeth. It was like listening
to somebody else speak. It was not "me" who was invoking
Changó. It was not the conscious part of my personality, the
familiar ego I identify with. It was some primitive and alien entity
I had no control over or conscious knowledge of. I sat up in bed,
fully awake and badly shaken. Changó is the patron of fire,
thunder, and lightning, as I have already explained. He is one of
the most powerful deities of the Yoruba, and is used in Santería
to overcome enemies, as well as for works of passion and desire.
Although Oshún is the acknowledged patroness of love and
marriage, Changó is the one who brandishes a lightning bolt to
overcome recalcitrant lovers. I realized at once that I had been
working subconsciously to bring back Peter through the power
of Changó. My knowledge of Santería and my past experiences
with the beliefs and practices of the religion made me feel certain
that Peter would come back that Sunday. Feeling more assuaged
and relaxed than I had felt in months, I went back to sleep
without any further mishaps. This happened on a Tuesday, which
is Changó's appointed day in Santería. On the following Sunday I
woke up feeling very calm and collected. I dressed carefully and
sat down to wait. Around six in the evening, a light rain started
to fall, and I could hear soft peals of thunder vibrating in the
distance. By nine, the rain had almost stopped, and Vienna was
in the clutches of the most magnificent and breathtaking electri-
cal storm I have ever seen. Lightning and thunder followed each
other in rapid succession across a starless sky. I opened the
French windows of my living room and walked out onto the
balcony, oblivious of the weather and of the danger of becoming
the recipient of a lightning bolt. I stood alone in the dark, my
long robe billowing around me in mad swirls, my hair raging
with the wind. Every few minutes a shaft of lightning pierced the
darkness, framing my silhouette with fingers of fire. I was in a
trance. I felt the mighty power of Changó surging through me
and around me. I knew the tempest was the orisha's answer to
my invocation. Peter did not come that night, but I was not

disappointed. I knew there had to be a reason for his failure to appear. Next evening I had an early dinner and lay down for a short nap. At that precise moment the doorbell rang. I knew before I opened the door that it was Peter. He offered no explanation for his absence or for his return. I asked for neither. But I was curious to learn why he had not come on Sunday. He volunteered the information. He told me he had been in Italy over the weekend for business reasons and had just arrived in Vienna a few minutes before.

I showed my gratitude to Changó for his intercession by buying a large red candle in his name and a fresh shiny apple. I had no need to invoke him again after this, at least not consciously.

A common protective measure used by an omo-Changó against someone who wants to harm him is to buy some bananas for the orisha and a big white dish with a red border. He invokes Changó and asks the god to protect his omo-orisha and to punish the enemy. He covers one of the bananas with manteca de corojo and ties it with a red ribbon. He repeats this action with three more bananas, making a total of four, the number sacred to Changó. Every time he ties a knot in a ribbon, he repeats his invocation to Changó. He places the four bananas thus tied on the dish, lights a candle, and calls on Saint Barbara (Changó) and offers her the bananas, repeating his request. The bananas are left to rot at the feet of her image. When the bananas are entirely rotten, he wraps them in a piece of paper and brings them to a palm tree. He walks away in the complete certainty that Saint Barbara-Changó-Alafi-Abakoso will protect his omo-orisha and will take good care of the enemy with the orisha's usual swiftness. The santeros say that the genuine omo-Changó is the one who is born already marked by the orisha. The mark is usually a cross on the roof of the mouth. Very often at the hour of birth of an omo-Changó, there is a thunderstorm, and lightning flashes across the sky. In some parts of Cuba, the hair of these children is not cut until puberty, regardless of sex. Usually the omo-

Changós can predict the future with uncanny accuracy. They are able to touch fire with impunity and will not get burned. At a güemilere in New York, I saw an iyalocha, a daughter of Changó, possessed by the orisha, wash her arms with alcohol up to her elbows and set them on fire. With her flaming hands she "cleansed" several people present at the ceremony, without burning their clothes or their skin. When she finished, she shook her arms a few times and the flames died out, without leaving any trace of a burn on her arms.

Since Changó is the god of lightning and thunder, nothing could be more natural than to invoke him when there is a severe thunderstorm. At this time the santeros recommend burning some of the palm leaves given by the Catholic church on Palm Sunday, as this will pacify Changó, and the tempest will abate. These palm leaves are known as *güano bendito*.

Most of the santeros use Changó in cases where it is necessary to overpower an enemy. Oggún is also used, but usually when the purpose is attack rather than defense. Changó's great strength is used most effectively in spells where fire is one of the principal ingredients. The owner of a well-known nightclub in New York told me the following story. Shortly after he purchased his place of business, he started to receive a series of anonymous telephone calls threatening his life if he did not sell out or rid himself of his newly acquired nightclub. It did not take him long to discover that the source of the calls was the owner of a rival nightclub in the vicinity. There was only one way my friend could avoid serious trouble, and that was to consult a santero. A few weeks later the other nightclub was devastated by fire. According to the police and the fire department, the fire was caused by faulty wiring. But my friend is firmly convinced that the real cause of the fire was a spell cast by a santero with the help of Changó. This was accomplished by mixing several magical powders together: *polvos de zorra, polvos voladores, azufre, sal pa fuera, mielda de chango, precipitado rojo*, and the ashes of a cigar. The mixture was wrapped in a piece of red silk and then scattered at the suspected enemy's door at the stroke of midnight. A red candle was then lit in Changó's honor and a photograph of the other nightclub was burned in its flame.

The use of magical powders is very popular in Santería. Some of the powders are used to banish enemies and others for love spells. A common practice is to slip the powders in a person's clothing, preferably the shoes. *Precipitado rojo* is used for works of destruction and for protection against enemies. It is one of the most powerful powders used by the santero. Its efficacy and evil qualities are believed to be so strong that the santeros do not like to touch it with their bare hands. It is likened by many to dragon's blood, a hard, resinous substance well known in European witchcraft, but I think the differences between both substances are marked. A very popular spell that has this powder as the main ingredient is used to get rid of an enemy in a matter of hours. A lemon is cut in half and a small piece of paper with the name of the person one wishes to be rid of is placed over one of the lemon halves. A tiny pinch of *precipitado rojo* is sprinkled on the paper, which is then covered by the other half of the lemon. The two halves are then held together by fifty new pins that are placed all over the lemon in the form of a cross. The lemon is then placed at the bottom of a wide-necked black bottle filled with an equal mixture of urine, vinegar, and black coffee. The idea behind the spell is that in the same way (sympathetic magic) that the lemon and vinegar are sour and unpleasant to the taste, so will the life of the person bewitched "turn sour and unpleasant." The black coffee is intended to darken the life of the enemy and the urine is used to "dominate and humiliate him." (Incidentally, urine is used very often in spells of domination by the santeros.) The black bottle with the lemon is then thrown into the river, preferably from a bridge or a high position. The moment the bottle comes in contact with the water the spell comes into effect. Great care must be taken, according to the santeros, as long as the bottle remains in the possession of the one casting the spell. For this incantation is so potent that it can easily backfire unless the bottle is promptly thrown into the river.

One of the most common practices in Santería to attract good luck is to take special flower and herbal baths known as *despojos*. Often the santero recommends to his clients a series of nine baths to dispel evil influences. After this preliminary cleansing, a second series of despojos is advised to attract good vibrations and help solve the problems of the consultant. The most popular plants used to dispel negative vibrations are *pasote, álamo, yerbabuena, mejorana, tártago,* and *albahaca*. The plants are boiled for at least one hour in a large container filled with several gallons of water. The resultant liquid is strained into a clean basin, where it is allowed to cool. After the bath has cooled for several hours, it is usual to add to it several magical substances to strengthen its cleansing powers. Ammonia is considered a superb cleanser of unnatural and vicious spiritual forces, and several drops of this powerful-smelling liquid are invariably added to the despojos. Some other substances used, usually in liquid form, are *bálsamo tranquilo, menta, lavándula roja, sal de violeta, esencia de dinero,* and *esencia de la buena suerte*. The bath is then divided into nine portions, which are individually used during nine consecutive nights. The usual procedure is to stand in a bathtub or shower stall and pour the despojo over the shoulders. Very often a special prayer, invoking one of the orishas, is said after the bath by the light of a color candle. The color of the candle must be the same attributed to the orisha who is undertaking the cleansing. Saint Claire, Saint Michael, and Saint Barbara are invoked very often in this type of despojo. Our Lady of Mercy (Obatalá), the patron(ess) of purity, is also used by many santeros. After the nine baths are completed and the person is considered cleansed of evil influences, he is advised to undertake the next bath series, which is usually only one or three. These new baths are made of flowers and sweeter herbs, of the kind attributed to the orisha who is being invoked. Magical aids are also added to the new baths, the type of substance to be used depending on the needs of the believer. These old-fashioned despojos are becoming so popular that they are being mass produced and sold in eight-ounce bottles. The most popular of these pre-bottled baths are those of Saint Claire, the Seven African Powers, *rompezaragüey*, and Saint Michael. There are also pre-bottled despojos for love, money, and general good luck. New in the market are also special soaps bearing the names of some of the saints, especially the Seven African Powers and Changó. There are soaps for love, for gamblers, and for a variety of purposes. The labels on these new products are printed in Spanish and English, which gives an indication of the growth of Santería in the United States.

Another common practice to dispel bad influences utilizes *sahumerios* and *riegos*. Sahumerios are a mixture of incense, storax, mastic, garlic skins, and brown sugar, which is burned over live coals. The resulting fumes are allowed to fill all the corners of the house, especially those in darkened closets and behind doors.

Riegos are undertaken to rid a house of lurking evil spirits. The santero recommends boiling some plants in water, particularly, *paraíso*, *tártago*, and *rompezaragüey*. The liquid is then sprinkled throughout the house. The best days for both riegos and sahumerios are believed to be Tuesdays and Fridays.

In the house of the santero, and of most practitioners of Santería, there is always present a mysterious bottle full of half-dried plants that crowd each other amid a greenish liquid. This liquid is usually Florida Water, to which certain powerful plants and some special substances have been added. After some time, the Florida Water is tinted green with the chlorophyll of the plants. The santero uses this liquid to rub his forehead and limbs whenever he is tired or ill, or when he believes he is under psychic attack. The unusual power of this liquid is so marked that it can dispel common headaches, dizziness, and the pain of aching limbs with just a brisk rub. The effects are reputed to be fast and lasting.

The use of specially prepared perfumes for good luck is also very popular in Santería. The santero asks his client to bring to him any favorite scent. To this he adds a number of magical essences, depending on the type of problem being faced by the querent. For love, he may add musk, *lirio, amor, amanza guapo, atractiva*, and *vente conmigo*. He may also use a bit of coral, patchouli, cantharides, brown sugar, a stick of cinnamon, and some rose petals. The resulting fragrance is very heady and musky, and also very effective.

The Jericó rose (*rosa de Jericó*) is very often recommended by the santeros to bring good luck into a person's life. The rose is a botanical curio that is purchased dried, with tightly closed leaves, but which opens fully and regains its green color when it is immersed in water. The rose is believed to be most effective when used in conjunction with the oil that bears its name. A few drops of the oil are placed on the center of the rose, which is then allowed to remain in water for a week. On Fridays, this water is sprinkled throughout the house and fresh water is replaced in the container where the rose is kept. Some santeros believe it is a good practice to write a petition on a small piece of paper, which is then tightly folded and placed on the center of the rose. Such petitions are believed to be granted by the spirit that guards the rose.

Many of the people who come to the santero are elderly and infirm, or ailing with some chronic or unusual disease that has been declared incurable by medical doctors. A competent santero is usually able to eradicate all sorts of pathological disorders, ranging from common colds to cancer and epilepsy. The treatment and cure of several types of cancer have been known in Santería for many years. An *iyalocha* who has cured countless malignant tumors in her lifetime told me of a remarkable cure she made in New York several years ago. It seems that one morning, as she was starting her daily chores around her house, she was visited by a young woman dressed in black, whose haggard face showed signs of intense suffering and distress.

When the santera inquired the motive of the woman's visit, she was told that the latter's father was desperately ill with a malignant tumor in the lower intestines, and that doctors had declared him a hopeless case. His daughter had heard of the santera's miraculous herbal cures and had come to see her as a last resort. The iyalocha sat down in her small living room and wrote down one word on a piece of paper and gave it to the girl. The word was *higuereta*, which is a tropical plant known in Latin as *Ricinus communis*, from which castor oil is processed. The santera instructed the girl to boil the plant in a large container of water and to use the resulting liquid to give her father a series of warm enemas. These enemas were to be administered every three days, and no other medicines should be given to the patient. The iyalocha asked the girl to report her father's reaction to this treatment within a month's time. At the end of this time, the girl returned to the santera's house, brimming with enthusiasm. Her father's condition had improved miraculously. He was able to eat for the first time in months, instead of being fed intravenously. The tumor had been dissolved and the pain had disappeared. He was still weak from his long confinement but could already walk around his room without help. He was visibly improving every day. The doctors, who were still checking on the man's condition, were unable to explain his incredible recovery, and were full of theories. The santera told the girl to stop the enemas, as she felt sure the girl's father was cured. She refused to accept payment for her help but was happy to receive instead a beautiful statue of Babalú-Ayé, patron of the sick in Santería.

Although *higuereta* has been used as a cure for cancerous growth by santeros from time immemorial, it was only recently that a scientific investigator discovered the effectiveness of the plant in destroying cancer cells. Dr. Garth Nicholson of the Salk Institute, La Jolla, California, informed the Science Writers' Seminar of the American Cancer Society that the proteins of the castor-oil plant (*higuereta*) have the ability to agglutinate cancer cells, producing their destruction, and thus halting their multiplication patterns. These findings were possible by means of powerful electronic microscopes. These technical details would be meaningless and confusing to the santeros, who, nevertheless, have known of the curative properties of *higuereta* for centuries.

The santera who told me this story has cures for practically every disease known to science, as well as for some that may not be so well known. Her remedies are simple but effective. For recurrent or acute headaches she recommends compresses of black coffee on the forehead, while the patient is lying down. For earaches, she squeezes into the eardrum a few drops of the juice of a large leaf known as *yerba bruja*. She bathes sensitive or irritated eyes with the juice of another leaf known as *malá*. Strong stomach cramps caused by severe indigestion or colitis are relieved at once by drinking a tea made with *yerbabuena, ajenjo*, and orange peel. She cures typhus, a plight of the tropics, by giving the patient enemas made of the cactus plant, *malva, flaxseed*, and a few drops of olive oil. The high fever that is characteristic of this dread disease is lowered by applying to the sole of each foot a strong piece of paper covered with a special grease known as *sebo de Flandes*. The greased paper is held in place by a heavy sock. According to this santera, the grease "pulls" the fever out of the person's body, while the enema cleanses the body of the disease.

Hot cactus compresses to which olive oil has been added are used to alleviate inflammations of the ovaries. To calm nerves, this same santera recommnends frequent teas of *yerba mora* (*Salanum nigrum*) or sarsaparilla. The latter is also very popular in the treatment of syphilis. She also cures acute cases of dysentery by boiling a leaf known as *melembre* in a quart of milk. After the milk boils she lets the mixture cool and then dips into it a red-hot iron. She adds some coconut milk and a substance known as *nitro dulce* and places the resulting liquid on her windowsill overnight so that it may "catch the night dew." She feeds a cupful of this brew daily to her patient, who is generally cured by the third day.

In the tropics, where the sun can burn blisters on sensitive skin in a matter of minutes, the danger of sunstroke is omnipresent. In severe cases, the santeros give a purge prepared by boiling the following herbs in a large pan of water: *caña fístola, coitre blanco, maná, paretaria, verdolaga* (purslane), and cactus. The liquid is divided into several doses, which are administered daily until the person is fully recovered.

Another santero can cure even open wounds and broken bones with the help of a few herbs. He told me that a few years ago a young man was brought to his house by two of the young man's friends, who were with him when he became involved in a barroom brawl. In the course of the fight, the boy of the story was stabbed repeatedly in the chest and on his left arm and was bleeding profusely and was very weak from loss of blood. He did not want to be taken to a hospital because he was afraid he would get in trouble with the police. One of his friends knew of the santero's reputation with herbal cures, and he suggested that they come to the santero's house and ask for help. The santero did not bother to ask any questions. He helped accommodate the wounded man on his couch and set to work right there. He bathed the wounds with warm water and dried them. Then he applied a plaster of crushed chicory leaves and sugar to the wounds and held them in place with strips of clean cloth. He gave his patient a cup of strong black coffee laced with rum and told him to try to sleep. The chicory leaves and the sugar helped coagulate the blood so the bleeding was stopped and helped promote the healing of the wounds with a minimal risk of infection. The wounded man remained at the santero's house for two weeks, and during this time the santero changed the plaster twice daily. At the end of the two weeks, the wounds were practically healed and the man was able to leave the santero's house.

The same santero mends broken bones with another plaster made by crushing an herb known as *suelda con suelda* and mixing it with a sandy substance called *pedrega*. He applies the plaster directly on the skin over the broken bones and holds it tightly in place with several strips of clean linen. The plaster adheres rapidly to the skin until it is impossible to remove it. It hardens to the consistency of light cement within an hour. The afflicted member must not be moved until the plaster falls off on its own, which usually takes place within several weeks. When the plaster falls off, it indicates that the broken bones have mended.

The santeros often use a curative system known as *santigüo*, especially when a young child is the sufferer. *Santigüo* is a Spanish word that means "to bless," "to heal by blessing," and that is exactly what the santero does. He blesses the body of the sick person, usually concentrating on the solar plexus or the abdominal area. Generally, persons who undergo the santigüo are believed to be bewitched or under the influence of the evil eye. Chronic or intestinal diseases are also cured with the santigüo. In the latter cases, the santero rubs the stomach with olive oil and *sebo de Flandes*, with a curious flexing of the fingers, which are pressed hard and deep into the stomach and then brought downward to the lower intestines. A candle is lit in the honor of Saint Luis Beltrán, and every few minutes the person doing the santigüo stops to bless the stomach and to say a special prayer to the saint. After the santigüo is finished, the abdominal area is covered with a warm piece of flannel. The persons thus treated, usually small children, generally recover from the illness within a few days.

Although the magic of the santeros may seem at times phenomenal, it pales in comparison with the feats of the orishas themselves, either during possession or during direct communication with one of their initiates.

18.

Orisha Power

Contrary to popular belief, the practice of Santería is not the exclusive domain of the ignorant and the uneducated. Some of the most devoted followers of the Religion are people with extensive educational and cultural backgrounds. There are famous actors and personalities who measure their every step by the throwing of the Diloggún. There are psychologists, sociologists, doctors, writers, lawyers, physicists, and college professors who pay foribale at the feet of the orishas and undergo cleansing rituals with blood and honey. Some conduct the rituals themselves because they were initiated in the ceremony of the asiento.

In recent years, an increasing number of black and white Americans are becoming involved in Santería. Many of these new initiates are professionals with solid educational and financial backgrounds. Irwin and Martha Hochberg are well-known designers on New York's fashionable East Side. He is a Changó initiate and she is an initiate of Yemayá. Together they head one of the largest and most respectable houses of Santería in New York, most of whose members are Jewish.

Gene and Constantine Bailly have been married several years and have a two-year-old daughter who has already received the necklaces of Santería. Gene has a masters in Education and teaches at a junior high school. Constantine is a college professor, a writer, and an editor with a Ph.D. in Asian studies. One of Gene and Constantine's closest bonds is the fact that they are both santeros. He is a Yemayá initiate and she has just been initiated into Oshún's mysteries.

Sandra Reindl-Schweighofer is a black American who works as a trilingual secretary for the United Nations. She has received the necklaces and the Warriors and hopes someday to make the saint.

The power of the orishas is not an intangible, mystical force nurtured by the faith of the believers. It is not something sublimely ethereal that sustains the soul and gives it strength through faith. It is raw energy, awesome power visually and materially discernible. One does not pray to God through the orishas on bent knees and hope they will somehow convey the message. One speaks to the orisha *directly* and asks for what is needed. And because the orisha is a direct manifestation of God, he or she can say at once whether or not your wish can be granted. But the orishas are not mere pawns of human beings in their search for wealth and power. The orishas are the mouthpieces of the Godhead, and through them God makes his wishes and designs known to mankind. The orisha is always willing to help and to guide, but also ready to chastise when God's laws are broken. The worship of the orishas is not easy because they demand strict obedience and total surrender to their will. But it is worthwhile because obedience and acceptance are rewarded, often in the most extraordinary ways.

The orisha worshiper knows that he cannot win every battle or get every wish. Strife and its subsequent overthrow are the great builders of human character and the testing grounds of the soul. What the orishas provide is protection and sure help in times of need. Fulgencio Batista knew it was time to surrender his power when Fidel Castro took over Havana. But he was not killed in the revolution, and he lived the rest of his life in perfect safety and Arabian splendor, in spite of all the efforts to destroy him. He was a typical child of Changó, all of whom undergo severe ordeals but are always protected and sometimes rewarded with the highest pinnacles of fame and fortune. One of the most typical of Changó's children was Ludwig van Beethoven. Changó is fire and thunder. So was Beethoven and his music. Everything in Beethoven's life shows the orisha's firebrand. A fire sign, he was born in Sagittarius, with a soul as tempestuous as his ruling orisha. The number six—Changó's number—was evident throughout the great composer's life. His *Pastorale* Symphony has a famous movement in which the instruments simulate the sounds of a storm. One can hear the peals of thunder, the crash of lightning, and all the elements raging with Changó's fury. Beethoven called it Symphony Number 6. Beethoven died in Vienna on March 26, 1827. One of his contemporaries, Anselm Hütten- brenner, described the scene: "There was suddenly a loud clap of thunder accompanied by a bolt of lightning. Beethoven opened his eyes, raised his right hand, and, his fist clenched, looked upwards for a few seconds. . . . As he let his hand sink down onto the bed again, his eyes half closed. The great composer's spirit had fled from this world of deception into the kingdom of truth. It was six o'clock in the evening."

If Beethoven was the son of Changó, Mozart, with his typically playful and childish personality, was most likely the child of Elegguá, just as the exquisite and romantic Chopin was undoubt- edly the child of Oshún.

One of the strongest beliefs of Santería is that every human being has a ruling orisha, even if that person never learns his orisha's name or practices Santería. It is not difficult to discern the identity of an individual's orisha. All that is necessary is to be a keen observer of human nature and notice each individual's character and personal traits. These are invariably similar, in some greater or lesser degree, to those of his ruling orisha. It is only when a person decides to undertake one of the Santería initiations that his orisha is formally determined by the santero or the babalawo. But usually a santero has a very good idea who rules an individual without the need of the seashells or the babalawo's Table of Ifá.

Because the orishas are the embodiment of very real human archetypes, they have personal characteristics that make them easy to identify. Following is a list of these characteristics.

Elegguá—risqué, fun-loving, playful, outrageous, tricky, smart, unfathomable, and variable (fate)

Obatalá—wise, clever, kind but stern, peaceful, mystical, magnanimous, generous, idealistic (peace, fatherhood)

Orúnla—wise, creative, quiet, serene, gentle, self-controlled, shrewd, sagacious (wisdom)

Aganyú—stubborn, fiery, aggressive, harsh, indomitable, hard to please, determined (stubbornness)

Changó—fiery, proud, passionate, reckless, daring, fearless, domineering, dashing, sensual (passion)

Oggún—revolutionary, unforgiving, direct, honest, brave, rough, militant, devoted, hardworking (labor, war)

Ochosi—just, strict, severe, unswerving, moral, ethical, wise, impartial, honest (justice)

Yemayá—loving, maternal, gentle, kind, generous, dignified, lofty, but terrible in anger (womanhood)

Oyá—fiery, tempestuous, fascinating, shrewd, mystical, cool and detached, yet with hidden passions (adversity)

Oshún—seductive, tender, gentle, kind, irresistible, insatiable, flirtatious, loving, sweet, generous, ambitious, soft yet tenacious, dangerous, unforgiving, unforgettable (love, wealth)

Some of the orishas share certain qualities, such as Changó and Aganyú, who are father and son (fire and volcano). Oggún and Ochosi also have some similar qualities because they always work together. Most people display the characteristics of two of the orishas, male and female, because, as we have already seen, everyone has a mother and a father among the orishas, But it is the strongest characteristics of a person that denote his ruling orisha.

Persons with markedly negative personalities can be identified by considering the negative or extreme aspects of their orishas.

The orishas protect their children fiercely and often punish their enemies harshly, even with death. A very well-known santero of New York told me this story. Several years ago, one of his godchildren brought a friend to this santero for a registro. The santero told the man that the orishas were angry with him because he was dealing drugs and conducting other illegal activities. He had to stop all his wrongdoing and make the saint if he wanted the help of the saints. The man agreed immediately to do what the orishas ordered and asked the santero to conduct the asiento. But the babalocha, who knew the man was dangerous, was reluctant to accept him as his godchild. To dissuade him, he told the man the initiation was too expensive and that furthermore he had no time at present to undertake the initiation. The man insisted and offered to pay the santero double the price of the initiation. The santero's godchild added his pleas to those of his friend's, and finally the santero agreed to do the asiento. He only charged the man the correct derecho for the initiation.

About two years after the ceremony, the santero received a court citation. The man he had so reluctantly agreed to initiate was suing him for fraud and illegal practices. The case was very notorious at the time and received full coverage in all the New York newspapers. But the santero was not worried. He knew he had acted in good faith and had behaved in accordance with the orishas' laws. He consulted the Diloggún, did the prescribed ebbós, and went to court with the complete assurance that Changó would take good care of his opponent, who was now his godchild, and who was guilty not only of defamation of character, but also of offending his godfather.

The verdict was swift, clearing the santero of all wrongdoing. But that was not enough for the babalocha. He wanted his godchild punished for his affront. A few weeks after the trial, the man, who lived in Miami, was visited by the police, who suspected him of drug dealing. The man went suddenly berserk, barricaded himself inside the house, and opened fire against the police. He was finally captured, and when he went to trial, he was sent to prison for twenty years. The santero was not happy with the news, but saw his godchild's downfall as Changó's punishment for his behavior.

Another santero—also a son of Changó—told me of an experience he had with his orisha while he was still living in Cuba. The santero had been initiated for only a few years when he received a visit from a *palero*, a priest of the sect known as Palo, which we will discuss in the next chapter. The palero told the santero that one of his godsons had died recently, leaving instructions that his *prenda* (the equivalent of an orisha in Palo) should be passed on to a son of Changó. As the santero was the only son of Changó in town, the palero had decided to ask him if he would take the prenda. The santero was not very familiar with the workings of Palo, although he knew the paleros worked with the dead and often did some ferocious black magic. He asked the palero to explain how the prenda worked. "That is easy," said the palero. "Is there anything that you would like to have?" The santero thought this over for a few minutes, and then said that he and his family were interested in buying the house next door to theirs, but that his neighbors refused to sell. "That's very easy," said the palero. "You simply take a bit of the powder that is inside the prenda, mix it with a bit of wax, and throw a few pellets of the mixture on your neighbor's roof. Then wait until the sun melts it." He proceeded to prepare the mixture and handed the pellets to the santero, who threw them onto the roof of his neighbor's house. This happened about eleven in the morning.

At noon the family, who worked nearby, came to the house for lunch. By this time the fierce tropical sun had long since melted the wax pellets. Within minutes after their arrival, the various members of the family began to quarrel. Very soon they were at each other's throats, creating such a turmoil that the other neighbors, fearing a tragedy, called the police. By the time the police arrived, one of the members of the family was dead, and all the others badly wounded. The terrified santero witnessed this with open mouth, wondering whether the spell cast by the palero had really caused the tragedy. The palero confirmed his suspicions by smiling archly. "Now," he said with a wink, "you can have the house for a song."

"But I did not want it this way," said the santero.

"It makes no difference," the palero answered. "It is done."

As the palero had predicted, the next day the owner of the house, who had not been present during the fight, came to the santero to ask him if he was still interested in buying the house. He was so desperate to sell it, he offered it to the santero for a fraction of its value.

Although the santero was horrified by the tragedy, he was still young enough to be thrilled at the idea of having such power at his fingertips, so he decided to accept the prenda.

For the sake of clarity, I have to explain here that the palero's prenda is kept inside a large cauldron where the guardian spirit of the prenda is said to reside. Since I will discuss this in some detail in the next chapter, I will only say here that there are pieces of human bones inside the cauldron and various types of earth, including earth from a cemetery.

The night he received the prenda, the santero was instructed to sleep naked in the room where the cauldron was. If he saw or noticed anything unnatural, he was to get up and throw a pail of water out the door. In the meantime, the palero was going to be in his own house, sending all the spirits of the prenda to the santero's house, where they were to take up new residence. All night long the santero was visited by horrifying specters that even the most fertile imagination could not conjure. Stark naked, his hair standing on end, and dripping cold sweat, he was kept busy all through the night, throwing pail after pail of water out the door.

Several days after he received the prenda, his padrino came to visit. This was a renowned babalocha who had tremendous powers and a direct link to the orishas. As soon as he came into the house, he made a beeline for the room where the santero had placed the prenda. This was quite visible, standing all by itself in a corner. But with the terrible power of the spirits within it, the cauldron made itself invisible to the babalocha. The old santero was not fooled. He moved slowly around the room, sniffing in every corner like a hound on a hot trail. But he could not see the prenda. Finally he turned to his godson and said, "You have something to do with witchcraft in this room. It is powerful and it is black and very evil. It has hidden itself from me, but I know it is here. Changó is asking me to tell you that since you think this prenda is better and stronger than he, you can keep it because he is leaving you. From now on, you're on your own. And the only reason I don't leave you also is that I haven't seen it. But as far as Changó is concerned, you're no longer his omo-orisha."

The santero paled at these words and did his best to deny that he had the prenda, but his padrino just shook his head and left the house. Terrified at the thought of losing Changó's protection, the santero called the palero and asked him to come and remove the prenda. As soon as the prenda was gone from his house, he made a long series of elaborate ebbós to pacify his enraged orisha.

The very next day his padrino returned to the house. Again he went into the room and walked slowly around it for some time.

"So you got rid of it," he finally said. "But it doesn't matter. Changó says he appreciates your efforts in trying to appease him, and he will remain with you, but he's not going to forgive the offense or forget it. He won't do anything now because he doesn't want me to suffer, as he knows how much I love you. But as soon as I die, he's going to burn this house down and the house next door, which you acquired through such evil powers. The only thing he's going to leave standing is your bakery, because he knows that's your livelihood, and he doesn't like to see his children begging."

A few years later the babalocha died. The very next day, both the house where the santero lived and the one next door caught fire. Only the bakery was spared. All the santero could think of was to save the main emblems of Eleggua and Changó. Ignoring the cries of his neighbors, who tried in vain to stop him, he rushed inside the flaming house and threw open the door of the room where the orishas were kept. He swears that as soon as he entered the room, he saw Changó himself, in a tower of fire, reach out and embrace him. When he staggered out of the house, he was covered in flames. As he collapsed on the ground, his hands opened. In one of them he was holding the symbol of Changó and in the other that of Eleggua.

But this is not the end of the story. The santero spent several months in the hospital, fighting desperately for his life. When he finally came out, his face and the upper part of his body were covered with red blotches, dreadful reminders of his ordeal.

A few weeks later, during a tambor in Changó's honor, two iyalochas became possessed by Oyá, who is one of Changó's paramours. Through the possessed santeras, Oyá informed the santero that Changó was ashamed to see him looking like a spotted leopard and had therefore asked her to cleanse him. The two santeras proceeded to lick the santero's face and upper body in the typical cleansing ritual of an orisha. The only place they missed was a small spot on the back of his neck that was covered by his hair. Within days after the cleansing, the terrible scars faded away, leaving no trace on the santero's body, except for a red mark on the nape of his neck.

Perhaps the most impressive of orisha communications is the one that takes place during possession. For at that time one is actually face to face with the orishas themselves. One of my friends, who is a practicing physician at one of New York's hospitals, had an unforgettable experience with Eleggua. She attended a tambor in honor of the orisha, to whom she is very devoted. Soon after the ceremony began, one of Eleggua's omo-orishas became possessed by the saint. It was the first time my friend saw that particular santero, and there was no way he could know anything about her life. But before the tambor ended, while he was still possessed by Eleggúa, he took her aside and asked her, without any preamble, where her son was. As she has two sons, my friend asked the orisha to which one he was referring. "The one who is away from here, in another state," answered the orisha. My friend was staggered. Her oldest son was living in Texas at the time, where he was collaborating with a friend on a screenplay. She had not heard from him for some time and had been very worried about him. She told Eleggúa about her concern and the orisha said, "In a very short time your son is going to call you and ask you to send for him. When he calls you, do as he asks, because if you don't, you're going to lose him. As soon as he arrives, tell him I said that I am not very happy with him because he has been doing some things that are very wrong. He'll know what I mean. But also tell him that I am going to give him a last chance. If he changes his ways, I'm going to make his dearest wish come true. If he doesn't, I'm going to remove him from this world."

Naturally my friend was quite shocked by these pronouncements, uttered so coolly by the lips of a complete stranger. For the next few weeks she waited with the worst forebodings to hear from her son. His call came one night after she had gone to bed. The young man was calling from the middle of the highway, halfway between Houston and San Antonio. He told his mother he had no money, his plans for the screenplay had failed, and he wanted her to call one of the airlines, prepay a ticket, and have it waiting for him at the nearest airport, as he wanted to come home. Under ordinary circumstances, my friend would have refused to do what her son was asking, thinking that he deserved a good lesson. But, remembering Eleggúa's warning, she immediately agreed to send for her son.

When he arrived at Kennedy Airport, he told her that when he had called her he was so desperate that he did not know what he was going to do. He felt her swift response to his call for help was a sign that things were about to turn for the better. She then told him what Elegguá had said at the tambor, carefully stressing the orisha's warning. The young man did not share her belief in Santería, but he was so shaken by the story that he promised to try to mend his ways. Shortly afterwards, he was asked to adapt a best-selling book to the screen. The screenplay is now in production and will star one of Hollywood's best-known actors.

One of the most common ways to offend an orisha and to put oneself on the receiving end of his or her rage is to fail to observe one of the prescribed rituals. I had a personal experience with Elegguá concerning a forgotten ritual, for which I still bear a scar. Every Monday, as I have already explained, those people who have the initiation of Elegguá and the Warriors must conduct a minor ceremony. This requires an offering of water, some rum, a cigar, a small dish of candies, and a white candle. This must be done every Monday morning without fail, as soon as the person awakens.

Several years ago, while I was still living in Vienna, I returned to the Austrian capital after a short visit to New York. I arrived early on a Monday afternoon, but I was so busy unpacking and straightening out my flat that I completely forgot about Elegguá. I kept his image and implements in a small cabinet with a square metal handle, near the front door. In my hurrying back and forth through the flat, I kept passing the cabinet but still failed to remember Elegguá. On one of those little trips, one of the corners of the cabinet's handle caught suddenly on my knee. I was wearing a thick pair of jeans, but the hard metal bit through them and deep into my skin. When I pulled back my leg, the door of the cabinet swung open, and there, looking up at me with aggrieved eyes, was Elegguá's image. When I rolled up the pant leg, I saw the metal had cut through to the bone. The end result was a very visible and ugly scar that I will carry as long as I live. Needless to say, I have never again forgotten that Mondays belong to Elegguá.

It is this sort of personal and dynamic interrelationship between the orishas and the believers of Santería that makes the power of the saints seem so real and so deeply comforting. It is as if one had many fathers and many mothers, all of whom are protective and yet stern, like any good parent should be. Herein lies the power of the orishas.

Unfortunately, in our overly permissive societies, a "good parent" is often expected to give and forgive ad infinitum. Santería teaches that a child must also give to a parent, that promises are inviolate, that parents are entitled to receive as much as they are expected to give. The orishas are generous, loving, and protective, but they are also strict disciplinarians. Perhaps if all parents taught their children a little more discipline, we would be faced with a better society.

19.

Palo ///

Witchcraft and Santería

Brujería or witchcraft is not a common practice of Santería. This type of magic is known as Palo Monte or Palo Mayombe. Monte and Mayombe are the names of two different sects that practice *palo* or witchcraft. In this book we will concern ourselves only with the beliefs and practices of Palo Mayombe.

Palo is a Spanish word that means "branch" or "wooden stick." It is used to designate the sect because its practitioners work with pieces of various woods and many herbs to do their magic spells. The initiates of Palo Mayombe are known as *paleros* or *mayomberos*. Both men and women are initiated into the sect.

There are two branches of Palo Mayombe, one that is "good" and one that is "bad." The "good" branch is called "Christian" Mayombe and the "bad" is called "Jewish" or "unbaptized" Mayombe. This differentiation is made by the paleros because the "Christian" cauldron in which their secrets are kept is sprinkled with holy water and the "Jewish" one is not. To the practitioners of Palo who, like the santeros, are steeped in Catholic tradition, anyone or anything that is not baptized is evil and does not belong to God. Because the ceremony of baptism utilizes holy water for the rejection of the devil, everything that is sprinkled

238

with this liquid is considered by the paleros to be "baptized" and purified. Evil spirits are believed to be frightened away and "burned" by the touch of holy water.

The palero or mayombero who is "Christian" works with the forces of God, whom they call Sambia, a corruption of the Kongo name for the deity Nsambi. The "unbaptized" or *paleros judíos* work with Kadiempembe, the name given to the devil by the Kongos, the tribe from which the Congo (now Zaire) derived its name. (In Santería the devil is known as Olosi.)

All paleros work with the spirits of nature, such as trees, plants, rain, river water, and animals. "Christian" paleros also work with the spirits of the dead, but only with "good" spirits. "Unbaptized" paleros work exclusively with the spirits of suicides, criminals, and evil witches (*ndoki*). The name of the spirit "living" inside the cauldron is *Mpungo, Nkisi, Nkita,* or *Fuiri.* The chants used for its invocation are known as *mambos*. This is also the name given in Haitian Voodoo to the high priestess of the religion, which underlines the interaction of the various African tribes in the Caribbean.

The palero is *rayado,* that is, "cut" in Palo. This term means that the individual has had the initiatory designs of Palo cut with a razor on his skin.

The source of the palero's power is the *prenda* (jewel) or cauldron where the spirit or spirits of the dead used by the palero are said to reside. The African name of the prenda is *nganga,* a Kongo word that means "dead," "spirit," or "supernatural force." Within the nganga are kept the human skull, bones, graveyard dust, crossroads dust, branches, herbs, insects, animal and bird carcasses, and hot spices that are its foundation. Upon these ingredients are rooted the forces of the spirits who inhabit the nganga or prenda. The palo initiate is known as *Mpangui* and also as *Nganga Nkisi* or *Tata Nkisi* (father of the *nkitas* or "spirits").

Palo is reputed to be faster (for magical results) than Santería. This is because one can order the dead inside the nganga but not the orishas or saints, who are the ones who issue the orders and who have to be obeyed.

The nganga does what its owner orders it to do. To work with the nganga is called "playing" with it. When the spirit of the nganga carries out its owner's orders, he or she gives it the blood of a rooster as an expression of gratitude. Ashes (*mpolo banso*) are rubbed on the hands before and after a ritual, for purification.

The ceremonies of Palo are simpler and less costly than those of Santería. Also, the palero always works secretly, behind closed doors. The santero opens his doors during a tambor to everyone, including those who have not been initiated in the Religion. The palero cannot do this because he includes human remains inside the nganga, something that not everyone will accept, especially the civil authorities.

Unlike the santero, the palero does not use a bell or a maraca to call the spiritual entities with which he works. Nor does he use fancy clothes to dress those who become possessed by an entity, or fans (agbebe) to refresh them, or tools. When the palero wants to "play" with his nganga, he simply grabs a tibia (*kisengue*) or a horn and uses this to invoke the spirit. He does this by sitting on his haunches, facing the prenda, and spraying it with rum and cigar smoke. He hits the floor three times with his fist, then draws a sign on the floor with chalk, which he covers with three small mounds of gunpowder, known as *fula*. He lights them and begins to chant the mambos to invoke the spirit and coerce it to obey him.

Among the many names of God used by the palero are Sambiapunguele, Sambia Mpungu, and Pungun Sambia. Sambia created everything there is. He also created a couple, but their names are unknown. Man is known as Yakara and woman as Nkento. Father is Tata and Mother is Yaya or Mame.

Sambia made *menga*, blood, to give life to the first man and woman. Then, through their ears (*nkutu*), he blew in intelligence so that they could know and understand things. He taught this first couple everything they had to know in order to survive. He also taught them how to prepare an nganga to work either good or bad. So, presumably, Sambia left this decision of choosing between good and evil to man and woman. But he reserved for himself the right to punish the practice of evil, and this practice he punishes with death, which he created to inflict on mankind for the sin of disobedience.

After his creation, Sambia left the world and went very far away; but even from that remote distance he is very attentive to what is happening on earth and keeps on ruling everything, no matter how insignificant. The paleros do not make any offerings to Sambia. He does not "eat," but he is very much revered and respected.

The paleros also revere their ancestors, all the dead, and the spirits of nature. Changó is the orisha most actively worshiped by the paleros, who claim that the orisha comes from the Congo instead of Nigeria. They call him Nsasi, which is also the Kongo name for the palm tree, one of Changó's attributes. The paleros prepare an nganga they call Siete Rayos (seven lightning bolts), which is said to be presided over by Changó in his Kongo aspect.

I must emphasize that the practices described in this chapter are those of the "unbaptized" mayomberos, or paleros judíos. I must also add that many of the "Christian" paleros with "baptized" ngangas often do positive works for the good of the community, especially in the treatment of difficult and often incurable diseases. Following are some of the terms most commonly used among the mayomberos or paleros:

Bilongo—magic spell
enkangar—to cast a spell
ezulu—heaven
kisanguele—a species of snake used by the mayombero in some of his spells
kuna—place
makutoresguardo, or protection against evil
malembe—care, cautiousness

masango or **uenba**—evil spell

mbua—the evil spirit used in a bilongo

mpambu—the four cardinal points, the crossing of four ways; this is the place where the masango is sent to the victim

nganga—a big spell to "tie" or destroy a person; this term is also used to describe the mayombero's cauldron with all its magical elements

ngau—term used by the witch to call his familiar or protective evil entity

nkisi—spirit

npaka—an animal horn filled with a special liquid, used to force the nkisi to manifest itself

nsambi kuna ezula—God is in heaven

nsambi kuna ntoto—God is in earth

ntoto—earth

Tata Nkisi—title given to the witch doctor or mayombero

telemene—to spy

telemene nkisi—an order to an evil spirit to spy upon a person

ya njila—an apology

yaya—mother, the term of endearment used by the mayombero to call the nkisi

Before his initiation into the palo mayombe, the neophite must sleep during seven nights under a ceiba. At the end of this period he takes some new clothes and brings them to the cemetery, where he buries them in a previously chosen grave. The clothes remain buried during three Fridays, or twenty-one days. During this time, the candidate takes a series of purifying baths prepared with several strong herbs, including some leaves from the ceiba. When the twenty-one days are over, he returns to the cemetery, disinters the clothes, and puts them on. He is then taken to a ceiba by his teacher and initiator, and other mayomberos who serve as witnesses. They invoke the spirits of the dead and the spirit of the ceiba to witness and approve the initiation. The initiate's forehead is encircled with a crown of ceiba leaves. The leaves are believed to attract the spirits of the dead, who take possession of the new mayombero, making the initiation a success. A white dish upon which a candle has been lit is placed on the initiate's hands, and he is also given a human tibia wrapped in a black cloth, which is the macabre scepter (*kisengue*) with which he will rule over the powers of darkness. He is then declared a full-fledged mayombero, and is able to conduct all the fearful ceremonies of the cult.

Before the initiate can really call himself a mayombero, he must prepare, for his use and protection, the nganga of the Kongo.

MOON INFLUENCE

Under no circumstances must any serious work in witchcraft be undertaken during the waning period of the moon. In this respect, Kongo witchcraft does not differ from European witchcraft, which also hinges strongly on the influence of the moon.

In an African myth, the sun married the moon and they had many children. The daughters are the stars (*irawo*), and they never went anywhere without their mother. The sons decided to follow their father, and the sun, annoyed by the persistent company of his children, told them sternly to return home at once. The small suns lost their way and fell into the ocean, where they drowned. That is the reason why the sun always appears alone in the sky, while the moon is always accompanied by the stars, her daughters.

The waning moon is known as *ochukwa aro*. She is very much feared by the mayomberos, for she is believed to be associated with *ikú* (death). The waxing moon, on the other hand, is believed to be beneficent, and newborn babies are usually presented to her after the fortieth day following their birth. It is believed that the moon's rays will protect the child during all its life.

THE MAKING OF AN NGANGA

The mayombero waits until the moon is propitious, and then he goes to a cemetery with an assistant. Once there, he sprinkles rum in the form of a cross over a pre-chosen grave. The grave is opened, and the head, toes, fingers, ribs, and tibias of the corpse are removed. The mayombero usually knows the identity of the cadaver, which is known as *kiyumba*. They are usually recent graves, as the mayombero insists on having a head in which the brain is still present, however decayed. He believes that the brain of the kiyumba can think and thus "act" better. The choice kiyumbas are those belonging to very violent persons, especially those of criminals and of the insane, for the purposes of the mayombero are generally to commit acts of death and destruction. The bodies of white persons are also greatly favored, as the mayombero believes that the brain of the *mundele* (white person) is easier to influence than that of a black man and that it will follow instructions better. Still, some mayomberos prefer to have the brains of both a white and a black person, to ensure that they will be able to attack anyone, regardless of skin color.

After the macabre remains are removed from their graves, they are wrapped in a black cloth and the mayombero and his helper return to the witch's house. The mayombero lies on the floor. His assistant covers him with a sheet and lights four tapers, which are placed on each side of the mayombero's body, as if he were dead. On the blade of a knife he places seven small heaps of gunpowder, known as *fula*. The body of the mayombero becomes rigid and then goes into convulsions as the spirit of the kiyumba takes possession of him. The assistant asks the spirit if it is willing to work for the mayombero. If the spirit agrees, all the heaps of gunpowder will ignite spontaneously and simultaneously. If the gunpowder does not burn, the answer is negative and the body remains must be returned to the cemetery.

Once the spirit accepts the pact, the grisly ceremony is ended.

The mayombero writes the name of the dead person on a piece of paper and places it at the bottom of a big iron cauldron, together with a few coins, which are the price of the kiyumba's help. The body's remains are added to the cauldron, together with some earth from the grave. The mayombero then makes an incision on his arm with a knife that must have a white handle, and lets a few drops of blood fall into the cauldron, so that the kiyumba may drink and be refreshed. Some mayomberos do not think it wise to give some of their own blood to the spirit, as it may become addicted to human blood and thus become a vampire and eventually destroy the mayombero. These cautious witches think it is safer to sacrifice a rooster to the spirit and thus avoid trouble later on.

After the human or animal blood has been sprinkled on the remains, the mayombero adds to the cauldron the wax from a burnt candle, ashes, a cigar butt, and some lime. Also added to the mixture is a piece of bamboo, sealed at both ends with wax, and filled with sand, sea water, and quicksilver. This gives the kiyumba the speed of the quicksilver and the persistence of the sea tides, which never rest and are forever in movement. The body of a small black dog is also added to the cauldron to help the spirit "track down" its victims. Next to the dog, a variety of herbs and tree barks are placed inside the cauldron. The last ingredients to be added are red pepper, chili, garlic, ginger, onions, cinnamon, and rue, together with ants, worms, lizards, termites, bats, frogs, Spanish flies, a tarantula, a centipede, a wasp, and a scorpion.

After the nganga is ready, it is brought back to the cemetery (nfinda kalunga) where it is buried and left for three Fridays. Then it is disinterred and taken to the woods, where it is again buried for another three Fridays, this time by the side of a ceiba, or any other magical tree. At the end of this combined period of forty-two days, the nganga is taken home by the mayombero, where he again gives it some fresh blood and adds some rum with pepper, dry wine, and Florida Water. The nganga is finished and ready to work.

In some Latin American countries, "unbaptized" mayomberos still prepare the nganga or prenda from human remains stolen from opened graves. In the United States, where cemeteries are patrolled, it is practically impossible to rob graves. The paleros are therefore forced to purchase the human skulls and bones they need for their prendas from people who acquire them illicitly from gravediggers. In Miami's Dade County, the office of the Chief Medical Examiner is kept constantly busy by the findings of human skulls smeared with blood and feathers. Through careful examination of the remains, the department has learned that they are not the result of grisly murders or ritual human sacrifice, but rather the work of the paleros and their ngangas. Included in this book are photographs taken by members of the office of the Chief Medical Examiner in Dade County, especially by Dr. Charles Wetli, who has done considerable research on the subject of palo practices.

Sometimes the mayombero prepares an nganga without a cauldron. This is called a *boumba*, which is wrapped in a large sheet or placed inside a burlap sack. This sack, with its macabre contents, is known as a *macuto*, and it is kept hanging from a beam of the ceiling in the darkest room of the house.

The mayombero believes that his nganga is like a small world that is entirely dominated by him. The kiyumba rules over all the herbs and the animals that live inside the nganga with it. The mayombero in turn rules the kiyumba, who obeys his orders like a faithful dog. The kiyumba is the slave of the mayombero and it is always waiting inside the cauldron or the macuto to carry out his commands.

When the nganga is ready to work, the mayombero tests its powers in several ways. First he takes it to the woods, where he buries it under a tree and instructs the kiyumba to dry all the leaves in the tree within a certain period of time. At the end of this time, the mayombero returns to pick up the nganga and to ascertain whether or not is has carried out his instructions. If the leaves are dried, he proceeds to test the nganga further by asking it to destroy a specific animal. If the nganga obeys his command again, the mayombero is satisfied and puts the cauldron or macuto away in a safe place until it is time to use it.

USE OF THE NGANGA

How is the nganga used? Suppose a woman comes to the mayombero and asks him to kill her husband, who is throwing away all his money on other women. The mayombero agrees, for a price. He then goes to the cemetery, where he "buys" the life of the man with a silver coin, maybe fifty cents. He pays for the man's life by making a hole in a dark corner of the cemetery and burying the coin inside. This hole becomes the symbolic grave of the man who is to be killed. The mayombero takes some of the earth from this hole and wraps it in a black rag. He takes it home, where he lights a taper that he has previously stolen from a church. He heats a pin, which he uses to run through the body of a live centipede that has been tied with a black thread. He then calls the man's name aloud three times and places the earth from the cemetery into the nganga, together with a piece of clothing of the victim that has been recently worn by him. He takes the nganga and the pin with the centipede to a large tree, where he sticks the still-squirming animal to the tree bark. He again calls the victim's name aloud and commands the kiyumba to kill the man and to make him suffer the same torments as the centipede pinned to the tree. Invariably, a few days after this frightful spell has been cast, the intended victim dies suddenly, usually in a violent way.

The mayombero does not always use the nganga to kill a person. Sometimes he kills without the nganga. In a typical form of this type of killing, the mayombero goes to the woods, where he finds a large tree, perferably the aforementioned ceiba. He sprinkles rum on the tree roots and buries a few coins near it to pay for the work required. He then stabs the tree trunk with a knife and states that just as he is stabbing the tree trunk, so will the victim be stabbed in the heart and thus killed. The tree is usually stabbed on its four cardinal points. A black candle is then lighted by the tree's roots and allowed to consume itself. The wounds received by the tree will soon be received by the mayombero's victim.

Another spell uses a frog (*chula*). A piece of paper with the victim's name is placed inside the frog's mouth with some salt. A handkerchief of the intended victim is then sewn to the frog's mouth. The frog is put inside a large-necked bottle and left to die in the cemetery. The victim will die at the same time as the frog.

The palm tree is also especially revered by the mayomberos, who use it just as often as the ceiba for their evil spells.

A typical bilongo, used to kill, is known as the *nkangue* of death. With a brand-new knife, the mayombero opens the breast of a live black chicken and sprinkles the wound with rum. He puts into the wound pepper and garlic mixed with sulfur and graveyard dust and then wraps the bird in a black cloth. All during this process he is cursing his victim and invoking the spirit of the palm tree (*nsasi*) to kill the unfortunate person in the cruelest and slowest way. He then buries the chicken still alive, under the roots of the palm tree, leaving the head outside the hole. With a new broom (*kamba*), he hits the trunk of the tree so that Nsasi (Changó), angered at the punishment, will hasten to destroy the intended victim.

A story is told of a mayombero who took revenge on his wife because she had been unfaithful to him with one of his neighbors. He waited patiently until the woman thought he had forgiven and forgotten the offense and then came to her house late one night with a wide-necked bottle in his hands. He knocked at her door three times, and when she asked from within who was at the door, he captured the sound of her voice inside the bottle and, closing it tightly, hurried away from the house. (This is a common practice among the mayomberos, who believe that the voice is the breath of life of a person and can be used to kill.) The mayombero of the story went to the palm tree with the bottle, which he promptly buried under the roots of the tree. He then lit four candles and pinned a live black chicken to the tree trunk with a new knife, all the while invoking Nsasi to destroy the woman. The very next day the woman responded to the spell by dousing herself with gasoline and setting her body on fire.

THE ZARABANDA

Very similar to the fearful nganga is another "*prenda*," very popular with the Kongo, called *zarabanda*. The basic difference between an nganga and a zarabanda is that while the nganga works directly with the kiyumba, the zarabanda has as its spiritual entity a powerful Kongo deity also known as Zarabanda, who is the equivalent of the Yoruba orisha Oggún. This Zarabanda is a typical case of a Yoruba god syncretized as a Kongo deity (*mpungo*).

The zarabanda is prepared in a manner similar to that of the nganga, but it must always be made inside an iron cauldron, never in a sack, like the boumba.

THE NDOKI

Perhaps the most evil of all the ngangas is the infernal ndoki, which is prepared by boiling a black cat alive, after torturing the animal for some time. After the cat has boiled for a while, it is removed from the pot and buried for twenty-four hours. It is then disinterred, and from its carcass the mayombero removes a few bones, which he adds to seven phalanges from the little fingers of seven corpses and graveyard dust from seven graves. All these ingredients are placed in the cauldron with garlic and pepper. The mayombero sprinkles rum over the cauldron and blows the smoke of a cigar into its nauseous contents. He takes the cauldron to the woods, where it remains overnight. It is then ready to work. This ferocious nganga is an attribute of the devil and is used exclusively to kill and destroy in the most hair-raising ways.

Despite all his evil deeds, the "unbaptized" mayombero often dies a natural death, after a particularly long and busy life. Upon his death, the nganga is either given to one of his disciples or is brought to the woods, where it is dismantled and interred. The best place to bury the nganga thus destroyed is at a busy anthill. The nganga is buried, and the ground is sprinkled with rum and the blood of a black chicken. It is left there to return to the earth whence it came. Only after the destruction of the nganga is the work of the mayombero finally ended.

It is not uncommon in Santería for a palero to become initiated as a santero. There are also santeros who own a prenda, but who were never "cut" in Palo. The prenda may be inherited or given to the santero after the death of its owner, or it may be his own prenda, which he received before he made the saint. For it is very important to remember, according to both the paleros and the santeros, that once a person has made the saint, he cannot become a palero. He may inherit the prenda but cannot receive one of his own. The reason for this distinction is the old belief that the dead always go before the saint. Also, the orishas are highly evolved spiritual forces who will not have any contact with negative spiritual entities. Some orishas, such as Changó, expressly forbid their initiates to do any type of black magic or witchcraft or to work with an nganga. This is because Changó is said to be the greatest of all witches, and he will not tolerate the performance of witchcraft by anyone but himself.

Santeros and paleros usually have fairly harmonious relations and avoid interfering with each other's practices. The spirits of the dead are never allowed to take possession of anyone during any of the orisha ceremonies, as this is considered an offense to the saints. Once I saw a palera at a tambor, crying in desperate shame and apologizing profusely to the head of the house because one of her spirit guides had taken possession of her at the ceremony, without her being able to avoid it.

Very often, paleros are practicing *espiritistas* (spiritists), who seek in this manner to establish stronger links with their guiding spirits. But not all spiritists are paleros, and some of them condemn the practice as injurious to the spiritual forces used by the paleros. They believe these spirits are forced to remain earthbound, unable to seek higher spiritual evolution because they are obligated to serve human beings in their own selfish pursuits. The paleros counter these accusations with their belief that the spirits of the nganga acquire greater light and evolution through their help to human beings.

20.

Candomblé ///////////////////////////
The Religion in Brazil

The Yoruba tradition, which gave birth to Santería in Cuba, evolved in Brazil into Candomblé and Macumba. Although there are many similarities between Santería and Candomblé, there are also some very marked differences. (Candomblé must not be confused with the ritualistic dances of Rio de Janeiro, known as *afochés*, which are performed as tourist attractions.)

Like most Latin American countries, Brazil is predominantly Catholic. The city of Salvador, capital of the state of Bahia, has an astonishing 356 churches. "That's practically a church for every day of the year," boasts a proud Bahian. Like 90 percent of Brazilian people, he is a practicing Catholic who goes to mass every Sunday. But, between church visits, he is busy practicing Brazil's "other religion," the African-based Candomblé.

So extensive is the practice of Candomblé in Brazil that it is now officially recognized as the country's national religion. In Bahia, which is the center of Candomblé, there are almost four times as many Candomblé temples as there are Catholic churches. With an estimated 30 million people practicing Candomblé in the country, the Brazilian government has decided to teach the elements of the religion in the public schools.

The Yoruba deities are known as *orixas* in Brazil, and, as in Santería, they have all been identified with saints of the Catholic faith. The centers of Candomblé worship, known as *terreiros*, are headed by initiated priests and priestesses known as *pais* or *mais de santo*, fathers or mothers of the saints. There are no babalawos in Candomblé.

Each terreiro is a temple that functions as a congregation where members share the expenses of the rites and initiations. The terreiro is like a great community. Everyone who practices Candomblé belongs to a terreiro. Some temples may have only five or six people as members, while others may have hundreds. The beautiful clothes worn by the initiates and by the various priests and priestesses are sewn by the members of the terreiro. The costly fabrics, laces, and beads used in the construction of the clothes are bought with the contributions of the members. In this way, everyone is assured a beautiful costume during the ceremonies, and no one dresses better or worse than anybody else.

The oldest and largest of the terreiros, Casa Branca (White House), has recently been brought under the protection of the Brazilian government's historic preservation law. So accepted is Candomblé in Brazil that pictures of the orixas are used on postage stamps. People from all levels of society practice the religion, and the terreiros are traditional stops in the campaigns of politicians, who openly seek the aid of the orixas during the elections.

The reason for Candomblé's great popularity is that it offers solutions for all sorts of human problems. Business deals, political campaigns, love affairs, broken marriages, illnesses, persecution by enemies, and all kinds of personal difficulties can be brought to the feet of the orixas for prompt and happy resolutions. Like Santería, Candomblé has literally thousands of rites and spells that are reputed to make everyone's wishes come true.

Each mai or pai de santo—the equivalent of the santera or santero—is a revered figure who heads a terreiro, sitting on its throne until he or she dies. The other members of the temple follow the priests and priestesses' leads in the practice of the religion. The mai or pai de santo is chosen by the orixas themselves for their exalted positions, and sometimes they lead congregations in which there are members three times their own ages. These people are invariably quite psychic, with extraordinary healing and magical powers. The most famous of the mais de santo in Brazil was Mother Menininha de Gantois, who died in 1985 at a very advanced age.

The most important of the orixas or saints worshiped in Brazil are Exu (loosely identified with the devil), Ogum (Saint Anthony in Bahia and Saint George in Rio de Janeiro), Xangô (Saint Jerome), Oxossi (Saint George in Bahia and Saint Sebastian in Rio), Oiá-Iansã (Saint Barbara), Oxum (Our Lady of Candeias), Oba (Saint Catherine), Iemanjá (Our Lady of the Immaculate Conception), Omolu (Saint Lazarus in Bahia and Saint Sebastian in Rio), Nana Buruku (Our Lady of Mount Carmel), and Oxalá (Our Lord of Bonfim). It is easy to recognize the dieties worshiped and syncretized in Candomblé with those of Santería, although the spellings and the syncretisms vary.

All Candomblé ceremonies begin with an offering to Exu so that he will not hinder the rituals. Each of the orixas has his or her own special ceremonies, celebrated on specific dates. Among the most popular are the Waters of Oxalá (Obatalá in Santería), the Mortar of Oxalá, the Fogueira or Fire of Xangô, the Apeté of Oxum, and the Feijoada of Ogum.

The most spectacular of the rites devoted to the orixas is undoubtedly the one celebrated on January 2, in honor of Iemanjá— also known as Dona Janaina, *rhaina do mar* (queen of the sea), and *mai d'agua* (mother of the waters). The day is a legal holiday in Brazil, and in Bahia, thousands of flower garlands are placed on wooden rafts and floated out to sea. The beaches are crowded on this day by thousands of devotees and curious onlookers. The air is fragrant with the scent of fresh flowers, and the sea breezes carry throughout the city the monotonous, rhythmic sound of hundreds of *atabaques*, the ritual drums that are played in honor of the orixa. (The batáa drums are not used in Candomblé.) Initiated priests and priestesses—known as *filhos* and *filhas de santo* (sons and daughters of the saints)—dance to the drumbeat, dressed in colorful costumes. Some of the dresses worn by the *filhas* are stunning. The long, voluminous skirts are usually of heavy satin or brocade, richly embroidered by hand and trimmed with many yards of exquisite lace. The wide over-blouses are topped by wide satin bands that are tied in large bows over the breasts, Yoruba-style. Both priests and priestesses wear crowns made of the same materials as the costumes, heavily beaded or trimmed with white feathers. Female orixas demand that their priests and priestesses wear veils of beads hanging from their crowns, half covering their faces, a tradition common among Nigerian kings. Of the male orixas, only Xangô wears a beaded veil, a show of his vanity about his legendary beauty. Xangô's priests, also following a Nigerian tradition, sometimes braid their hair to one side, another of Xangô's characteristics.

As in Santería, each of the orixas represents both an aspect of nature and a human pursuit. Ogum (Oggún), who represents the woods, is also the ironworker and the patron of policemen, surgeons, and all those who work with metal implements. Oxum (Oshún) represents the river waters and is also the patron of love, gold, and marriage. Xangô (Changó), the symbol of fire, thunder, and lightning, represents passion and the overcoming of obstacles through power. Oxalá (Obatalá), the most important and revered of the orixas, is a symbol of peace and purity. All white objects are sacred to him. As in Santería, the orixas have special foods, numbers, and colors assigned to them. They also have beaded necklaces that are conferred upon the devotees during initiation ceremonies.

Like Santería, Candomblé is an initiation system. There are minor and major initiations, each of which confers upon the initiate, in varying degrees, some of the power (axé) of the orixas.

Some Candomblé ceremonies are open to the public and are

even photographed. Others are so secret that not even some of the members of the terreiro can see them. The reason for this strict secrecy is that there is a progressive series of initiations. After an individual receives the initiation that makes him a *filho de santo* (the equivalent of an asiento), he must undergo several other initiations. One is received three years after the initial ceremony; the next, five years later; another, seven years later; and the last, nine years later. After this last ceremony, the filho can open his own terreiro if he so desires, but this does not make him a priest or pai de santo. Only the orixas can decide that. Sometimes the filho does not know if he is meant to be a priest for many years. This is because there may be as many as three hundred people in a temple, of which only ten may be called into the priesthood.

After every initiation the individual receives a title. For example, after the five-year ceremony he becomes a second-class priest, known as an *ebomin*. This initiation entitles a person to wear shoes in front of the priests; ordinarily, the lesser initiates must be barefoot in the presence of the mai or pai de santo. Ebomins usually wear an undershirt with a robe over it. The way they tie their turbans also indicates their rank. After the seven-year initiation the ebomin becomes a *bagan*. After the nine-year initiation he becomes a *babalorixa* and can open his own terreiro.

Another member of the temple, the *ekedi*, is the one in charge of the iyawós or initiates. The ekedi is usually a woman, and comes into this title as soon as she receives the initial initiation. She assists the priests and priestesses during the initiations, and is in charge of those who fall into trance. She also cooks for the orixas and has the secrets of the shells and of the herbs used in the rituals. The ekedi always wear white clothes, a large apron, and many petticoats.

The first initiation is the most complicated. At this time the iyawó receives the secrets of the orixa believed to be his father or mother. But this cannot happen unless the iyawó becomes possessed by his orixa. At this time he receives cuts with a razor on his tongue, back, arms, and legs. (Santeros only cut the tongue.) The cuts are then stuffed with an herbal concoction that would make the iyawó scream in agony if he were conscious. Because he is under possession, he is not aware of any pain.

The first initiation process lasts a little over a year. For the first three months after the ceremony, the iyawó remains in the temple, where he assists the priests and prays day and night in Yoruba. He prays early in the morning, at noon, and at six in the evening. He also prays during each meal and thanks the orixas for all he owns, including the clothes he wears. During this period the iyawó is known as *abian*. To identify him, he wears an armband of Nigerian raffia, braided and tied very tight, so that when he finally removes it, the mark remains for a very long time. As the abian is considered a sacred slave, he also wears a chain with a ball tied around his ankle, presumably so that he cannot run away. His head is also shaved during the initiation, and he must wear white for a full year. Female initiates are forbidden the use of makeup and jewelry, except the bead necklaces sacred to the orixas.

The initiations and rituals dedicated to the orixas invariably include animal sacrifices. As in Santería, the blood of the animals is poured directly over the otanes of the orixas. During the initiations, the decapitated heads of the animals are offered to the possessed novices, who drink deeply of the animal blood and then clamp the head between their teeth and parade for a few minutes around the terreiro. This is an indication that the iyawó's orixa has accepted the blood sacrifice.

The term *Macumba* is often associated with Candomblé, but they are not the same thing. Brazilians say that Macumba was created to take care of the evil that Candomblé once used to do. Macumba is divided into Umbanda, or white magic, and Quimbanda, or black magic. But today there is very little difference between the two. Macumba in general is a mixture of black magic, white magic, Spiritism, Kongo magic, and some Angolan practices. Macumba is so closely associated with Spiritism that when Brazilians are going to attend a séance, they say they are going to a Macumba. There are definite similarities between Macumba and Palo practices, undoubtedly because of the influence of the Kongo people in both.

The attitude of the Catholic Church on the subject of Candomblé is curiously ambivalent. Although the rituals and magic practices are officially condemned by the Church, the Catholic clergy actually allow some of the rites to be conducted inside the churches. In fact, the major initiation, when an individual becomes a filho de santo, culminates in a Sunday-morning mass. There are even priests who have been initiated into Candomblé. One of the best known of such cases is that of Father François de l'Espignay, a middle-aged priest who is also an initiate of Xangô. Father de l'Espignay claims that he has never felt that his two faiths were in contradiction. He says his intention was to show the Catholic Church that Candomblé is a religion that was not invented in Brazil, and whose traditions are so old that they cannot even be dated. To him, the basis of Candomblé is the revelation of God, very much like the Christian scriptures.

Even Bishop Boaventura Kloppenburg, of the diocese of San Salvador, who is one of Candomblé's strongest opponents, admits that "they have abundant ritual and ornamentation, as the Church does. They are strongly traditional and give great value to authority figures, as we do. As for the orixas, we have saints and angels, and have always operated on the basis of intermediaries. And what they call axé, their divine force, is like the Christian state of grace."

When Pope John Paul II visited Brazil in 1980, he publicly recognized the importance of Candomblé as an expression of the spiritual roots of the Brazilian people. He even underwent a ritual cleansing conducted by a pai de santo. While deploring the superstitions and magical practices inherent in Candomblé, he still recognized its social and spiritual values. His statements had such powerful repercussions that they made newspaper headlines, not only in Brazil, but all over the world.

To the average Brazilian, Candomblé is more than a religion. It is a way of life, something that is as much a part of him as the coffee he drinks and the carnival he loves. In many ways, Candomblé is Brazil.

21.

Itutu ///
The Death of a Santero

Like the asiento, the lugubrious ceremony of the itutu extends for a whole year. It is divided into three parts. The first of the three rituals is celebrated on the same day the santero dies, the second nine days after his death, and the third a year later.

When a santero dies, his family immediately informs several santeros, who should number at least nine—the number of Oyá, owner of the cemetery. The santeros gather together in the mortuary chamber where the body lies. Locking all the doors, they proceed with the ritual, which is a form of appeasement to ensure that the dead person's soul departs and will not remain behind to hunt the living.

The santeros sit down in a circle. One of them—preferably an oriaté—asks each of the ikú's orishas whether they want to "depart" with the dead person or remain on earth. For this purpose, all the dead santero's soperas (with the otanes he received during his asiento) are opened, and each orisha's cowrie shells are used for the questioning. Eighteen cowrie shells are allotted to each orisha, except Elegguá, who owns twenty-one. But as usual, only sixteen are used for the reading of each orisha's wish.

While some choose to remain behind, other orishas opt to leave with the ikú. Immediately after the orishas have "spoken," the oriaté breaks the soperas of the orishas who wish to leave with the dead. A white plate and one of the necklaces of each of the departing orishas are also broken. The otanes, together with the orishas' implements and attributes, are either thrown in a river or buried with the dead santero. If the orisha decides to stay on earth, the oriaté questions him or her until he determines with whom—among the family, friends, or ahijados of the dead santero—the orisha wishes to remain. Once the heir has been established, the orishá's otanes and various attributes pass immediately into that person's possession, who must purify them as soon as possible to rid them of the dead santero's influence, but must never use them, as they are meant only as means of protection.

But the otanes and seashells are not the only sacred objects to be disposed of. The hair cut during the dead santero's asiento, the scissors and shaving blade that were used, the head dyes, the four pieces of cloth in the colors of the orishas that were placed on the santero's head, and the comb used to comb his hair prior to the asiento, must all leave with the dead.

The santeros dress the corpse in the clothes he wore during his initiation. The seashells of the departing orishas are laid upon the corpse's breast, encased in a white bag, together with bits of opossum, smoked fish, and a few grains of corn. The hair is placed next to the body in the coffin. The other objects are placed in a large gourd that has been previously covered with two pieces of cloth, one white and one black, in the form of a cross. Within the gourd, all the santeros deposit handfuls of dried corn silk, bits of dried okra, and ashes. Then they all turn their backs to the gourd and the oriaté kills a black chicken, which he puts over the ashes. The gourd with this symbolic ebbo is placed next to the coffin. It must enter the cemetery before the body, and must be thrown into the grave so it will come to rest at the head of the coffin.

Several hours before the burial, all the santeros begin to chant in Yoruba and dance around the coffin, calling the dead santero by his initiation name, and all the dead santeros mayores and other ikús to come and attend the ceremony. The oriaté marks the compass with a beribboned palo. Then the orishas are called, one by one, starting with Elegguá, to come and cleanse the body of all impurities.

The orishas arrive at the itutu by taking possession of their children, and cleanse the dead santero with colored handkerchiefs that they pass all over the corpse. The orishas do not speak. They just moan, and make low, guttural sounds through which they express their grief. Yewá, who must precede all the dead to her lonesome abode, also possesses one of her children and purifies the body with an iruke, a sort of scepter made of a horse's tail.

When the purification ritual is completed, the santeros who are not possessed place those mounted by their orishas with their backs against the wall and hit the wall with their fists three times. This dismisses the orishas, who now leave to accompany the dead person to his last resting place. The doors of the mortuary room now open, and the coffin is removed. Once in the street, a small clay vessel is broken behind the funeral car, and plenty of cold water is thrown by its side so the dead person will start "refreshed" upon his final journey.

A santera told me a terrifying story of what took place during the itutu of a friend of hers, an initiate of Oyá, the cemetery owner.

The itutu was almost over. The santeros were beginning to line the possessed santeros against the walls to dismiss the orishas. The santera, who had been staring disconsolately at her dead friend's face, saw the corpse's eyes open slowly until they were staring straight at her.

"I nearly fainted," she told me. "My heart jumped so hard in my chest I thought it would come out of my mouth."

"There are various natural reasons why a corpse may open its eyes," I told her, "such as an uncontrolled movement of the lid mechanism. It has nothing to do with the supernatural."

"Maybe so," she said. "But what is the natural explanation of the fact that when I turned around to tell the other santeros what I had seen, I found myself face to face with the dead santera?"

"What do you mean, 'face to face'?" I asked incredulously.

"I mean she was standing by my side, as clear as day." The santera shivered a little and rubbed her arms briskly. "She was dressed in black, and her eyes had a fixed, vacant stare. I moved slowly away from her, and she made no move to follow me. Soundlessly—for I could not have spoken if I had tried—I shook the arm of the oriaté and pointed to the dead santera. I saw immediately from the look in his eyes that he could also see her. One by one, all the mamalochas and babalochas in the room became aware of the presence of the specter. Without a word, we all formed a circle around the coffin, next to which stood the ghost of the deceased. We joined hands and began to pray once more, calling the name of the dead santera, and asking her to recognize that she was a spirit and that it was time for her to leave the material world. Very slowly, the ghost began to dematerialize until only a smoky wreath was left floating over her coffin. After a while this too disappeared, and we were able to breathe normally once more."

"What happened afterward?" I asked.

"Nothing much," said the santera. "But I dreamed of her almost every night after the itutu. Only nine days after her death did the dreams end."

The funeral mass, said in honor of the dead santero nine days after his death, is known as *oro ilé Olofi*—prayers in the house of Olofi (the church). After the mass, the santeros meet once more and "offer coconut" to the dead santero. During this second part of the itutu, the santeros ask the spirit if he is satisfied with the rites and purifications, and if there is anything he requires for the total peace of his soul. The dead santero's wishes are carried out meticulously, as soon as possible after the ritual.

A year later, the third and last part of the itutu is carried out. During this, the most complicated part of the ceremony, a four-legged animal, usually a pig, is sacrificed to the dead.

Prior to the ceremony, which is called *levantamiento del plato* (removing of the plate), all the santeros paint the three yeza of the Yoruba upon their cheeks so that Oyá will spare their lives and will not take them with her. The derecho of the ikú is placed by each santero on its basket by the side of a table, and the ritual begins by covering the table with a white sheet. Upon this improvised altar is placed the plate that the deceased used to eat from. Another plate, filled with salt, is placed on the table, next to a large bottle of Florida Water, two lit candles, and the images of Saint Peter (Oggún) and Saint Theresa (an aspect of Oyá). On the wall behind the table the santeros hang another white sheet, with a black cross in the center.

During the coconut offering preceding the sacrifice, all the santeros look away from the pieces of coconuts as they fall on the floor. This is done so that the ikú will not demand the life of an observer together with the animal sacrifice.

As the head priest sacrifices the animal offering, all those present chant in Yoruba, praying to all the dead, starting with the santeros mayores. Outside the house, one santero acknowledges each prayer by making a line in chalk on the ritual palo used to call upon the dead.

As during all animal sacrifices, the head of the dead animal is separated from its body and placed on a white plate. The head, together with a gourd filled with the animal's blood, is placed under the altar, where the dead may partake of them.

Around midnight, the tambor begins. Contrary to the happy atmosphere of the orishas' tambors, a tambor dedicated to the dead is sad and melancholy. Everyone sings and dances, but the action is perfunctory. There is no joy in the santeros' voices or movements. During these somber festivities, the orishas do not descend to earth, with the exception of Elegguá—who opens all doors, including death's door—Oyá, and Yewá.

Shortly after the beginning of the tambor, at the stroke of midnight, two of the santeros bring some of the ritual food of the dead to the cemetery. If they cannot enter within, they leave their offering by one of the cemetery's corners. The food, prepared with rice and some of the sacrificed animal's meat, is unsalted, as are all of the ikú's foods. The santeros accompany the dead in this funeral meal, which they call *osún*.

Before sunrise, the sacrificial animal's head and its blood are removed and brought either to the cemetery or to the woods. The tambor continues until early the next morning, when all the santeros and the members of the family of the deceased attend a mass said in his honor.

When the santeros return from the church, the house where the tambor took place is ritually cleansed. Some of the food is thrown around the house and then swept out of doors, so that "the dead will leave, following the food." The floor is then scrubbed with special herbs and clear water.

The final act of the itutu, and the one that gives the ceremony its name, occurs when four santeras clear the altar and lift the sheet that covers it, placing it folded on the floor with the plate of the deceased on top. This is the ritualistic "removal" of the plate, which is then taken to a street corner and shattered into many pieces. When the plate is broken, so are the last ties the dead santero had with the material world, and his spirit is finally free. This ends the itutu.

22.

The Church
and Santería

The Catholic Church is of paramount importance to the santero, who considers himself a practicing Catholic in spite of his involvement with the African orishas. The santero usually refers to the deities as *santos*—saints—but calls them by their Yoruba names. Elegguá, Changó, Orúnla, Obatalá, Oshún, and all the other orishas are santos and are referred to as such by the santero.

The santero denies that the orishas and the saints are the same thing. He maintains that each saint is an aspect, a path, an "avatar" of a particular orisha. Saint Barbara, for example, is *not* Changó. She represents a force that is identifiable with the orisha because it has the same characteristics. The Catholic image of Saint Barbara shows a young girl wearing a white gown with a red mantle and a golden crown shaped like a turret. In her left hand she holds a sword, and in her right a golden goblet. There is a small castle at her feet. Red and white are Changó's colors. Saint Barbara's goblet is a symbol of Changó's mortar, the vessel in which he prepares his powerful spells. The sword the saint holds in her left hand is also a symbol of Changó's double-edged ax. The castle symbolizes royalty, as Changó is said to have been the fourth king of Oyo.

Legend says that Saint Barbara lived in the fourth century. Although her actual life is obscured by many contradictory legends, most sources seem to indicate that she was the daughter of a barbarian king and that she secretly pledged her life to Christ. Her father had her imprisoned in the highest turret of his castle because of her Christian beliefs and her refusal to marry according to his wishes. One tempestuous night he went up to her tower and renewed his demands that she marry one of his chieftains. Her refusal to do his will filled him with such fury that he drew out his sword and beheaded her. At that moment he was struck down by a bolt of lightning, thus creating the legend that gives Saint Barbara power over thunder and lightning. The analogies between the virgin martyr and the orisha Changó are so marked that they helped create the syncretism that binds them both.

Interestingly, although Saint Barbara is the saint most commonly syncretized with Changó, she does not appear as any of his *caminos*—paths— in Santería. As we have already seen, there are other Catholic saints—all male—identified with Changó's various aspects. Among them are Saint George, Saint Mark, and Saint Jerome.

As the belief in Changó's identification with Saint Barbara grew, two other representations of the saint became popularized. In one of these, Saint Barbara is shown on horseback, with several of Changó's attributes along her horse's path. Typical of these is a large bunch of green bananas, which is one of the orisha's favorite foods. The other representation of the saint is that of the "African" Saint Barbara (*Santa Barbara Africana*), showing the saint as a young black woman with European features and the tribal yeza of the Yoruba on her cheeks.

On the other hand, there is a *Changó Macho*, a "male" Changó, which emphasizes the difference between Saint Barbara as a "female" Changó and the true identity of the orisha in all his virility. This last image, available in printed form as well as a statue, is that of a handsome young Nubian prince, crowned, holding a large tray of precious stones in his hands. The image was obviously copied from a famed wooden sculpture by the baroque sculptor Balthasar Permaser, which was brought to Europe in the sixteenth century.

In spite of the obvious syncretism between Changó and Saint Barbara, the santero worships them separately, but in the same way. This is also true of all the other orishas. Yet, to the santero, both Saint Barbara and Changó are saints and he often speaks of them interchangeably.

To illustrate the Catholic overtones of Santería, there are prayers printed in loose form or in prayer collections, all of which refer to the orishas as Catholic saints. One of the most popular of these prayers is that of the Seven African Powers (*Las Siete Potencias Africanas*), an awesome septet formed by Elegguá, Orúnla, Obatalá, Oggún, Changó, Yemayá, and Oshún. The image representing the Seven African Powers shows a circular chain interspersed with the seven medals of the Catholic saints identified with these orishas, but with their Yoruba names inscribed on the medals. At the bottom of the chain are the seven implements of Oggún. In the background there is a crucifix with all the various known elements of the crucifixion. The name at the feet of the cross is Olofi, showing the accepted identification of Jesus with the Yoruba supernal deity.

Another Catholic element common in Santería is holy water. All the cleansing baths, the ritual omiero—as well as the liquid used in all the initiations and most of the ebbós—contain holy water as a purification substance. Traditionally, all Santería initiates should be baptized Catholics, but with the influx of Jews into the Religion, this rule is not as strenuously observed as before. But there are still many casas de santo that will not initiate anyone unless that person has undergone the ceremony of baptism.

In spite of the guarded attitude of the Catholic Church about Santería, there are many parish priests who, aware of the need for holy water in Santería, bottle it and sell it to the botánicas, which, in turn, sell it to the general public. But most santeros do not trust the sale of holy water, because they believe it loses its grace when it is sold. They prefer to acquire it themselves from the containers available to the faithful in most churches.

Perhaps the most traditional connection between the Church and Santería is the Holy Mass. Santeros are among the most assiduous worshipers at mass services, and they always recommend to their followers that they attend mass as often as possible. As we have seen, the itutu ceremony ends with a funeral mass dedicated to the soul of the dead santero. Candles lit in church are also believed to be of great power, especially when dedicated to the eggun. Masses are always said in honor of the orishas, especially on their birthdays. As we have already seen, one of the most popular of these masses is that celebrated in New York's St. Patrick's Cathedral in honor of Our Lady of Charity (Nuestra Señora de la Caridad del Cobre), patron of Cuba, and Oshún in Santería. The priest who usually celebrates this mass is Cuban, and he invariably refers to the saint as "our beloved Cachita," one of Oshún's pet names in Santería. The mass is celebrated on the eve of September 8, and after the liturgical services are over the image of the saint is paraded around the church, while those present wave yellow handkerchiefs in the air.

While the New York Archdiocese maintains that the mass of September 8 is celebrated to honor the patron of Cuba, who is a revered aspect of the Virgin Mary, their clergy are very much aware of the syncretism between the saint and Oshún. This apparent tolerance of Santería by the Church is part of the many changes that have been taking place in its internal structure since the Second Vatican Council in the mid-1960s.

Deeply concerned with the stagnation of the Church's development and the increasing indifference of Catholics to traditional teachings, Pope John XXIII decided to bring together all the princes of the Church to discuss how they might revive the flagging Catholic spirit. The result was the Second Vatican Council, better known as Vatican II, which was held between 1962 and 1965.

During the reign of Pope John XXIII, and later, during that of Pope Paul VI, the Church experienced the most climactic and staggering changes of its two-thousand-year history. Seeking for new ways to reach the decreasing numbers of practicing Catholics, the clergy instituted many changes in the mass liturgy that only compounded the problem instead of alleviating it. Gone was the traditional Latin that had graced the mass for centuries, bonding Catholics from all parts of the world together. The mass began to be conducted in the native language of each church. The position of the altar changed, so that the priest now faced the congregation. The Eucharist was dispensed either directly on the tongue, as always, or into the extended hands of the parishioners. There was singing of hymns and an exchange of peace between the worshipers halfway through the mass. New groups, such as the Charismatics, developed within the Church. (The Charismatics sing songs during services and sometimes fall into trances, during which they are believed to be possessed by the Holy Spirit. Often during the trances, they "speak in tongues.")

Also among the changes were new rules to govern nuns and priests. Nuns forsook their traditional long habits and began to wear ordinary clothes. Sometimes they wore a short veil over their heads in lieu of the heavy draperies that had shrouded them for centuries. They were also allowed to wear makeup. Priests also began to wear ordinary garb, and one of the most surprising photographs ever taken of a pontiff was that of Pope Paul VI in a white suit.

Some of the changes did help the Church in its bid for renewal and revival; others were less successful. Notable among the latter was Pope Paul VI's edict reversing the sanctified status of more than five hundred saints in the Catholic calendar. Millions of Catholics around the world were saddened and shocked to learn that some of the saints to whom they had been devoted for centuries were saints no more. One of these desanctified saints was Saint Barbara. Santeros were not the only Catholics who were shocked by the news. Saint Barbara is one of the Church's most popular saints, the acknowledged patron of soldiers and miners. There are basilicas all over the world erected in her name. One of the most beautiful is in New York, in the borough of Brooklyn. In Vienna, her image is found in the world-famous Votivkirche and in one of the city's underground mines, which is renowned for its lovely caves and underground lakes.

Pope Paul's edict did not affect Catholics in the least. Ignoring the Pope's decision, they continued their devotions to the saints of their choice, regardless of their status in the Church's calendar. And even though Saint Barbara's name no longer appears in the calendar, her devotees still honor her on December 4, which had always been her allotted day in the Church.

Vatican II was exemplary in its concern for the spiritual needs of Catholics throughout the world. But it would have been vastly more effective if many leaders of the Church had provided their congregations with a better indoctrination and catechetical explanations of the staggering changes that were taking place. Bewildered and confused, many Catholics found themselves lost in the new masses, uncertain as to the meanings of the changes and how they would affect their faith. As Father Juan J. Sosa, of the Miami Archdiocese, said in a recent article, "To the limited religious preparation of the people was unconsciously added a loss of interest for the new emerging symbols. Confronted by this loss, the easiest alternative [for the people] was to look for other symbols, close at hand and well known to them. Santería, with its extreme devotion to saints, became a singular alternative."*

Father Sosa goes on to emphasize the need for the Church to incorporate "popular religiosity" (such as Santería) in the liturgical celebrations of ecclesiastical communities. He warns, however, that:

---

*Sosa, Juan J., *Popular Religiosity and Religious Syncretism: Santeria and Spiritism* (Miami: Southeast Regional Office for Hispanic Affairs, Inc., 1982).

1. Popular religiosity should be intimately joined to the common mission of the Church today: evangelization.
2. All priests, deacons and lay persons should understand the difference between the positive and negative aspects of popular religiosity.
3. The Church should take this mystical and transcendent experience outside its walls, to those who wait outside for a sharing in this new spiritual development.

Father Sosa is not alone in this call for a fusion between the Church and popular beliefs such as those typical of Santería. In the pastoral conference that took place in Washington in 1977 (II Encuentro Nacional Hispano de Pastoral), the members urged that "bishops allow for greater flexibility and creativity in Hispanic liturgies, so that these be authentic expressions of the cultural values of our Hispanic people."

Both Popes Paul VI and John Paul II recognized popular religious beliefs as an intrinsic part of the culture and the spiritual roots of nations. John Paul II made his views clear with his words and actions when he visited Brazil in 1980.

It is nevertheless clear that while the Church ponders the possibility of a fusion with popular religiosity, it does not consider every element of popular religiosity liturgically acceptable. This means that whereas the Church may accept some aspects of Santería, it does not accept others.

To the santero this ecclesiastical controversy means very little, because to him Santería and Catholicism are both expressions of his religiosity. They are not the same, and they never were. One continues where the other leaves off. They both answer very definite spiritual needs and are perfect complements of each other. The santero does not experience any spiritual strife in the blending of both beliefs, perhaps because they are both an intrinsic part of his soul.

Ultimately, Santería can be seen as an extension of the Catholic

Church, embracing all of its practices while suffusing it with rich and powerful new beliefs. It may or may not ever be totally accepted by the Catholic Church, but it will always remain a part of it.

23.

Santería
and Spiritism ⚡⚡⚡⚡⚡⚡⚡⚡⚡⚡⚡⚡⚡

There seems to be a great deal of confusion in the minds of many people as to the differences and similarities between the beliefs and practices of Santería and those of Spiritism (Espiritismo). The first thing that must be emphasized is that all santeros are spiritists (*espiritistas*), but not all spiritists are santeros.

Spiritism should not be confused with Spiritualism, as there are many basic differences between the two.

Spiritualism was born in the United States in 1848. In this year, three young sisters named Leah, Kate, and Margaret Fox were able to communicate with the dead by means of wall rappings. The girls, who lived with their parents in a small cottage in Hydesville, New York, had been hearing the mysterious rappings for some time. One night they decided to start a conversation with their unseen visitor. One rap for yes and two raps for no. The dialogue began on March 31, 1848, which is the date regarded as that of the birth of Spiritualism. Through the ghostly communications the girls were able to learn that the spirit with whom they were "speaking" was that of a murdered peddler whose body had been buried underneath their cellar. When their father decided to dig up the cellar to verify the girls' story, he and the men who helped him with the work found hair and fragments of human bones buried under a mound of charcoal and lime. Nearly fifty-six years later the rest of the body was found, surrounded by the implements of a peddler's trade.

All three sisters grew up to be world-famous mediums, the first in a long line of spiritualists who claimed they could communicate with the dead. From the United States the movement spread to Europe, particularly to England and France, where it soon became the rage in exalted social circles. Queen Victoria became involved with Spiritualism, in her desperate search to establish contact with the spirit of her beloved Prince Albert. Many famous personalities throughout the world became fascinated with the fad. Edison, Marconi, Sir Arthur Conan Doyle, Harry Houdini, and President Lincoln were all interested in Spiritualism and attended many séances. The practices of Spiritualism were simple. Séances were conducted by special invitation (for a price), and the guests sat around a table and waited for the medium to begin a demonstration of her or his powers. These ranged from table rappings, levitation, materialization, and communication with spirits to automatic writing, the playing of ghostly instruments, and the favorite trick of all, the producing of ectoplasm, a vaporous, luminous substance that allegedly emanated from some mediums' bodies during a trance.

Naturally there was much fraud connected with Spiritualism, but there were also many well-documented cases of true mediumship. Among these was the famous Scottish medium Daniel Douglas Home. He was much admired during his time, and among his many followers he counted Elizabeth Barrett Browning and Napoleon III.

While Spiritualism is mostly concerned with the demonstration of a medium's psychic powers and his or her abilities to communicate with the dead for the benefit of her or his clients, Spiritism has loftier ideals.

Spiritism evolved out of a mixture of Spiritualism and the beliefs of a French philosopher called Hippolyte Leon Denizard Rivail, better known under the pseudonym of Allan Kardec.

Kardec believed that spiritual progress could only be achieved through a series of progressive incarnations. He maintained that God assigned each individual a group of spirit guides as his protectors. These are known as guardian angels and protecting spirits. Kardec stressed the importance of communicating with these enlightened spirits to acquire their help with our human problems. He adapted the practices of Spiritualism to those of Christianity, composing a series of special prayers and lectures, all of which were based on strict moral and ethical codes of behavior. He claimed that all of this material was received from several spiritual entities through the various mediums he used for his communications with the spirit world. All of these teachings were collected into several books; two of the most famous are *The Book of the Spirits* and *The Gospel According to Spiritism.* The type of Spiritualism practiced by Kardec was therefore more concerned with spiritual evolution and material prosperity through proper behavior than with the more materialistic endeavors of spiritualists. It eventually became known as Spiritism.

Kardec's books were swiftly translated into several languages, including Spanish and Portuguese. In the late nineteenth century, several copies of his works made their way as contraband into Latin America. Among the Latin American countries most deeply influenced by Kardec's teachings were Brazil, Argentina, Cuba, and Puerto Rico. In spite of the severe prohibitions of the Catholic Church against spiritualist beliefs, Spiritism spread swiftly throughout these countries. Brazil and Argentina have the largest concentrations of spiritists in the world, and close to 90 percent of all Cubans and Puerto Ricans are fervent believers in Spiritism.

The type of Spiritism practiced by Latin Americans is very special. Espiritismo, as it is most commonly known, teaches the importance of realizing one's spiritual essence and of disdaining material values and pleasures (*la materia*) in an effort to come closer to God. A typical Spiritist séance (*sesión espiritista*) is conducted with several mediums, both male and female, all dressed in white, sitting around a table. Those present at the séance who are not mediums sit on chairs behind the mediums. A large bowl of water, a vase of white flowers, a bottle of Florida Water mixed with curative plants, and a lit white candle are all placed on the table, which is always covered with a white tablecloth. At the head of the table sits the person who directs the séance, usually a man. He is known as Presidente de Mesa.

There are several types of mediums (*mediunidades*) in Espiritismo. Among them are *mediunidades videntes* (mediums who can see the spirits), *mediunidades clarividentes* (mediums who can see the future), *mediunidades auditivas* (mediums who can hear the spirits speak in their ears), *mediunidades de comunicación* (mediums who become possessed by spirits), *mediunidades de arrastre* (mediums who can take on evil spirits and banish them), and *mediunidades de transporte* (mediums who are able to project their consciousness to other places, including the realm of the spirits). Automatic writing is also very common in Espiritismo.

The séance begins with everyone standing up, as the Presidente opens the sesión with a special prayer from Kardec's *Gospel According to Spiritism*, known as the *Evangelio*. After the opening, they all sit down again, and the Presidente begins to read several lectures, prayers, and poems from the book. This is a very lengthy procedure, and often one of the mediums begins to show signs of possession before the Presidente finishes the prayers. Sometimes one of the *videntes* or the *auditivas*, the mediums who can either see or hear the spirits, starts to describe his or her visions or the messages he or she is receiving. These are generally concerned with one or more of the persons present at the sesión. Some of the visions and messages describe so accurately the special circumstances of the person in question that he or she is moved to tears.

During an ordinary sesión, several spirits usually manifest; some are enlightened spirits who bring messages of hope to those present; others are low spirits (*espíritus atrasados*) who come to express their hatred and persecution of someone at the sesión. Many of these negative entities are trailing a person who injured them in a previous existence and are now making that person the recipient of their spirit's vengeance. A ghostly revenge may express itself in all sorts of human suffering and misfortunes, especially in love matters. Sometimes an evil spirit torments a person through the machinations of another individual who has been engaged by the entity to harm his enemy by means of an *enviación* or "sending." Enviaciones are very popular forms of revenge in Espiritismo and are very difficult to undo. Usually at the séance, the *mediunidad de arrastre* or *transporte* banishes the evil spirit with the help of other, higher spirits, who then put the spirit in "chains" and bring him to spiritual schools to learn better manners.

Espiritismo teaches that there are many spiritual levels. Each spirit has its own special vibratory rate pertaining to its own level. While higher spirits may descend to visit the lower spiritual levels, the lower spirits cannot ascend to the higher ones because the vibrations are too powerful and would disintegrate them.

Each medium has his or her own guides (*guías*) who prepare his or her mind to receive them and other spirits, while at the same time protecting against evil or demonic entities. The guides call the medium a *casilla* (little house) or *caballo* (horse) because they "enter" or "mount" his mind. When a person at a sesión is very burdened with negative vibrations (*cargado*), the medium may rid him of these undesirable emanations by means of hand passes (*pases*). The medium inhales very fast as she is doing the cleansing, and passes his hands very fast over the person's "aura," a few inches away from the body. He asks the person to turn around and continues the cleansing from head to foot, all the while exhorting all evil spirits to leave the person and invoking his guardian angel to come to his aid. Every few seconds the medium stops the cleansing and taps his hands briskly on top of the water bowl. By the time the cleansing is done, the water bowl, which is present to receive all negative vibrations, is filled with millions of tiny air bubbles, a sure indication to the medium that the cleansing worked. After he has finished his exhausting work, the medium rubs himself with some of the Florida Water and does *pases* all over his own body to dispel any remaining evil forces.

When the Presidente, who is seldom "mounted" by spirits, feels it is time to end the sesión, he indicates his intention to "close" the reunion. If the other mediums agree, everyone stands up and the Presidente proceeds to recite the closing prayers from Allan Kardec's book.

Sometimes spiritists hold Centros (Centers) on specific days and at specific times, either at their homes or in specially designated "temples." These are formal meeting places where the séances are held. The Centros always have a Presidente de Mesa and also vice-presidents or auxiliary mediums. Sometimes the Presidente or one of the auxiliary mediums holds private sessions or *consultas* with the members of the Centro or visitors. During the consulta, the medium may use the Spanish playing cards to ascertain the problems facing the individual, or he may use a glass of water and a white candle or any of a number of other methods. Once he learns the needs of the client, the medium proceeds to give him or her a *receta*, which is a sort of prescription giving detailed instructions on what steps must be taken to alleviate the situation. These may range from herbal baths and prayers to the dead to complicated cleansing rituals undertaken by the medium on behalf of the client. Sometimes the medium discerns that a *trabajo*—a magic spell—is needed by the person. He suggests the type of spell required, and names the price of its preparation. Costs vary according to the type of spell needed; it may be a few dollars or several hundred.

Naturally, this sort of practice engenders the possibility of fraud and extortion, and this sometimes happens in the practice of Espiritismo, as it does in Santería; but there are many mediums and santeros who are very devoted to their beliefs and would not dare to defraud the public because of fears of retaliation from their spiritual guides.

There are also many spiritists who work on their own, conducting consultas for a few special clients. So ingrained is the belief in these consulting "espiritistas" within Hispanic communities that a renowned espiritista in the Bronx charges $250 for her cleansings and consultations, and gets it without complaints. But this particular espiritista is so uncanny in the accuracy of her predictions and spells that her clients consider any money they pay her for her services well spent.

In recent years, a singular fusion or syncretism has taken place between some of the elements of Santería and Espiritismo. Previously, the spiritist worked with his own spiritual guides. Typical among these protective spirits were *Madamas* (West Indian mammies), turbaned and rotund; *Gitanas* (gypsies); *Indios* (Indians); *Piratas* (pirates); and *Congos* (Africans). Each of these colorful but highly evolved entities spoke with his or her own distinctive accent and style, and was invariably welcomed with joyful and affectionate greetings by those present at the séance, who were well familiar with each entity. Recently, however, to these better-known spiritual "characters" have been added others, not so well known in spiritist circles. These new entities are the orishas or saints worshiped in Santería.

Not only are the spirits now "working" with the orishas, but they are also wearing the beaded necklaces of the saints *and* giving them to some of their clients. Some spiritists I know even go so far as to give the image of Elegguá to their clients, and use the coconut as a divination system. The spiritists, however, are careful to stress that when they give Elegguá or the necklaces to a person, they do not conduct any special ceremony of initiation, and simply use these Santería symbols as talismans of good luck.

Many of the new Centros do not have a Presidente as head of the séances. The leader of the Centro is now known as the padrino (godfather) and his wife as the madrina (godmother), titles clearly borrowed from Santería. The members of the congregation are naturally their godchildren. The Centros are also growing larger; whereas a few years ago the average Centro had no more than a few dozen members, today its membership may be counted in the hundreds. In most Centros, visitors are not charged an entrance fee, but members are expected to help in its maintenance.

Among the most popular orishas claimed as guides by the new spiritists is the redoubtable Changó, and many of the padrinos and madrinas of the Centros wear his red and white necklace during the séances and consultas.

Another staple of Santería used by the Centros is the cigar. Some Centros have also introduced rum during the séances, in case an African spirit manifests itself.

As we have already seen, the séance conducted by the santero is known as a "spiritual mass" (*misa espiritual*); and although it has some elements of Spiritism—such as the use of Allan Kardec's prayers—it has some elements all its own. The most notable difference between the two kinds of séances is that the spiritists sit around a table, while the santeros use the table as an altar, sitting in front of it as in a church. Also, spiritist séances may be conducted during the daytime, while the santero's *misa* is usually done at night. The *misa*, unlike the séance, is invariably followed by a large dinner party, where all of those present are provided with plenty of Latin food and as much drink as they want.

In spite of all the elements of Santería that have been incorporated into the Centros, the basic practices and beliefs of Spiritism have not changed. The sesión is still conducted around a *mesa blanca* (white table), the cleansings (*despojos*) are still done with hand passes, and the mediums still prognosticate the future and eradicate evil spirits with the help of their guides. The new syncretism has not transformed Spiritism; it has simply brought it closer to Santería.

24.

The Botánica ⟋⟋⟋⟋⟋⟋⟋⟋⟋⟋⟋⟋⟋⟋⟋⟋⟋⟋⟋⟋⟋

On New York's 116th Street, near Park Avenue, stands a religious-goods store called Otto Chicas-Rendón, owned by a Guatemalan of the same name. His store features large statues of Catholic saints, some of them exquisitely carved in wood and ornamented in gold leaf. It also sells a huge variety of candles in all colors and sizes, exotic herbs and roots, special incenses, magical oils and powders, bead necklaces, all sorts of amulets and talismans, and other magical paraphernalia. Such stores, known as *botánicas* in the Hispanic communities, cater mostly to the basic needs of santeros and espiritistas.

Understandably, the owner of the botánica must be well acquainted with his customers' magical beliefs and practices. Often called upon to provide solutions for a variety of problems, he usually has a keen understanding of human nature. Otto Chicas is no exception. A competent herbalist and spiritualist and a shrewd self-styled psychologist, he is quite well known in the community, and his name is a household word to most Hispanic families throughout New York. In fact, one could say that Otto is something of a celebrity. He and his family have been the subject of several articles in *The New York Times*. A graduate student working with the late Margaret Mead has produced a film about Santería, featuring Otto prominently. Mead herself, working at the time with the Museum of Natural History, also expressed an interest in Otto's rare talents, and was preparing to make a study of his work before she died. Even Mayor Ed Koch of New York City has visited Otto on several occasions, as have a large number of other political and entertainment personalities.

Very often the owner of the botánica is a santero, a palero, or a spiritist, and conducts registros or consultas for his clients. If he does not do consultations, he invariably knows someone who does.

The origins of the botánica can be traced to the 1920s, when one of Otto Chicas's uncles, a pharmacist named Alberto Rendón, returned to New York after serving in World War I. Mr. Rendón found work at a local drugstore in East Harlem, and soon noticed that many West Indians and black Americans came to the pharmacy looking for herbal remedies, essences, perfumed oils, and plants. It was clear to Mr. Rendón that "magical powers" were associated with some of the plants.

Possessing a creative turn of mind and extensive chemical knowledge, Mr. Rendón decided to open a small shop where he would sell his own herbal and chemical formulas and perfumed oils. He began by making arrangements with one of the domestic airlines to bring him daily shipments of fresh plants from Puerto Rico. He then built a small laboratory in the back of his shop, where he prepared a series of herbal formulas and prescriptions for a variety of purposes. So successful was his idea that he soon found himself at the head of a thriving business. The name he gave to his store was West Indies Botanical Gardens.

In the 1940s, Puerto Rican immigration to the United States began to increase significantly. Most of the Puerto Ricans who came to New York established themselves in East Harlem, which eventually became known as El Barrio. As Mr. Rendón's store was located on 116th Street, between Park and Madison avenues, in the heart of El Barrio, he soon became one of the most popular merchants in the area. The Puerto Rican immigrants, who spoke little or no English, quickly shortened the store's name from West Indies Botanical Gardens to Botánica.

Deeply steeped as they were in the practices of magic and spiritism, Puerto Ricans found a haven in Mr. Rendón's store. There they could find love perfumes and oils, essences to bring money and good luck, incenses, and fresh herbs for their lustral baths or despojos. The West Indians and black Americans for whom the store was originally conceived still came to the shop, but they were soon vastly outnumbered by large numbers of Puerto Ricans clamoring for spiritual relief from their problems of adaptation to their new homes.

After the Puerto Ricans, other Hispanic groups came to New York, all of whom shared similar magical beliefs and practices. With the arrival of Cubans came the santeros. Mr. Rendón's business was booming.

This paradisiacal state of affairs was not destined to last. By now, other enterprising individuals had begun to notice the great potential of the botánica. Very soon a host of competitors appeared all over El Barrio. The number of botánicas grew, and they soon spread to other parts of the city, and from there to other states where large Hispanic communities could be found. Today there are literally hundreds of botánicas in the New York metropolitan area, as well as in Miami and Los Angeles.

In 1945, Otto Chicas arrived in New York. After working with his uncle for several years, he learned the botánica business so well that he decided to open his own store on 115th Street. When Mr. Rendón died in the late 1970s, his nephew took over the original store, where he is still located. Because he is the major importer of fresh herbs in the business, Otto is the main supplier of this staple need to other botánicas in New York.

Besides herbs, essences, oils, and incenses, botánicas now sell all the various implements of Santería, Palo, and Spiritism, including books on magic, special prayers, images of saints, talismans, magic roots, a huge variety of colored candles, snake skins, ouanga bags, and magic soaps and bottled despojos (baths) for every possible human need.

The three major botánicas in New York are listed below.

Otto Chicas-Rendón 60 East 116th Street, between Park and Madison avenues. This is the best known of New York botánicas, doing a brisk wholesale and retail business. It is one of the few botánicas that manufacture and package their own products.

Original Products 2486 Webster Avenue, Bronx. This is a large but unpretentious botánica, which has one of the most varied stocks of magical ingredients in New York. It sells wholesale, retail, and mail order, and caters specifically to the needs of Santería. The two owners, both of them Jewish, speak fluent Spanish and are very knowledgeable about the magical practices of Latin Americans.

El Congo Real 1789 Lexington Avenue (at 111th Street). This is probably one of the best stores for the typical spells of both Palo and Santería, with some of the most exotic ingredients in the market. It has a marked folkloric flavor. Both of its two owners are initiated santeros, well known and highly respected in the Santería community.

For a comprehensive list of botánicas in any major city in the United States, the reader may look under Religious Goods Stores in the classified telephone directories.

25.

Santería and the Community/////////////////

It is clear that the work of the santero, like that of the espiritista, is helpful to the Hispanic community. Latin Americans are so involved with magic and folk healing practices that their mental and spiritual health are directly connected with their beliefs. A Hispanic often has more faith in the home remedies prescribed by a santero or a spiritist than in those of an accredited physician. And it is not uncommon for a person to visit a doctor only because the santero has advised it. Once, while I visited a santero in the Bronx, a woman came in for a registro. She asked the santero if her daughter, who was gravely ill with cancer, should be operated on as her doctor suggested. The santero consulted the seashells and told the woman that her daughter could not be saved, because the disease was too advanced, but that an operation would prolong her life for a few months. In his opinion, she should listen to the doctor's advice and agree to the operation. The woman cried disconsolately all during the registro, but as soon as it was over she asked permission to use the telephone. She wanted to call her daughter's doctor and tell him he should go ahead with the operation as soon as possible.

Some of the most popular doctors in New York are those who

are also practicing santeros or espiritistas. One of the best known has a flourishing practice in the Bronx, where he sees as many as a dozen patients a day. Every morning there is a line outside his office, waiting for the doors to open. This doctor uses his spiritual powers to diagnose his patients and determine the adequate prescriptions. He is an internist as well as a surgeon, and his accuracy is said to be phenomenal.

Miracle cures are very common in Santería. At a recent tambor, one of the santeros present related that a man had been brought to him a few weeks earlier with a paralyzed arm. The man had been seen by several doctors who had said the paralysis was permanent because the arm's nerves had been severely injured. The santero prepared an obra, and within minutes the man could feel sensation in the arm. A few days later the arm was completely healed. The man's doctors could not understand the cure and asked him to explain the treatment he had undergone, but he would not tell them that he had been cured by a santero.

A santera at the same tambor told an even more incredible story. She said that one of her clients, who is a hematologist, came for a registro one day, very worried because he burst out crying each time he examined one of his patients, a man whose gangrenous leg was about to be removed. The doctor feared that he was losing his medical objectivity; doctors are not supposed to cry in front of their patients, no matter how ill they may be. The santera told the doctor that the reason he cried over this patient was that the doctor's spiritual guide wanted to cure the man and the doctor would not let him. The santera advised the doctor to let himself be possessed by his guide the next time he was with the patient. The very next time the doctor saw the sick man, he closed his eyes and let his spirit guide take over. As soon as he was in possession of the doctor, the spiritual entity proceeded with the cure. The end result of this unorthodox treatment was that the man's leg healed and did not have to be amputated.

Many of the santeros' cures are affected through their astonishing knowledge of herbal remedies. This great herbal expertise is being carefully studied at present by several medical researchers.

Social workers, psychologists, and psychiatrists are also beginning to realize that the santero's magical and spiritual practices are of great therapeutic value in the treatment of mental illness and social displacement among Hispanics. Some psychologists liken the work of the espiritista to group therapy (the séance) and to individual therapy (the consulta). The work of the santero is seen as individual therapy (the registro), but on a more advanced "technical" level.

Aware of the importance of Santería in the Hispanic community, social workers and psychotherapists are turning to the santero in increasing numbers for help in their assessment of difficult cases. A well-known santero from the Bronx, Eduardo Pastoriza, an initiate of Changó for over forty years, works on a regular basis with a psychiatrist from Bellevue Hospital. Each time a Hispanic with a severe mental problem comes to her attention, the psychiatrist asks her patient if he or she would like to be referred to a santero for help. The patient is invariably relieved at the suggestion and agrees rapidly to the doctor's suggestion. The psychiatrist then calls Eduardo Pastoriza for an appointment and refers the patient to him. This unusual alliance has proven very successful, and there are dozens of cases where the combined efforts of the psychiatrist and the santero have been able to help a severely disturbed person find his or her way back to society.

Eduardo Pastoriza's case is only one of many unusual partnerships between santeros and psychotherapists. In New York, some psychotherapists at both the Columbia Presbyterian Medical Center and Lincoln Hospital are actively engaged in mental therapies involving the cooperation of santeros.

In spite of the obvious social value of Santería, it is still largely unaccepted by most American communities. The secrecy with which the santeros surround their practices is largely to blame for the antagonism facing the Religion. People tend to fear what they do not know. It is not so much the animal sacrifices, tambors, and magical practices that trouble Anglo-Americans; what is most disturbing to them is the fact that Santería is shrouded in deep mystery, that it is heavily cloaked in impenetrable silence. So much secrecy is bound to be regarded as suspicious.

It is difficult for the average American person to understand the four-hundred-year-old tradition that binds the santero to secrecy. The rigorous oaths of silence created by the Yoruba slaves to ensure the survival of their faith are now haunting the santero in his own bid for survival in a hostile environment. The santeros are aware of the problem, and many casas de santo are trying to dispel some of the negative publicity surrounding their practices. They understand the importance of letting the world into their mysteries. But many of the elders still cling to the ancient traditions, and since there is little union between the various houses, it is difficult for the santeros to reach a common agreement.

The secrecy in Santería also makes the Religion easy prey for extortionists and charlatans, who take advantage of the ignorance of the public about the practices of the santeros and charge outrageous prices for useless implements and initiations. A woman in the Queens section of New York conducted more than a half-dozen asientos at seven thousand dollars each before it was discovered that she was not a santera. There are cases of persons charging up to five hundred dollars for one necklace or twenty thousand dollars for a bogus initiation. If the public were better informed as to the beliefs and practices of Santería and the average costs of initiations and ebbós, the dangers of extortion would be considerably reduced.

Fear and discrimination are the two worst problems faced by the santero. In Hialeah, Florida, a santero who tried to build a temple in honor of Saint Lazarus (Babalú-Ayé) met with severe opposition from the leaders of the community.

"It is possible that these people may be witches," said a reporter from the Hialeah Home News. "The sacrifice of animals is a barbaric custom."

"They behead animals and drink their blood," said a member of a civic group in town. "The North American culture is in danger in Dade County."

Even Cubans who wish to be accepted as members of the community attack the practices of Santería and insist that the santeros do not represent the Cuban religious point of view. This rejection of cultural roots is very common among Hispanics in Florida. I was recently invited to participate in a discussion of Santería on a CBS television program in Philadelphia. I was part of a panel of three, which included a Southern Baptist minister and one of the cast members of the film *The Believers*, which deals obliquely with the subject of Santería. The minister, who was from Florida, was born in Puerto Rico, of Puerto Rican parents. He spoke with a thick Southern accent and brandished a gilt-edged Bible as if it were a sword. It was fascinating to watch how his prejudice colored his every action and word. Since he was Puerto Rican, his self-entrenchment was like a desperate bid to disassociate himself from anything even remotely connected with his roots. This quest for acceptance in established communities has led many Hispanics to abandon their cultural heritage.

26.

María //
A Spiritual Beginning

Arecibo, tucked in a fold of Puerto Rico's northeastern coast, is one of the oldest towns in the western hemisphere. Originally an Indian village ruled by a Taino chieftain called Aracibo, the present town was founded by the Conquistadores in 1616.

When I was three years old my mother hired María, a black woman of mammoth proportions, to be my nanny. María's skin was like shiny mahogany with almost iridescent tones, and her smile was radiant. I never saw her angry or sad, and if she was ever prey to these dismal human moods, she was quite adept at hiding them from me. I thought her very beautiful, and soon I would take my meals only if María ate with me, and would not fall asleep unless María sat by my side.

María took me everywhere she went. To the marketplace where she did our daily shopping, and to the shantytown where her large family lived; to daily mass, for she was a devout Catholic; and to the neighborhood store where she placed her occasional bets with the numbers. My mother took a dim view of these escapades, but I was so healthy and happy in María's care that my mother eventually relented and let her take full charge of me.

Each morning María would put me in a frothy sundress with a matching sunbonnet, white sandals, and socks that she bleached daily to ensure their whiteness. Underneath the bonnet, my long black hair would be meticulously braided and tied with silk ribbons matching the color of my dress. María was partial to the scent of Parma violets, and all my clothes exuded a faint violet fragrance.

Once my morning toilet was finished, María would march me proudly into our dining room, where my parents and grandparents would make proper sounds of praise and admiration at my dazzling pulchritude. Then, under María's watchful eyes, I would sit down to breakfast without wrinkling my skirts or soiling my ruffles. After a substantial breakfast, María sailed majestically out of the house with me in tow, her long, immaculate skirts crackling with starch. On her shoulder was a huge parasol to protect us from the fiery Caribbean sun, while from her wrist dangled a fan to bring us relief from the stifling heat. Since air conditioning had barely made its appearance on the island, the fan was more than an ornament. But female vanity had long since turned a necessity into a thing of beauty, and fans had become the objects of both pride and delight, some of them made of fine sandalwood and hand-painted with exquisite landscapes by renowned artists. Others were of peacock or ostrich feathers, or Chantilly lace embroidered with seed pearls. María had purchased her fan from a merchant marine sailor who had brought it from Spain. Its unusually wide span was of ebony, carved with intricate flowery designs and highlighted with delicate touches of color that made the flower patterns dance with light.

It was María who first taught me that with a flick of the wrist and the opening and closing of a fan, a woman can tell an admirer that she is angry or jealous, that she welcomes his advances or finds him a crashing bore. María taught me all this and more during the twelve years I remained in her care.

I was thrilled at the idea of going to school, which opened the day after I turned five, and talked about it incessantly with María. My mother had promised me an especially nice party to celebrate my birthday, and my grandfather had a famous designer in San Juan make a special dress of pink organdy, hand-embroidered with tiny flowers and musical notes. The shoes and socks were also pink, as were the silk ribbons for my hair. But early in the morning, María dressed me in an old white dress and took me to mass. She did not take me in to my family to have breakfast with them. I kept questioning the departure from our daily routine, but María said to be silent and do as I was told.

After mass was over, María brought me to an altar over which stood a statue of the Virgin Mary. While I knelt down before the image, María pulled from her capacious handbag a large wooden rosary, and proceeded to pass the beads. She stood behind me, praying in muted tones, with her hand on my shoulder as if she were introducing me to the Virgin.

Even if you don't pray the litanies, a compilation of fifty-three Hail Marys and seven Paternosters is a lengthy business if you are a child of five. My stomach was empty. My knees ached and throbbed and threatened to buckle, and I had to keep balancing my weight first on one knee, then on the other. I must have presented a most unhappy picture to Our Blessed Lady. But not once did I think to complain to María. One did not question her orders.

It was already midmorning when we left the church. My knees were functioning again after María rubbed them briskly with her handkerchief, but my stomach was grumbling louder than ever.

"María, are we going to the marketplace or back home?"

"I know you're tired and hungry," she said evasively, opening her parasol and pulling me under it. "But you must never let your body tell you what to do. It must obey you, not the other way around."

I trotted obediently by her side. "But how does my body tell me what to do?"

"By making you feel things," she answered. "It makes you feel hungry, so you eat. Tired, so you sit down. Sleepy, so you go to bed. Sometimes it makes you feel angry, so you scream and yell and stamp your feet."

My face colored, remembering my occasional temper tantrums.

"But, María, then my body isn't good."

"Oh yes it is, *florecita* [little flower]. Because of your body, you can see the sky and the sun and the sea. You can smell the perfume of the flowers and sing and play, and love your mother and father."

"And you," I added, drawing closer to her.

"And me." She laughed her great throaty laugh. "But you see, *florecita*, your body is like a little child. It must be taught good habits and to obey. It must learn we can't always eat when we're hungry or sit down when we're tired or sleep when we're sleepy. And the best way to teach your body these things is by sometimes not doing the things it wants you to do. Not always," she emphasized. "Only sometimes."

"Like now?" I asked.

"Like now."

We reached the bus stop. With delight, I thought we were going home, where I could eat some breakfast and play before my party in the afternoon.

"But I will only eat a little," I promised myself, remembering María's words, "and I will play with only one doll."

But I was not to eat a little breakfast or play with any dolls that morning.

The bus chugged along the country road to our home. Palm trees and banana plants heavy with fruit grew profusely on both sides of the road, as did the brilliant blossoms of the hibiscus, the poinciana, and the bougainvillea. To our left, gently sloping hills alternated with narrow valleys carpeted in a dazzling variety of greens. To our right, the Atlantic melted with the sky in a majestic display of aquamarine and gold. A few peasant huts, known as *bohíos*, were scattered on the hillside, while on the ocean side rose elegant, luxurious *quintas* of white stucco ornamented with costly mosaics and Spanish ironwork.

We were still about ten minutes from home when María pulled the cord to get off. Before I knew what was happening I found myself standing by the road, watching the bus disappear in the distance. María opened her parasol and gathered her parcels together.

Directly in front of us was a rough path, largely overgrown with vegetation. María and I trudged along this path until we emerged directly onto a part of the beach hidden from the main road by a series of large boulders embedded in the sand. Among the dunes grew a profusion of tropical sea grapes, their hard, bitter fruit shining like amethysts among their harsh round leaves. Some palm trees bent their trunks so close to the sand that one could easily grab the clusters of coconuts growing among the fan-shaped leaves.

We stopped under the shadow of a palm while María removed my shoes and socks, her own heavy brogans, and the thick cotton stockings she always wore. Thus, barefoot, we trampled through the warm sand.

I did not bother to ask María the reason for our detour, being used to going along on all her outings. I had the vague feeling that this surprise visit to the beach I had always admired from a distance, but never had walked on before, was María's birthday present to me. Intoxicated by the sharp, tangy smell of the sea, I wanted to stay on the shore for the rest of my life.

When we finally arrived at the water's edge, María set her parcels down, closed her parasol, and then calmly proceeded to tear the clothes from my body.

I felt no shame. María washed and dressed me every day and put me to sleep every night. I had stood naked in front of her many times before, and I had not yet learned to be ashamed of my own body. But her action had a certain ominous authority that made me feel destitute and vulnerable beyond description. Deprived of more than my old clothes, I felt stripped of identity, of a sense of being. It was as if I had died somehow, standing there on the golden sand, when the sun like a halo around me and the taste of salt water on my lips. I stood there in shock and utter humiliation, tears rolling steadily down my cheeks. I did not understand María's actions, but I knew there was always a reason for everything she did. (Many years later I would find an echo of María's teachings in the philosophies of some of the world's greatest religions, especially Zen Buddhism. When María tore my clothes off and left me naked facing the sea, without any sense of ego or identity, she was echoing Zen's concept of the perfect initiate, who must be "devoid of selfhood, devoid of personality, devoid of identity, and devoid of separate identity.")

Out of her handbag's unfathomable depths, María extracted a bottle of sugar-cane syrup and the red handkerchief, tied in a knot, where she kept all her loose change. Only then did she turn to look at me, all at once the picture of consternation.

"Ah, my little flower, don't cry. You afraid of María? You think María can hurt you?" She rocked me gently against her bosom as she spoke her soothing words. "Why, *mi florecita*, María would cut out her heart for you. María could never hurt you."

Slowly my tears stopped flowing. I lifted my wet face from her shoulder. I felt I could question her now.

"Why, María?" I asked with trembling lips. "Why did you do that?"

"Because I want you to be protected from all harm. Now that you're going to school, you'll be alone, *florecita*, without María to watch over you. You need protection, and only God and the Blessed Lady can give it to you. That's why I bring you to the Lady in church, so she can know you and give you her blessings. And now I bring you to the Lady and her true power, the sea."

As she spoke, María opened the bottle of sugar-cane syrup. Tasting it with her forefinger, she anointed my temples, lips, wrists, and ankles with the thick liquid. I automatically licked the heavy, cloying syrup on my lips.

"It's too sweet," I grimaced. "I don't like it."

"It has to be sweet for the Lady, as sweet as possible. Nothing can be too sweet for her."

María undid the knot of her red handkerchief. Counting seven pennies, she pressed them in my hand.

"Here, *florecita*," she said, closing my fingers around the coins. "This is the payment, *el derecho*, of the Lady. I give you seven pennies because seven is her number. You remember that. Seven is the number of the Lady, of Yemayá."

"Of *who?*" I asked, staring at the pennies. "What Lady are you talking about, María? The Blessed Lady is in the church and in heaven."

"Yes, *florecita*, but her true power is in the sea and the sea water. She stands in heaven, but where the bottom of her mantle touches the earth, it turns into the ocean. The waves and the sea foam are her ruffles and her lace. And here, in the sea, her name is Yemayá."

She enunciated the strange name carefully so that I could grasp its melodious rhythm. "Say it, *florecita*. Ye-ma-yá."

I repeated it after her. "It is the prettiest name I ever heard, María!"

"The prettiest name in the whole world," María laughed delightedly. "It is the name of the Lady in African, in Yoruba. My mammy taught it to me. And now, my little flower, your black mammy teaches it to you." She took my hand gently and guided me to the water. "Come, let me show you how to salute Yemayá."

Lifting her voluminous skirts so that the waves would not wet them, she turned her body to the left and forced me to do the same. We both stood ankle-deep in the water, our bodies at right angles to the sea.

"See, *florecita*, you never enter into the ocean facing front. To do so is a challenge to Yemayá. It's like saying, 'I'm here, come get me.' So then maybe she does. Always, always enter on your side, better the right side. Then you say, '*Hekua, Yemayá, hekua.*' Say it, little flower."

I looked dubiously at the water, then at María. Like most Puerto Rican children, I had been raised as a very strict Catholic, and I had the vague feeling that our parish priest would not approve of what María was saying. But my trust in her had been firmly reestablished and I did not want to offend her. *"Hekua, Yemayá, hekua,"* I repeated.

As soon as I repeated these words, I felt relieved and relaxed, as if an unseen link had been established between the sea and myself. My soul was overwhelmed by a great love for the sea that has never stopped growing within me. I have never bathed in the sea again without remembering that incredible feeling of love illuminating my entire being.

"See, *florecita*," María said joyously. "Yemayá blesses you, she accepts you. She will always protect you now."

I looked up at her with wondering eyes. "Is that what *hekua* means?"

"Yes, *hekua* means 'blessings.' And see how Yemayá blesses you?"

María pointed to the water frothing softly around my feet. Small whirlpools of foam enveloped my ankles, then my knees. Then suddenly an unexpectedly huge wave rose from the sea like a great green arm. As the wall of water collapsed over my head, I heard María cry out, "The coins! The coins! Let go the coins!"

I felt myself being drawn out to sea inside a glimmering cocoon, with the rushing sound of a thousand crystal bells. I opened my arms to embrace the sea, and the seven pennies fell from my fingers. Almost immediately, the water receded and the waves resumed their usual gentle motion. I stood as before, ankle-deep in foamy water, blinking at the morning sunshine.

I recall little of what happened inside the water. The lingering memory is one of silky green depths, of sun rays shining through the water, of softness, warmth, and safety. It was almost as if I had returned to the womb of the world, and felt reluctant to be born anew. This episode at the beach was my first initiation into Santería.

María used to tell me that the presence of Yemayá is always much stronger in very deep waters. Off the north coast of Puerto Rico, in an area known as Bronson's Deep, the ocean floor plunges down to 27,000 feet. Measured from this depth, the mountains of Puerto Rico would be among the highest in the world, with an approximate height of 31,500 feet. Anything that falls within these waters is lost forever—says the legend—unless Yemayá is offered a prize in exchange for her bounty. Truly, her demands are modest. Seven shiny copper pennies, a bit of sugarcane syrup, and sometimes a few candles are enough to please her. Perhaps it is not the value of the gift that Yemayá really wants, but the faith with which it is given.

In these same waters, on August 16, 1977, off the coast of San Juan, an incident took place that was fully reported in the San Juan *Star*. For several weeks I had been in one of the hotels lining El Condado Avenue, working against a deadline on one of my books. One afternoon a friend went snorkeling in the deep waters off the San Juan coast. When he returned several hours later, he had a tragic story to tell.

A family from nearby Santo Domingo had come to visit Puerto Rico for the first time. Their thirteen-year-old son disregarded the warnings concerning the dangerous undercurrents surrounding the coast of San Juan, and the great depth of the waters, and he swam out far from shore. Probably too weak to fight against the currents, the boy suddenly sank under the water and did not surface again. Local lifeguards and members of the police rescue squad tried to locate his body, but all their efforts proved fruitless.

The story spread throughout El Condado, and all the hotels sent out search parties to find the body. The boy's mother was determined not to leave her son's body in the sea, as she wanted to bring it back to Santo Domingo for proper burial. But late in the afternoon of the following day, the authorities called off the search. All the desperate entreaties of the boy's mother fell on deaf ears. The police were sure the powerful undercurrents in these waters had driven the body toward the ocean floor or wedged it in one of the reef's many underwater crevices. But the mother asked to go along with a search party—the very last one, she pleaded. If the body was not found during this last search, she would not insist any further.

After some consideration, the authorities agreed. As the story unfolded in the San Juan *Star*, she brought along four white candles. When the boat had gone sufficiently out to sea, she asked the officers to stop the engines. Here, she felt, they would find her son's body. More to humor her than for any other reason, the rescue squad officers stopped the boat's engines.

The mother then approached the boat's gunwale and began an impassioned plea to the sea. Kneeling on deck, her hands linked together in prayer, tears streaming down her face, she called out to the sea to return her son's body to her. Reminding the sea that the boy was dead, she proposed that it exchange his body for the candles she had brought along. Since four candles are burned around a coffin, these also represented her dead son.

As she spoke, she pulled the candles from her handbag and threw them overboard. A few minutes later, the rescue squad officers aboard the boat watched, aghast, as the boy's body surfaced at the same spot where the candles had sunk into the water.

Had María been aboard the boat, she would not have been at all surprised. Without any doubts she would have stated that Yemayá, the Great Supernal Mother, had taken pity on another mother and had accepted the exchange willingly, and with her blessing. As to the apparent cruelty of the sea in taking the boy's life, María would probably have answered that the sea had been kind, saving him from a life of suffering and giving him eternal life instead.

María held the view that life was an illusion. So, for that matter, was death.

"It's just another way of life, *florecita*," she would say. "A far better way of life."

I would wrinkle my forehead. "But, María, then why do we

live this life? Wouldn't it be better to die and live a better life in the other world instead?"

"No, *florecita*, we're here for a reason. We're here to learn, to become better so that we can enjoy that other, better life. If we're bad here, we don't go to the better life after this one. Instead, we have to come back, again and again, until we learn to be good."

This simple explanation is exactly the same as the theory of reincarnation expressed by Buddha to his disciple Subhuti in the Diamond Sutra:

"Furthermore, Subhuti, if it be that good men and good women . . . are downtrodden, their evil destiny is the inevitable retributive result of sins committed in their mortal lives. By virtue of their present misfortunes, the reacting effects of their past will be thereby worked out, and they will be in a position to attain the Consummation of Incomparable Enlightenment."

The Consummation of Incomparable Enlightenment was the same concept expressed by María as "a better life in the other world."

After she took me out of the water, María dried me and braided my hair and tied it with pink silk ribbons, and then dressed me in the pink organdy dress my grandfather had given me for my birthday. She seemed in very high spirits and hummed a popular tune. When I told her I was happy to have come to the sea and hoped that she would bring me back again, she laughed and hugged me.

"We'll see, *florecita*, we'll see," she said, putting the finishing touches on a satin bow. "But I'm happy that Yemayá has accepted you. Now you can go to school without María and no harm can come to you."

To my lips came a question that was burning in my mind. "María, why did you tear my clothes?"

She looked at me briefly. Her smile widened, and she returned her attention to my hair.

"Why? Because you had to be presented to Yemayá without

clothes, like a newborn baby. I tore the clothes to tell Yemayá you gave up your old life and wanted to start living again with her as your mother."

"And now my mother is not my mother anymore?" I asked in alarm, my eyes filling with tears.

María hugged me again, brushing away my tears with expert fingers.

"Of course she is, *florecita*. But she's your mother on earth, while Yemayá is your mother in heaven and in the sea."

"But who is Yemayá? The sea?" I asked, still confused.

"Yemayá is the Yoruba name of the Virgin Mary, *florecita*," María explained patiently. "She's the mother of all, of whites and blacks, of yellows and greens, of everybody. But in Africa she's always black because the people there are black, and she wants them to know she's black too."

"But, María, the Virgin is not black, she's white. I've seen her in the church."

"No, *florecita*, the Virgin is like your ribbons. She has many colors. Sometimes she's white, sometimes yellow, sometimes she's red, sometimes black. It depends on the color of the people who adore her. She does this to tell the world she loves everybody the same, no matter what their color is. To the Yoruba she's always black because they're black."

"Who are the Yoruba, María?"

María paused in the middle of a braid, her eyes lost in reverie.

"The Yoruba were a great black people." She continued her braiding. "My mammy was Yoruba," she said, with evident pride. "She come to Puerto Rico in 1872, the year before abolition."*

When she spoke of her mother, which was often, María reverted to broken Spanish, with African words interspersed. "She come with two hundred fifty Yoruba from Ife, that's the name

*Slavery was abolished in Puerto Rico on March 22, 1873.

of Yoruba land in black country," she added. "Come from Africa, they did, in them slave boats. In chains they brought them, the mean slave merchants—*los negreros*. Many of the black people die on boat, of hunger and sickness, but mostly of broken heart. Yoruba is proud people. Don't like white man."

"I'm white, María," I reminded her sadly.

"No, you aren't, *florecita*," María cried, holding me tight against her. "You aren't white, and you aren't black. You're like the sun and the stars—all light, no color."

She finished tying the last ribbon and stood up with great effort from her stooped position. Her usually immaculate clothes were drenched with sea water and covered with sand, but she paid no attention to them.

"Old María is not as strong as she used to be," she grunted, flexing her back. "Not like my mammy. My mammy real strong," she said with relish. "She only ten when she come to island. But white man leave my mammy alone. She knew how to talk to the *orishas*."

"What is 'orisha,' María?" I asked.

"Orisha?" she mused. "Yemayá is orisha. Elegguá is orisha. Changó is orisha. Orisha is a saint, a force of the good God. But come," she added, taking me by the hand. "It's no good to ask too many questions all at once. Later, I tell you more."

"But, María," I insisted. "Are there many . . . orishas?"

"As many as the grains of sand on the beach. But I only know a dozen or two. There are too many. Someday you'll know them too. But now is time to get back home, *florecita*, or your mammy will be really worried. And then your cake will be eaten, your presents gone, and the ice cream melted."

The thought of the promised birthday party came rushing back to my five-year-old mind, erasing all thoughts about the shadowy orishas, the Yoruba, and even the black Virgin known as Yemayá.

The pink shoes and socks remained in María's handbag until we emerged from the sand onto the path that led back to the road. Free from their confinement, I ran ahead of María toward the

bus stop, oblivious of my fine embroidered dress, pigtails dancing in the sun, my small feet encrusted with wet sand. She followed behind me slowly, dragging her heavy brogans, her parcels,
and her parasol, tired but always smiling.

I remained in María's care until I was fifteen. All during the
years she stayed with us, she spoke to me about the orishas and
their legends and the ancient African traditions that were still
practiced in the small town of Loiza Aldea, on the eastern tip of
the island. Her teachings would tend to dispel the views of many
anthropologists and sociologists who study Santería who believe
that the Yoruba traditions did not survive in Puerto Rico. When I
was a young child on the island, the Yoruba practices were
known as "the black religion" or "the African religion." It was in
Cuba that the syncretism between the orisha tradition and Catholicism took place, bringing about the birth of Santería.

María's teachings were the foundation of my research in Santería
and of my ever-growing interest in the Religion. I feel that my life
was enriched by the teachings of this woman, who did not know
how to read or write, but whose wisdom and understanding
surpassed those of many eminent scholars. I am a better person
for having known her, and I am grateful that she touched my life.
What she taught me was perfect and pure, and brought me closer
to nature and to God. This search for God, in nature and in
ourselves, is the true meaning of Santería.

Glossary

Abeokuta—city in Nigeria where Yemayá is worshipped

aberínkula—unconsecrated drums

abian—the iyawó in Brazil

abikú—a mischievous spirit who possesses a small child and sickens it until it dies

Abo-Faca—*Mano of Orúnla*; an initiation conferred only upon men by babalawos

abure—brethren

acuaro—pheasant

addele—the cowrie shells that arc not read

addimú—small offering to an orisha

afoché—ritualistic dances played for tourists in Rio de Janeiro

Aganyú—the orisha who owns the volcano, father of Changó

Agegun Orişa-Oko—Nigerian priestesses who become possessed by Orişa-Oko (Orisha-Oko in Santería)

Aggüeme—another aspect of Obatalá

ago—ritual robes worn in Nigeria

agogó—a ritual bell used to call an orisha

agüan—ceremony during which a person receives the initiation of Babalú-Ayé (Saint Lazarus) ahijado, ahijada—godson, goddaughter

Ajaba—another name of the orisha Dada, brother of Changó

ajé—witches

ajogún—forces of evil

akpetebí—handmaiden of Orúnla

akpwón—singer during ritual drum playing

akumí—"I am Aku," from which Lucumí (friendship) is derived

Alabwanna—The Lonely Spirit: Elegguá's mother according to a legend

Alafin, Alafia, Alafina, or Alafina Crueco—titles of Changó

Alagbaa—priest in charge of special ceremonies in Nigeria

alagbara—violent acts attributed to Oggún

albahaca—an herb belonging to Obatalá used in the omiero and lustral baths

aleyo—those who are not santeros

alforjas—knapsacks

Alláguna—an aspect or path of Obatalá

amala—Changó's favorite food, prepared with okra and cornmeal

amuluo—sixteen compound oddus of the divination systems

anamú—a very powerful herb used in baths, feared by some santeros

Añaqui—Elegguá's mother according to a legend

ankorí—answering chorus to the drums

apasote—a powerful herb used in lustral baths

apotí—the throne where the iyawó sits during the asiento

araba—chiefs of major towns in Nigeria

ara orun—a citizen of heaven

Arara—a part of Dahomey

arun—disease

asentado en ocha—Spanish for initiate of Santería

ashé—amen, power, blessings, energy

ashé Orúnmila—sacred powder prepared by the babalawo

asiento—the major ceremony of Santería

ASPCA—American Society for the Prevention of Cruelty to Animals, which monitors closely the activities of the santeros

avatar, avatares—paths or aspects of the orishas

awe merin—one of the divination aids

ayan—tree sacred to Changó

aye—another divination aid

ayugbona—assistant priest (priestess) to the padrino during the asiento

babalawo—high priest of Santería

babalocha—a santero who has initiated other santeros

babalorixa—equivalent of babalocha in Brazil

Babalú-Ayé—one of the most revered of the orishas

baba-Oru—ruling male orisha of a person, "heavenly father"

bagan—a priest of Candomblé

Bahia—a state of Brazil (São Paulo) that is Brazil's center of Candomblé

bajar a Orúnla—to bring down Orúnla in order to determine who is the ruling orisha of a person

Bantu—one of the tribes involved in the sect known as Palo

batáa—the sacred drums of Santería

batea—the wooden bowl where Changó's thunderstones are kept

Baumba—a path of Oggún

Bayanmi—another name of Dada, Changó's brother

Bellevue Hospital—a hospital in New York whose psychiatric department uses santeros in their treatment of mental illness

bembé—a ritual drum party in honor of an orisha

bendición—Spanish for blessings

bilongo—black magic spell

bohío—peasant hut in Puerto Rico

botánica—religious goods store that caters to the needs of the santeros

bóveda—the altar to the eggun, or dead

brujería—a magic spell; witchcraft

cabeza grande—a leader, head of state or of the orishas

cabildo, cabildos—temples of Santería in Cuba

camino—path

canastillero—the shelves where the tureens with the orisha's stones are kept

candelaria—a Catholic aspect of Oyá

Candomblé—Brazilian equivalent of Santería

canto de puya—chant used by the akpwón to needle an orisha to incite him or her to come to earth

caracoles—seashell divination

Casa Branca—one of the most famous temples of Candomblé

casa de santo—house of a santero

cascarilla—powdered eggshell, used in seashell divination and in many of the spells and rites of Santería

casilla—a medium

ceiba pentandra—kapok tree, the sacred tree of Santería

cencerro—cowbell used to call down Oyá

Changó—patron of fire, thunder, and lightning and one of the most popular orishas

Changó Ogodo—a path of Changó

chivos capones—neutered he-goats

city-kingdoms—divisions of Nigerian towns

clavos de línea—railway spikes

Cofá de Orúnla—initiation conferred only upon women by the babalawo

collares—the Necklaces, one of the initiations of Santería

Columbia Presbyterian Medical Center—a hospital in New York that works with the santeros in the treatment of mental illness

consulta—the consultation of a santero or espiritista

cowrie—type of seashell used in the seashell divination

Cuanaldo—initiation wherein babalawo receives the sacrificial knife

cuchillo—sacrificial knife

cundiamor—an herb belonging to Babalú-Ayé and used by the santeros in the cure of diabetes

Dada—brother of Changó

darle coco al santo—the coconut divination system

derecho—ritual fee paid to an orisha

desenvolvimiento—material and spiritual evolution

despojo—ritual cleansing

Dida obi—the kola nut divination system in Nigeria

Diloggún—the seashell divination system

ebbó—spell; offer to the orishas

ebbochure—a small offering to an orisha

ebbó de entrada—part of the asiento ceremony

ebbokun—a small offering to an orisha

ebomin—second-class priest of Candomblé

efun—cascarilla, or powdered eggshell

egba—paralysis

eggun—the dead of one's family

egungun—person possessed by an eggun

eja abori—special fish favored by Orisha-Oko

ekedi—priestess of Candomblé who is in charge of initiates

ekodidé—red feather from the tail of the African parrot, vital to the initiation of the asiento

eko tutu—cornstarch

el dia del medio—third day of the asiento, when outsiders may visit the iyawó on the throne

Eledáa—the guardian angel

Elegbara—another name for Elegguá

Elegguá—orisha who is the opener of the ways

elegun Changó—priest of Changó

elekes—the Necklaces

eleri-ipin—Orúnla's title as "witness of the ori," or guardian spirit

El Negrito José—an African eggun

endiosado—a santero who thinks himself superior to others

enu—larger head of the ritual drums

epe—curse

epó—*manteca de corojo*, palm nut oil

eriaworan—a divination aid

erindinloggun—Yoruba term for the seashell divination

eru tuché—seeds used in preparation of omiero

escoba amarga—ritual herb

Eshu, Eṣu—Yoruba name for Elegguá

Eshu Afra—a path of Elegguá

Eshu Alabwanna—a path of Elegguá

Eshu Anagüi—a path of Elegguá

Eshu Aye—a path of Elegguá

Eshu Barakeño—a path of Elegguá

Eshu Bi—a path of Elegguá

Eshu Elufe—a path of Elegguá

Eshu Laroye—a path of Elegguá

Eshu Ogguanilebbe—an aspect of Elegguá wherein he is the constant companion of Oggún

espanta muerto—herb used in baths to dispel evil spirits

Espiritism—Spiritism

espiritista—spiritist

espiritu travieso—a mischievous spirit

estera—straw mat

eucharist—holy communion

eupatorium odoratum—popular herb used in lustral baths

ewe—herbs, plants

eya aranla—music that is danced and sung by the participants at a drum party for the saints

eyerosun—a special powder used by the babalawo in the Table of Ifá

fadela—mixture of herbs and blood rubbed on drums for greater resonance

filho(-a) de santo—a santero or santera in Brazil

Florida Water—an herbal liquid very popular in Santería

Fon—an African tribe from Dahomey

foribale—genuflection in front of an orisha or elder

fuiri—one of the names given to the spirit living inside the palero's cauldron

fula—the piles of gunpowder used in Palo

fundamento de santo—initiation seen as a foundation of the asiento

Gbaye-Gborun—salutation to the babalawo; title of Orúnla

guano bendito—palms received at church on Palm Sunday

guemilere—drum party in honor of an orisha

guiro—a type of drum party given to an orisha where only one drum is played, accompanied by beaded gourds

Ibeyi—holy twins

Ibikiji Edumare—next in rank to Oloddumare, title of Orúnla

Ibo—an African tribe

Ibochichi—part of salutation to the babalawo

Iboru-Iboya—corruption of Gbaye-Gborun

Ico-Fa—Icofá, initiation given by the babalawo to women (*Cofá de Orúnla*)

idé, ildé—ritual bead bracelet received during an initiation

Igbo igbale—sacred groves in Nigeria where the eggun are invoked

Iggi-Olorún—name given by the kongo to the ceiba ("house of God")

igüi eggun—another name of the ikú achán

ikin—palm nut

ikin ifá—palm nuts used in Ifá divination

ikoidé—another name for the red parrot feather used in initiation

ikú—death

ikú achán—ritual staff used by the babalawo to invoke the dead

ilari—king's messengers in Nigeria, who were priests of Changó

ilé—home

Ile-Ife—the first city created by Obatalá according to one of the myths

Ilé-Olofi—the church, house of Olofi (God)

ilé-orisha—house of an orisha

inafa—*collar de mazo*; ritual necklace of the asiento made of many strands of colored beads

Inle—an orisha identified with Saint Raphael

Irawo—city in Nigeria

iré—good luck

irofá—deer horn used by the babalawo in the Table of Ifá

Iroko—sacred tree of the Yoruba, counterpart of the ceiba in Santería

ironworker—title given to Oggún

iruke—scepter made of a horse's tail, used by Obatalá and Oyá

italero—santero who is an expert in the reading of the seashells

Itán—major ebbó or offering in the iyanifá initiation

Itótele—one of the batáa drums

itutu—ceremony celebrated at the death of the santero

Iyá—mother

iyalocha—a santera who has initiated other santeros

iyá-Oru—ruling female orisha of an individual; "heavenly mother"

iyawó—initiate after the asiento

Jakuta—the Nigerian stone thrower, syncretized with Changó

Jimaguas—Spanish for the Ibeyi, or divine twins

Jutía—opossum, a staple powder used in Santería

Kabbalah—esoteric and magical tradition of the Jews

Kabiesi—a traditional salute to Changó

Kadiempembe—name given to the devil by the paleros

karioriocha—the asiento ceremony

Ketu—a city in Nigeria where Elegguá (Eṣu) comes from

kilase—a type of offering to an orisha

kisengue—a scepter made of a human tibia used by the paleros

Knife, the—the cuchillo, sacrificial knife

Kolonia 1800—a staple cologne used in some Santería spells and rites

Kongo—an African tribe

La Caridad del Cobre—patron of Cuba and saint syncretized with Oshún

La Colección—collection of prayers used by the spiritists

la prendición—part of the asiento ceremony

Larde—path of Changó

lariche—a part of the seashell divination

Legba—name given to Elegguá in Voodoo

letra—oddu or design in the seashell divination

letra del año—prognostications made by the babalawos at the beginning of each year

levantamiento del plato—part of the itutu ceremony

libreta—notebook received by the santero a year after his asiento containing prognostications of his future and prohibitions to observe

Loción Pompeya—a cologne used by the santeros and spiritists during spells and rites

Loiza Aldea—town in Puerto Rico where many Yoruba descendants still live

Los Guerreros—the Warriors; a major initiation wherein the initiate receives the protection of Elegguá, Oggún, and Ochosi

Lucumí—the Yoruba in Cuba

Macumba—spiritism in Brazil

macuto—a bundle, also a black magic spell

madrina—godmother

mai de santo—Brazilian santera

malanga—a yamlike root very popular in the tropics

mama Ungundu—a name given by the paleros and the Kongo to the ceiba

Mano de Orúnila—initiation given only to men by the babalawo

manteca de corojo—palm nut oil

mariwó—palm fronds

matanza—sacrifice of the animals during the asiento

mayombero—another name given to the palero who practices the regla mayombe, a type of palo

medio asiento—half of the asiento, the two initiations known as the Collares and the Guerreros

meduinidad de arrastre—medium who can remove evil spirits

mediunidad auditiva—medium who can hear the spirits

mediunidad clarividente—medium who can see the future

mediunidad de comunicación—medium through whom the spirits communicate with the living

mediunidad vidente—medium who can see the spirits

melli—twin

menga—blood

minestras—various mixed grains such as beans and corn

moyubbar—to pay homage to the orishas or to the dead during divination

Mpangüi—title of the palero

mpolo banso—ashes

mpungo—one of the names given to the spirit living inside the palero's cauldron

Nago—an African tribe, part of the Voodoo movement

ñangale, ñangare—a special ceremony of sun worship conducted by the babalawo

Necklaces, the—initiation wherein the five necklaces of Santería are received

New Oyo—city in Nigeria

ndoki—evil witches

nganga—the palero's cauldron

Nkisi, nkita—spirit living inside the palero's cauldron

nkunia casa sami—name given by the Kongo to the ceiba

Nsasi—name given to Changó by the paleros and Kongo

Oba—orisha said to be Changó's official wife

oba—king

Obakoso—"the king did not hang," title of Changó

Obaluayé—one of the names of Babalú-Ayé in Brazil

Obatalá—father of the orishas, creator of mankind

Obbamoro—an aspect of Obatalá

obe—machete

Obi—the coconut

obi abata—type of kola nut used in divination in Nigeria

obi güi güi—dry coconut

obí kolá—seed that is one of the ingredients of the omiero

Ocha—orisha; Santería

Ochacriñán—an aspect of Obatalá

Ochalufón—an aspect of Obatalá

Ochanlá—an aspect of Obatalá

Ochinchín—Oshún's favorite meal, an omelet made with shrimp and watercress

Ochosi—orisha who is patron of the hunt and of justice

Ochumare—the rainbow

oddu—a design in one of the divination systems

Oddúa—one of the more obscure orishas, seen by some santeros as female, by others as male

odduará—flint stones

Odduaremu—wife of Oddudúa

Oddudúa—warrior orisha

ofó—loss

Ofún-Mewa—one of the oddus of the seashells

Oggou—Oggun in Voodoo

Oggún—orisha known as the ironworker

Oggúndabedé—one of the oddus of the Table of Ifá

Ogún-Oniré—first king of Iré, title of Oggún

Ojubo baba—ancestral shrines for the invocation of the dead

Oju eggun, Oju orori—another name for ancestral shrines

Okónkolo—one of the batáa drums

Olire—king of Iré, descendant of Oggún

Oloddumare—God among the Yoruba

Olofi, Olofin—mankind's personal god

Olokun—deity at the bottom of the sea

olori-buruku—someone who is stupid

olori-iré—one who is very wise

Olorun Oloddumare—God Almighty

Olosi—the devil in Santería

omiero—sacred liquid of Santería

omi tutu—fresh water

omo—child

omokoloba—babalawo who has received the initiation of Olofi

Omolu—one of the names of Babalú-Ayé in Brazil
omo-orisha—child of an orisha
oñí—honey
oogun—herbal talisman
ooni—head of Ife
opelé—divination chain of the babalawo
opón-Ifá—the divining tray of the babalawo
ori—the head
oriaté—a santero who is an expert in reading of seashells
oriki—praise songs in Changó's honor
Orişa-nlá, Orichan-nlá—an aspect of Obatalá
orisha—Yoruba deity, syncretized as a Catholic saint
orisha fun-fun—white or "cool" orishas
Orisha-Oko—orisha who is the patron of agriculture
Orisha Tradition—the worship of the orishas in the New World
orogbo—bitter kola nut, said to belong to Changó
oru—heaven
orun—the sun; heaven
Orúnla—patron of babalawos, the holy diviner
Orúnmila—Orúnla, holy diviner, patron of babalawo
Osain—orisha who is the owner of the plants
Osainista—an expert herbalist
oshé Changó—Changó's double-edged ax
Oshún—orisha who is the patron of love, marriage, and money
Osowusi—night watchman is popular, a title of Ochosi
Osun—the tiny metal rooster who is said to be the guardian of the house in Santería
otá, otanes—sacred stone or stones representing the orishas
otí şeketé—favorite drink of Changó
Oyá—orisha who is the patron of lightning and owner of the ceremony
Oyo—city in Nigeria where Changó comes from

padrino—godfather
pai de santo—Brazilian santero

palero—priest of Palo

Palo—a sect based on the beliefs and magical practices of the Kongo

Palo Mayombe—a type of Palo

Palo Monte—a type of Palo

panaldo—ceremony conducted by the babalawo

Partenium hysterophorus—herb used in lustral baths

pataki—legend

pescado y jutía—smoked fish and opossum in powder, a staple in Santería

Petiveria alliacea—one of the most important herbs used in Santería

piedras de rayo—Changó's thunderstones

pilón—the wooden stand where Changó's wooden bowl (batea) is placed

pimienta de guinea—guinea pepper, popular in magic spells

Pinaldo—ceremony wherein the sacrificial knife is received

plumas—fowls; feathers

polvo de jutía—powdered opossum

prenda—the palero's nganga

prendido en el santo—a person who must make the saint

Quimbanda—the black magic aspect of Macumba

quita maldición—herb used to dispel evil spells

rayado—"cut" in Palo

registro—the consultation conducted by the santero

Regla—region of Cuba

Religion, the—Santería

resguardo—protecting talisman

ripiar—to crush (herbs)

rogación de cabeza—prayers to the head using grated coconut

rompezaragüey—herb used in lustral baths

sahumerio—"smudging," where a specially prepared incense is used to dispel evil

Sambia (Nsambe)—God among the paleros and Kongo

Santería—Afro-Cuban religion in which the orishas, or deities, of the Yoruba, syncretized with Catholic saints, are worshiped

santero, santera—priest and priestess of Santería

santeros mayores—elders of Santería

sarayeyeos—rubbing rituals used to rid a person of negative influences

şeeree (shere) Changó—gourd rattle used to invoke Changó

shékere—beaded gourd used in some drum parties as a type of maraca

Siete Rayos—one of the names given to Changó by the paleros

Şonponno—Babalú-Ayé in Nigeria

sopera—Spanish for tureen

Spiritism—the practice of invoking the dead through prayers and rituals using several mediums

Spiritualism—demonstration by a medium of his or her psychic abilities to an audience for a fee

suyeres—chants used during the asiento

Table of Ifá—the main divination system of the babalawo

tabonuco—a hard resin used in sahumerios

tambor—drum; drum party for an orisha

Tata—father

tcha-tcha—the smaller head of the batáa drum

tefar—to "write" or mark the oddus in Ifá

terreiro—temple of Candomblé in Brazil

thunderstone—naturally polished black stone, flat and triangular, believed to be formed as lightning strikes the ground. Thunderstones are extremely hard and cannot be burned or broken.

tingüi agüó—respect shown to an elder by paying foribale at their feet

toque—drum rhythm

toques de muerto—drum rhythms in honor of the dead

trono—the throne or display of the orishas' tureens during the tambor or the asiento

Umbanda—the white magic aspect of Macumba

Voodoo—Voudun, the Haitian religion based on the magico-religious practices of several African tribes, such as the Fon, the Arada, the Yoruba, and others

Wanaldo—initiation wherein the babalawo receives the sacrificial knife, known also as *Cuanaldo*

Warriors, the—initiation wherein the initiate receives the protection of Elegguá, Oggún, and Ochosi

Yakara—"man" in the Kongo creation myth

Yalodde—a title of Oshún (also *iyalode*), meaning "mother of nations"

Yansa—another name for Oyá

Yaya—mother, among the Kongo and paleros

yefá—powder prepared by the babalawo

Yemayá—orisha who represents the sea and motherhood

Yemmu—a female aspect of Obatalá

yerbero—herbalist

Yewá, Yegüá—the deity known as the "devourer of the dead"

Yeyeomo eja—title of Yemayá among the Yoruba, "the mother whose children are the fish"

yeza—the three tribal marks used by the Yoruba on each cheek; drawn in the color of the ruling orisha on the iyawó during the asiento

Yoda—a path or aspect of Changó

Yoruba—peoples of Southwestern Nigeria, whose magicoreligious practices are the basis for the Orisha Tradition in the New World, of which Santería, Candomblé, and Trinidad's Shango cult are part

Yroso—one of the oddus of the seashell divination

zapateado—a dance where feet are stamped hard on the ground, such as flamenco

zarzaparrilla—used in lustral baths and magic spells

Bibliography

Ajisafe, A. K. *Laws and Customs of the Yoruba People.* London, 1924.

Albertus Magnus. *The Book of Secrets.* London.

Aquinas, Thomas. *Summa Theologica.* Edited by T. Gilby. New York, 1969.

Awolalu, J. O. *Yoruba Beliefs and Sacrificial Rites.* London, 1979.

Babin, M. T. *Panorama de la Cultura Puertorriqueña.* New York, 1958.

Bascom, W. R. *Ifá Divination.* Indiana, 1969.

———. *The Yoruba of Southwestern Nigeria.* New York, 1969.

Bass, R. H. *The Story of Natural Religion.* New York, 1963.

Bastide, R. *Les religions Africaines au Brasil.* Paris, 1960.

Baxter, R. *The Certainty of the World of the Spirits.* London, 1961.

Binder, V., et al., eds. *Modern Therapies.* New York, 1958.

Blumber, M. F. *A History of Amulets.* Edinburgh, 1887.

Breger, L. *From Instinct to Identity.* New York, 1974.

Bromhall, T. *A Treatise of Specters.* New York, 1928.

Burland, C. A. *Myths of Life and Death.* New York, 1974.

Buxton, T. F. *The African Slave Trade*. New York, 1893.

Cabrera, L. *Contes Nègres de Cuba*. Paris, n.d.

———. *El Monte*. Miami, 1971.

———. *Ochún y Yemayá*, Miami, 1970.

Constant, A. *The Mysteries of Magic*. London, 1886.

Courlander, H. *Tales of Yoruba Gods and Heroes*. New York, 1973.

Dean, S. R., ed. *Psychiatry and Mysticism*. Chicago, 1979.

Dorsainvil, J. C. *Une explication philologique du voudou*. Port-au-Prince, 1924.

Eliade, M. *Rites and Symbols of Initiation*. New York, 1958.

Ellis, A. B. *The Yoruba-Speaking Peoples of the Slave Coast of Africa*. London, 1954.

Epega, D. O. *The Mystery of the Yoruba Gods*. Sagos, 1931.

———. *The Sacred and the Profane*, New York, 1957.

Farrow, C. S. *Faith, Fancies of Yoruba Paganism*. London, 1924.

Frazer, J. *The Golden Bough*. London, 1980.

Freud, S. *Totem and Taboo*. New York, 1952.

García Cortés, J. *El Santo (La Ocha)*. Miami, 1971.

Garrido, P. *Esotería y Fervores Populares de Puerto Rico*. San Juan, 1942.

Gleason, J. *The Gods of Yorubaland*. New York, 1971.

———. *A Recitation of Ifá*. New York, 1973.

González-Wippler, M. *Santería: African Magic in Latin America*. New York, 1973.

———. *A Kabbalah for the Modern World*. New York, 1974.

———. *The Complete Book of Spells, Ceremonies and Magic*. New York, 1978.

———. *The Santería Experience*. New Jersey, 1978.

———. *Rituals and Spells of Santería*. New York, 1984.

———. *The Seashells*. New York, 1985.

Graves, R. *The White Goddess*. New York, 1948.

Gross-Louis, K., et al., eds. *Literary Interpretations of Biblical Narratives*. New York, 1974.

Harwood, A. *Rx: Spiritist as Needed*. New York, 1977.

Hume, D. *A Treatise of Human Nature*. Reprint. New York, 1967.

Hurston, Z. *Voodoo Gods*. London, 1939.

Iamblichus, *De Mysteriis*. Reprint. London, 1968.

Idowu, E. B. *Olodumare: God In Yoruba Belief*. New York, 1963.

James E. O. *Origins of Sacrifice*. London, 1933.

————. *Sacrifice and Sacrament*. London, 1962.

Johnson, S. *History of the Yorubas*. London, 1921.

Jonas, Sulfurino. *El Libro de San Cipriano*. Mexico, 1952.

Jung, C. G. *The Interpretation of Nature and the Psyche*. London, 1955.

————. *The Structure of Dynamics of the Psyche*. New York, 1960.

————. *Mysterium Coniunctionis*. New York, 1963.

————. *Man and His Symbols*. London, 1964.

Kay, J. A. *The Nature of Christian Worship*. London, 1953.

Klein, H. S. *Slavery in the Americas*. New York, 1946.

Lachetenere, R. *Oh mío, Yemayá*. Manzanillo, Cuba, 1938.

————. *El Sistema Religioso de los Lucumís y Otras Influencias Africanas en Cuba*. Havana, 1940.

Lévi-Strauss, C. *Totemism*. New York, 1963.

Leyel, C. F. *The Magic of Herbs*. New York, 1925.

Lucas, J. O. *The Religion of the Yorubas*. Lagos, 1948.

Malinowski, B. *Magic, Science and Religion*. New York, 1954.

Mbiti, J. S., *Concepts of God in Africa*. London, 1970.

Michaelis, S. *A Discourse of Spirits*. New York, 1934.

Milburn, S. *Magic and Charms of the Ijebu Province*. London, 1932.

Montagu, A. *Man: His First Million Years*. New York, 1962.

————. *Man's Most Dangerous Myth: The Fallacy of Race*. New York, 1974.

Ortiz, F. *Brujos y Santeros*. Havana, 1938.

Paracelsus. *Selected Writings*. Edited by J. Jacobi. New York, 1951.

Pierson, D. *Negroes in Brazil.* Chicago, 1942.

Progoff, I., trans. *The Cloud of Unknowing.* New York, 1957.

———. *Jung, Synchronicity and Human Destiny.* New York, 1973.

Ramos, A. *Introdução a Antropologia Brasileira.* Rio de Janeiro, 1943.

———. *O Negro na Civilização Brasileira.* Rio de Janeiro, 1956.

Rhine, J. B. *The Reach of the Mind.* London, 1948.

Rigaud, M. *Secrets of Voodoo.* New York, 1970.

———. *Veve.* New York, 1976.

Ringgren, H. *Sacrifice in the Bible.* London, 1962.

Rogers, A. R. *Los Caracoles.* New York, 1973.

Rosario, J. C., and J. Carrion. *Problemas Sociales: El Negro en Haiti, Los Estados Unidos.* San Juan, Puerto Rico, 1940.

St. Clair, D. *Drums and Candle.* New York, 1971.

Simpson, G. E. *Shango Cult in Trinidad.* San Juan, Puerto Rico, 1965.

Sosa, J. J. *Popular Religiosity and Religious Syncretism: Santeria and Spiritism.* Miami, 1982.

Spinoza, B. *Ethics.* New York, 1959.

Thompson, R. F. *Voices of the Spirits.* New York, 1984.

Tylor, E. B. *Religion in Primitive Culture.* New York, 1958.

Van der Leeuw, G. *Religion in Essence and Manifestation.* New York, 1963.

Verger, P. *Flux et reflux de la traité de nègres.* Paris, 1917.

———. *Dieux d'Afrique.* Paris, 1928.

Weyer, P. *Primitive Peoples Today.* New York, 1960.

Williams, J. J. *Voodoos and Obeahs: Phases of West Indies Witchcraft.* New York, 1933.

Wyndham, G. *Myths of Ife.* London, 1921.

Index

Photos courtesy of the following: